*The Other Half*

# KENNETH CLARK

# THE OTHER HALF

# HALF

*A Self-Portrait*

JOHN MURRAY

Printed in Great Britain by
William Clowes & Sons, Limited
London, Beccles and Colchester
0 7195 3432 1

*To Alan*

# Contents

# Illustrations

# Illustrations

# Preface

I CALLED THE FIRST PART of my autobiography *Another Part of the Wood*, conflating the stage directions in *A Midsummer Night's Dream* ('Another Part of the Forest') with the opening of Dante's *Inferno*—'*Mi ritrovai per una selva oscura, che la diritta via era smarrita*' (I found myself in a dark wood where the straight way was lost). I also had in mind the old-fashioned proverbial saying "We're not out of the wood yet". The book ended when I was aged 36, and people who found it amusing asked me when I would publish a second volume. I used to reply "Never". The first volume had qualities that I knew I could not recover. The early part described a way of life so different from our own as to have a certain historical interest value. It was both touching and funny. In describing Edwardian *moeurs* I discovered a tone of voice, detached and slightly ironical, that I could use throughout the whole book, even in the chapter about London Society. A few readers did not catch this tone, and thought that my descriptions of Vanity Fair, which occupy only about 28 pages out of 278, were like Chips Channon with a less hearty appetite. A number of readers told me that the book had made them laugh out loud. One can't ask for better than that.

All this I knew I would not bring off in a second volume. It could not be in any sense a 'work of art', but only the record of a varied life, and it would not make anyone laugh. But after two years my son Alan talked me into changing my mind. I recognised that some of the episodes in which I had been concerned as the principal actor were passing into history—a very minor branch of history, to be sure, but one which would appear in footnotes.

As before, the book is written from memory. I have not consulted or (with two exceptions) quoted from letters. To have done so would have made it as cumbersome as the memoirs of a politician. Unfortunately my memory began to fail precisely at the moment when I started writing the book, so it is bound to contain a few mistakes, although I have done my best to avoid them.

As before, the book is unashamedly a self-portrait. In fact, since the tone is less detached, it probably contains more expressions of my feelings and prejudices than the first volume. Autobiography is a curious form. Excellent authors have felt themselves inhibited by it, and written dull autobiographies; duffers have written amusingly. Somerset Maugham said that no novelist could write a good autobiography as all his experiences had gone, thinly disguised, into his novels. This is true of Kipling, Conrad and Edith Wharton; but H. G. Wells's 'Autobiography' is one of the best I know. It succeeds because, when he wrote it, H.G. had not lost his appetite for life. After the age of 70 I began to lose mine. But I do not want to prejudice the reader against the book, which seems to me to contain a few amusing episodes, and records my impressions of some interesting characters.

This leads me to the question of 'name dropping', that abominable practice of which I was accused by reviewers of my first volume. If some of one's closest friends have been well-known people it would be ridiculous and unhistorical to omit their names simply because they have appeared in the newspapers. However, I have mentioned as few eminent people as is consonant with a true record of my life, and hope that this will be taken as a sign of grace by reviewers, although it may be a disappointment to the reader.

# I

## *Inglorious War*

I LEFT THE READER of *Another Part of the Wood* in the blackout on the first night of the war. The blackout was symbolic. It extended to every form of pleasure, recreation or enlightenment. Theatres and concert halls were in darkness, museums and galleries were closed, most art dealers shut up shop. It was as if the awful prospect of another war had to be marked by some sort of penitential ritual. Active people spent their time in evacuating children to the country in order to save them from an imminent air attack. The children, for whom the darkness of the country and the uncanny silence, broken only by the cries of animals, were quite as alarming as an air raid, spent miserable months, and gradually filtered back to London, in time for the raids that began a year later than had been anticipated.

I was fortunate in that I had an immediate, unquestionable duty: to see that the National Gallery pictures were in safety. England is full of large houses, and I thought it would be easy to find a proprietor who would have welcomed the quiet occupation of his house by famous pictures rather than by rowdy and incontinent evacuees. But in practice the difficulties were great. The house had to be near a town and station, but remote, as far as we could then suppose, from any target that might invite air attack. It had to be strong and dry; and above all it had to have one door, or window, big enough to allow the passage of the largest picture in the Gallery, Van Dyck's *Charles I on Horseback*. Almost the only house that passed all these tests was Penrhyn Castle, near Bangor.

The larger pictures went there, the smaller to the National Library of Wales at Aberystwyth. As I was also Surveyor of the King's Pictures, I included with the National Gallery pictures a selection from Hampton Court and Buckingham Palace; but I was defeated by the Raphael Cartoons, which are the property of the Crown. They had been in South Kensington since 1865 and the Victoria and Albert Museum had grown up around them. They could not be got out. They were too fragile to roll, so that the only course was to build a sort of air raid shelter for them inside the Museum.

Thanks to the efficiency of our scientific advisor, F. I. G. Rawlins and an admirable railway man called Inspector Bagshaw, the pictures arrived safely at Penrhyn Castle, and as soon as possible I visited them. Penrhyn cannot have been a cheerful setting for ordinary life, and with its dark walls covered by large, dark canvasses it was exceptionally dismal. The pictures, far from decorating the walls, appeared only as areas of discoloured varnish. I had already decided that this would be a good occasion to carry out a programme of cleaning, and had persuaded the restorer whom we most often employed, Mr Holder, that his war-work would be to come to Bangor and, for a tiny fee, set to work on this programme. It was a big risk, as Holder, the gentlest of men, had shown ominous signs of balancing some inner distress with the help of the bottle, and exile to the rather dismal atmosphere of Bangor might have pushed him further down the same slope. Kill or cure: in fact it cured him; throughout the war, in even more discouraging circumstances, he never showed a trace of addiction.

Holder was a restorer of the old, pre-scientific school. Gentleness and vast experience were his merits. To see him touch the surface of a picture with his swab of cotton wool was like watching a keeper picking up a baby partridge. The other restorer we had employed was the pioneer of scientific restoration in England, Helmut Ruhemann. He also agreed to work for the Gallery during the war, although on very different terms, and ultimately settled in Gloucestershire, where a number of the smaller pictures were housed in Lord Lee's gallery.

Now that almost every exhibited picture in the Gallery has been cleaned I am sorry that I did not carry my cleaning activities even further. The whole effect is incomparably more exhilarating than it was before the war, and the one picture that cannot be cleaned, the *Petrus Christus*, lent by Lord Verulam, looks like something out of an old attic. I doubt if a single picture has been damaged, much less 'ruined', although I confess that I liked Rubens's *Helena Fourment* rather better under her thin golden varnish. Cleaning is a battle won, and I can claim to have made, during the war, the first timid steps.

★    ★    ★    ★    ★

Most of the smaller pictures from the Gallery were in the National Library of Wales at Aberystwyth. This was a much more attractive town than Bangor, and the whole atmosphere was more humane. The chief drawings of the British Museum Print Room were also stored there, under the charge of A. E. Popham. He was a friend of mine, an admirable scholar and master of dry, ironical wit, spoken in the high accents of Bloomsbury. He had been through one war and showed no enthusiasm for a second. When asked what he was doing as war-work, he replied "making a catalogue of drawings by Parmigiano". It was a masterly catalogue, and will be remembered with gratitude when other forms of war-work are forgotten. There was another great scholar in Aberystwyth, Johannes Wilde, who had become a friend of ours when he was in the Kunsthistorisches Museum of Vienna. He was incomparably the most distinguished member on the staff of that institution but, as he had entered it late, he was junior to several mediocrities who were enraged when visiting scholars like Mr Berenson asked to see Wilde. I believe that everyone who knew him will agree that he was one of the sweetest and gentlest human beings in the world. The officials and employees of the Museum used to greet him with the obligatory "*Heil Hitler*"; to hear the accents with which he replied "*Gruss Gott*" was a beautiful experience. As he was married to a very boring Jewish lady he was bound to become a victim of the Anschluss, but his friend Antoine Seilern (the kindest of men) got him out, and he came to stay with us at Lympne, where my younger son taught him English.

Aberystwyth was a happy escape from the joyless atmosphere of London and the grim discomfort of Bangor. Unfortunately the blackout extended to Aberystwyth, and Wilde was arrested one evening returning from the Library, because a torch was projecting from his pocket. The Authorities decided that he was a dangerous alien, and must be deported to Canada. Many perfectly innocent scholars, scientists and men of letters shared the same fate, and not a few of them were drowned when their ships were torpedoed. I knew the Minister responsible, Osbert Peake, and innocently went to see him to ask that some kind of enquiry, at least, should be made before deportation was enforced. I should have realised that such decisions were taken in quite different quarters, and a Minister was, or believed himself to be, powerless to alter them. In time of war all countries behave equally badly, because the power of action is handed over to stupid and obstinate men. Fortunately Wilde survived, and returned to England after the war to become, through the Courtauld Institute, the most beloved and influential teacher of art history of his time.

When, in 1940, German air-raids began in earnest, it became clear that to put our pictures in apparently remote places like Bangor was no real security. A bombing force, returning from Liverpool, might easily have dropped its unexpended bombs on Bangor. I put the problem to my Trustees, some of whom advised sending the pictures to Canada. Arthur Lee, who had already given his own excellent collection of early goldsmiths' work to Toronto, was strongly of this opinion. I did not like the idea at all, and had already begun to look for shelter underground. This was not easy, as most underground shelters, tubes, mines, etc. were already occupied. Once more it was the indispensable Rawlins who saved the situation. He discovered a vast, abandoned slate quarry in the midst of a hill called the Manod, not far from the hellish town of Blaenau Ffestiniog in North Wales. It must have supplied half the roofs of Liverpool, and contained a cave called 'The Cathedral', which was on the scale of Karnak. When pressure was put on me to export the pictures I sent a short memorandum to Mr Churchill. It came back the same day, with a note in red ink "Bury them in the bowels of the earth, but not a picture shall leave this island, W.S.C.". Like a fool I never had this document photographed. I took it to the Treasury and the Office of Works, and they authorised me to look for a suitable hiding place. I returned with a report on the Manod caves and, since Mr Churchill's word was now law, they agreed on all the necessary action. It was not an easy job. The way to the Manod caves was up a disused mountain track, which had to be made good if it were to take vans full of large canvasses. When one got to the entrance it was only five feet high, and to reach the caves one had to go along a tunnel (called a level), stretching for about 350 yards, also five feet high. This tunnel had to be enlarged in order that the *Charles I on Horseback* could pass along it.

All this I discovered when I visited the site with Jane and Christabel Aberconway (we were staying with her at Bodnant). Jane was terrified by the drive up, and suffered from claustrophobia, but she and Christabel crawled along the level, led by a light which was frequently extinguished, and were duly impressed by 'The Cathedral'. In retrospect I am amazed that I had the courage to propose such an ambitious, expensive and hazardous scheme to a government department. More amazing still is the speed with which it was carried out. In peace time it would have taken seven years, spent in estimates, tenders, scientific tests, disputes about ownership and quarrels with the local authorities. In war time it took a few months. The level was hollowed out, and inside the caves were built huts, calculated to house the whole Gallery, plus the pictures of Mr Gulbenkian and a few from the Royal Collection. These huts were air-conditioned by a machine at the other end of the 'level'. We were very proud of it, and, in order to show how essential it was to the well-being of the pictures, we left one valueless work outside in the saturated cave. At the end of the war it was found to be in perfect condition, and looked rather healthier than the pictures which had been coddled by air-conditioning in their huts.

The time came for the transference of the pictures from Bangor and Aberystwyth to the Manod caves and once more it was Rawlins who organised the hazardous undertaking. He had thought of every detail, and had discovered that at one point the road passed under a bridge that took a local train from Bala to Blaenau. By hollowing out the road it would be possible for our largest cases to pass underneath. He miscalculated by half an inch, and the case containing *Charles I on Horseback* and Sebastiano del Piombo's *Raising of Lazarus* was stuck, irrevocably as it seemed under the bridge. We all stood silent, and I was reminded of the moment in Ranke's *History of the Popes*, when the ropes lifting the great obelisk in St Peter's Square began to fray. The crowd had been sworn to silence, but one sailor from Bordighera could not restrain himself, "Acqua alle tende" he shouted. Silence was broken. "Let the air out of the tyres" we all said in chorus. It was done and, grinding under, scraping over, the huge packing case passed through.

Introducers, wishing to commend me to an audience, used, in the days before *Civilisation*, to speak of me as the man who saved the nation's pictures during the war. This claim is entirely unjustified. The man was F. I. G. Rawlins. He received inadequate thanks from me and, as far as I know, no official recognition, not even an O.B.E. This was partly due to his diffidence, and partly because he was the most relentless bore I have ever known, and the kind of people who distribute honours fled from his approach.

We had built a studio for Holder, and he worked away uncomplainingly throughout the war, living somewhere in Ffestiniog. Near him, in a small isolated farmhouse, overshadowed by the Moelwyn mountains and surrounded by sycamores and fir trees, so that the sky was seldom visible from its windows, lived Martin Davies, who was the member of the staff in charge of the whole installation. He had always been a solitary character, and was said by his contemporaries in Cambridge to have emerged from his rooms only after dark; so this sunless exile was not as painful to him as it would have been to a less unusual man. In the morning he would emerge, thin and colourless as a ghost, and would be driven up to the caves, carrying with him a strong torch and several magnifying glasses. With these he would examine every square millimetre of a few pictures. In twelve years I hardly ever saw him look at a picture as a whole, but at a series of small areas of paint, which he usually found to be more or less damaged. The result of this scrutiny was noted, and he would then return to his retreat, in which he had housed most of the source-books from the National Gallery Library. These revealed to him how insecure was the evidence for all attributions in early art, and for the very existence of certain painters. It is indeed true that the history of art, like all history, is to a large extent an agreed fable, and perhaps only someone as passionately sceptical and as isolated as Martin Davies could have exposed so many convenient fallacies. The result of his relentless pursuit of the truth was a series of catalogues which, by their thoroughness, no less than their austerity, raised the standard of cataloguing in every country. Martin Davies's rejection of the easy-going assumptions of his predecessors sometimes led to a kind of perversity; but looking back at the old National Gallery catalogue by Collins Baker, which, to my great annoyance, was the standard work all the time I was at the Gallery, I am ashamed that I did not set Martin Davies to work on his catalogue the first week I was appointed director. Perhaps without the solitude of Ffestiniog he could never have achieved it.

I went to North Wales more frequently than was necessary. Naturally I visited the pictures in their caves, but for some reason I did not enjoy looking at them. Out of their frames, crammed close together, in no order except that imposed by the necessities of size they seemed to be dishonoured. Following the example of Martin Davies, I flashed torches at them and tried to study them in detail. But I could learn nothing, and realised that I am an incurable aesthete. Unless I enjoy a thing I cannot understand it. The real reason for my visits to the Manod was that I love the Welsh landscape. I dream repeatedly of a wide Welsh valley, twisting its way up to distant mountains, and wake in an ecstasy. In my old age I dream of it even more often than of food or girls, and it seems to play the dominating part in my unconscious mind. So a visit to North Wales was my escape from the war, made more overtly escapist by the place in which we stayed, a queer establishment named Portmeirion. This is a sort of hotel-village, where a rich architect called Clough Williams-Ellis had indulged his architectural dilettantism by building a number of cottages in different styles, and painting them different colours. They are arranged along the bank of a beautiful estuary with a genuine feeling for the picturesque. Only the shortage of food reminded one of the realities of the war. I was staying there, enjoying a brief escape, when I received a frenzied telephone call from the Welsh supervisor of the caves: "It's a crisis, it's a crisis. Come at once." He was not exaggerating. The rise in temperature and fall in humidity caused by the air-conditioned huts in the cave had so altered the consistency of the roof that large pieces of slate had fallen down, and it looked as if there might be a general collapse. The falling fragments had already hit the end of one of the huts and done considerable, although not irreparable, damage. The thought that the whole National Gallery might at any moment be buried under an avalanche of slate was not a pleasant one. The only course was hastily to erect steel scaffolding, from which to test the consistency of the ceiling, and to prop up those parts that

threatened to fall down. By a miracle there were no more falls
of any consequence.

★　　★　　★　　★　　★

Transferring the National Gallery pictures to what, with my
usual optimism, I believed to be places of safety was quickly done,
and I had to look for some full-time occupation. The Civil
Service had made a rule that none of its members should join the
armed forces. I could probably have persuaded them to make an
exception in my favour, as I was a Civil Servant only in so far as I
drew my salary from and made my reports to the Treasury, and
I was not the sort of civil servant who was likely to be of use in
wartime administration. I was not at all keen to join the Army. It
was not so much that I was afraid of being killed—where death is
concerned I am entirely fatalistic; but I dreaded the thought of
'going back to school', and joining the company of men with
whom I would have little in common. If I could not enter a club
without embarrassment, how much less could I enter a regiment?
I had got out of the habit of obeying orders, and I had visions of
hostile sergeant majors who would interpret my docility as
snootiness.

For anyone with my background there was an obvious source
of employment, the so-called Ministry of Information. This
notorious institution had been put together rather hastily when
the threat of war could no longer be ignored, and housed in an
enormous modern building, fortunately very solid, the Senate
House of London University. It was said to contain 999 employees.
The figure must have fluctuated with frequent comings and
goings, but it was basically correct. This large staff had been re-
cruited to deal with three or four different objectives. The first,
and most defensible, was censorship; the second the provision of
news; the third a feeble attempt at propaganda through various
media; and the fourth to provide a kind of wastepaper-basket into
which everyone could throw their grievances and their war-

winning proposals. It was the second of these activities that brought the Ministry into public disrepute, since hungry journalists believed that news was being withheld from them out of pure obstructiveness. There may have been some truth in this. The Ministry had been set up by the Treasury and staffed with civil servants drawn from various departments. Naturally these departments had been unwilling to surrender their best men, and there were a few obstructive individuals who confirmed the abuse, most of it unfair, that was levelled at the Civil Service. These were a small, but effective, element in the Ministry. Most of the 999 consisted of an uneasy mixture of so-called intellectuals, ex-journalists and advertising men, ex-politicians and discarded *éminences grises*. In this undirected orchestra it was necessary for each man to blow his own trumpet as loudly as he could. This alone seemed to disqualify me from joining the main section of the Ministry. Worse still, as I did not read newspapers, having been brought up by my father to believe that they were all lies, I had no conception of the sanctity that journalists attach to news. I therefore applied for a humble job in the censorship department, which, for sound reasons, kept itself apart from the chorus of boasting adventurers in the other departments. I was told that I would not be an appropriate member of the censorship division, and was asked to hold myself available for another appointment. After a day or two it came. I was to be the director of the Film Division.

It was an inexplicable choice, and was commonly attributed to the fact that in those days films were spoken of as 'pictures', and I was believed to be an authority on pictures. I had no qualifications for the job, knew absolutely nothing about the structure of the film world; and was not even aware of the difference between producers, distributors and exhibitors. I enjoy plunging into a new job, and learning about it as quickly as possible, but in this case I didn't know where to turn. There was nothing to be learnt from my predecessor in the job. He was a man named

Sir Joseph Ball, who had secured the patronage of Mr Neville Chamberlain because he owned a reach of the River Test, and asked Mr Chamberlain down to fish. I paid him a routine call, and found a small, fat man sitting behind an empty desk, with lines of cigarette ash stretched across the folds of his waistcoat. He cannot have moved for a long time. He did not bother to be polite to me, and when I asked him about his staff said that he had never met them. I then moved on to the Deputy-Director, who was a sad old Admiral. He did know the names of two or three members of his staff, but said that he never could make out what they did. The time had now come for me to be ushered in to meet the Minister. He was an old Scots dominie, named Lord Macmillan, who had been at Johnny Graham's school in Greenock with my father, and, although slightly younger, had, by his diligence, rapidly outstripped him. The thought of this made him look at me with favour. Finally, I visited Sir Kenneth Lee, the Director-General. He was obviously a man of perfect integrity and good sense. He, at any rate, had given some thought to the function of a Film Division, and said, slowly and deliberately, that we should make a full-length feature film which would indirectly describe the reasons why we were fighting the war. I feebly replied that such films were extremely expensive, but he said that this would be no difficulty: he would arrange for what he called a revolving credit, running into millions. I doubted if that idea would commend itself to the Treasury. When finally I met my small staff I understood the Admiral's bewilderment. They themselves did not know what they were doing. But one thing was certain; they did not want to become in any way involved with the film industry. I, on the other hand, thought such involvement absolutely essential, and, to the rage of my staff, who felt very much the same sense of betrayal as my staff at the National Gallery had done when I made friends with the Trustees, I invited all the leading members of the industry to meet me.

At that date films and film-makers were suspect. The extravagances of Hollywood were headline news, and had spread to England through the enterprise of Alexander Korda. It is true that there were some rather sordid characters among the far too numerous newsreel companies. But the leaders of the film industry were remarkable men, intelligent, easy to deal with, and, for the most part, public-spirited. Two of them are still alive, Michael Balcon and Sidney Bernstein, and I am glad of an opportunity to record my gratitude for all the help they gave me almost forty years ago. They actually offered to work in my department for no salary. But the Treasury has always disliked members of an industry being co-opted for government services, and declined to appoint them. Perhaps in the end this was a wise decision, as they would have found Civil Service restraints intolerable. As for the irresistible Korda, he was indeed one of the most charming men I have ever met. He had been brought up as a poor boy on a Hungarian farm, and told me that the only thing he minded was when the chicken mess got stuck between his toes. How he achieved a considerable culture, perfect manners and all the *allure* of a man of the world, I cannot imagine. Korda had in fact made a propaganda film for the Government, begun before the war, called *The Lion has Wings*, but for some complicated reason it had been rejected by the distributors, and was never widely shown—no great loss; and it taught me the danger of government-sponsored feature films. It was Korda who suggested the plan which was to become the chief activity of the Film Division, the making of films so short (two minutes) that the exhibitors would admit them into their programmes. In the days before television commercials people did not realise how rapidly they could be persuaded, and two minutes which, as we all know, is a long time to keep silent, was really all we needed to inform.

Before going any further into my film activities I must return to the politics of the Ministry of Information. Lord Macmillan obviously lacked the necessary energy, and early in 1940 he was replaced by Sir John Reith. It looked on paper like a good appointment. Reith had built up from scratch an analogous institution, and was believed to be a great administrator, with the ruthlessness necessary to bring order out of chaos and give the Ministry a direction.

For several reasons things did not turn out like that. The Ministry of Information was not really at all similar to the BBC. To begin with it was a government department. This meant that Reith was subject to Cabinet instructions, and in order to get his way had to be to some extent a politician. Reith hated and despised politicians; and he despised, almost equally, journalists, on whose co-operation the Ministry was ultimately dependent. Then, by a cruel stroke of irony, the independence of the BBC, for which he had fought so hard, became a major obstacle. Ideally the Ministry and the BBC should have complemented each other; but unfortunately Reith's bitter feelings about the BBC had, if anything, increased in the years since he resigned, and he had never disguised his low opinion of his successor, my old tutor Sir Frederick Ogilvie. He would not attempt the close daily co-operation that should have existed between them. Towering above all these difficulties was Reith's own extraordinary character. He has been described as a soul in torment. Perhaps; but it was a torment of his own making, the torment of an almost crazy ambition. He genuinely believed that God had destined him to lead the country in its hour of need, as de Gaulle was later to lead France; and it was partly with this in mind that he had left the BBC. In his diary he concedes that he would have accepted the Ambassadorship to Washington, or even the Viceroyship of India; and he was hurt when neither of these posts was offered him. To be Minister of Information was a comedown, which only his strong sense of duty led him to accept.

Such was the extraordinary being who battered on the door of my small office on January 3rd, 1940. He battered because he had made up his mind that the door would open inwards, and it actually opened outwards. By the time I had reached the door he was purple with frustration and physical exhaustion, and it was with some trepidation that I followed him to his office for a 'chat'. There followed the questions about my religious beliefs, which appear in all accounts of Reith, and must have been a pure formality; otherwise he would have had practically no staff at all. I managed to come fairly well out of these, as I am a persistent Bible reader, although my motives may not be the same as those of a Presbyterian minister. He then said to me suspiciously "You have an independent income". I admitted that I had. "That's bad", he said. I answered that both William Morris and Ruskin had independent incomes, and without them literature, design and the socialist movement itself would have been much the poorer. "It's all right for you", he said, "but it's not so good for me. I can't get you to obey me so easily." This was the first of many surprisingly frank things Reith said to me. "This place is a mess", he said. I agreed. "I want you to draw up a new form of constitution and let me have it tomorrow morning." This was a tall order, as there were many aspects of the Ministry of which I was entirely ignorant. But I said I would try. From all this it will be apparent that he had taken a fancy to me; and, to tell the truth, I had taken a fancy to him. He was so crazily independent of all accepted opinions, so totally unlike the standard public man. I returned next morning with the promised plan of a new constitution. As ill luck would have it I had included the post of Deputy-Director-General. "That is the post for you", said Reith. This was too much. I declined. Reith was deeply disappointed by my lack of enterprise, and asked me to think it over. I did not worry because I knew that the senior members of the Ministry would never allow Reith to make such a ridiculous appointment, and, as far as I can remember, the post of Deputy-Director-General was temporarily dropped. But Reith was determined on my aggrandisement and invented for me the post of Controller of Home Publicity, which I could not properly refuse.

This was the end of my usefulness to the Ministry. As Director of the Film Division I had had a definite job to do, and had done it fairly well. My new post, although it gave me more prestige, was shapeless and indeterminate. Various departments, including the Film Division, were nominally 'under' me, but, except on points of principle, their directors had to run them in their own way. I was fortunate in that my successor in the Film Division was my friend Jack Beddington ('Beddy-ole-man' of *Another Part of the Wood*), and he ran the Film Division excellently. One of the troubles about my new position was that I became head of the wastepaper-basket department; everyone with a scheme for saving the country, reforming the world, or, more modestly, spending vast sums of money on advertising campaigns with an unspecified aim, addressed themselves to me. They always said the same thing "All we want is a blessing". I knew that the faintest sign of benediction would have been interpreted as a promise of money. They went away unblessed and resentful, some of them actually in tears. Continually disappointing adventurers or crackpots, continually saying saying "No", is a depressing activity, especially to anyone like myself who likes saying "Yes".

The sensible, slow moving Kenneth Lee could not for long work in harness with Reith, and his place as Director-General was taken by a man who has been too rapidly forgotten, Frank Pick. He had been chief executive officer of London Passenger Transport. He was a brilliant administrator and, with the help of his friend, the architect Charles Holden, had made that institution the chief influence on applied art of its day. Buildings, posters and lettering (he gave currency to the type-face of 'Johnston's sans'), all conformed to an ideal of tidy, reasonable, and somewhat puritanical taste, which, in retrospect, does not look very exciting, except for the posters of McKnight Kauffer, but which showed a feeling of responsibility towards good design more admirable than the haphazard vulgarity of today. Pick came from Lincolnshire, and spoke very quietly, with a Scunthorpe accent. He had been a scholar at St Peter's School, York, but must have been largely self-taught, and he had made a good job of it. He was a great reader, and noted down things that struck him on slips of paper, written in green ink in a very clear hand. When I differed from him, which was seldom, he would send me back a note in green ink 'A just rebuke. F.P.' He was a close friend and admirer of Mr Bevin, and through him I owe my acquaintance with one of the few great Englishmen of our time. But he was not a friend for Mr Churchill. It was a classic confrontation of cavalier and roundhead. Pick is said to have told Mr Churchill that he would never countenance any form of propaganda which was not in accordance with the strict truth and his own conscience. After he had left Mr Churchill said "Never, never again allow that shanctimonious bus-conductor into my sight". As Reith loathed Mr Churchill to the point of mania (see his Diary *passim*) the Ministry was not well placed to solicit favours in the highest quarter; and I see from Jane's diary that I was occasionally called on to act as an intermediary. Several entries run: 'K all morning at War Cabinet', or 'K to Mr Churchill'. I have not the faintest recollection of these august occasions; but I do remember with pleasure making films or planning to make them. Three against careless talk, made by Michael Balcon at Ealing, were good short thrillers. We prepared a long film on minesweepers, and Graham Greene wrote an excellent script for a film on the Gestapo in England. I also planned to do a film on Anglo-French collaboration, with Leslie Howard and Danièle Darrieux in the leading parts, to be produced by René Clair. Everything was arranged, and I went to Paris with Leslie to see our brilliant producer. It was about a fortnight before the German advance. After the long faces of England everyone in Paris seemed very jolly, and I remember a delicious dinner with Noel Coward, who was doing some kind of liaison job. I naturally saw a number of my opposite numbers in the French Propaganda Ministry, and talking to them I suddenly realised why everyone in Paris was so jolly. The French were not going to fight. They had borne the brunt of the first war, both in losses of men and in occupied territory, and they did not intend to go through it again. When I returned home I reported my conclusions to Mr Churchill. This time I do remember the interview. He sat hunched up, and occasionally grunted and nodded. He did not speak. He knew it already.

I can see why at this point in the war Mr Churchill resisted the idea of propaganda. All the propaganda necessary he did himself; we could deal only in generalities. From Narvik onwards all our enterprises had been failures. We could not reassure people about our strength. We had, I believe, only seventeen tanks, and I was able to borrow three of them to show our great tank force grinding round Parliament Square, the number plates and drivers being changed for each circuit. We had really nothing to offer except a lot of hot air about our war aims, which, after lengthy discussion, we decided should be *democracy*. In fact we were fighting to save our skins; and we very nearly lost them.

Soon after the fall of Paris I received a visit from M André Maurois. I am an admirer of his biographies, and when I had met him in the past I had enjoyed his conversation. On this occasion the graceful raconteur was in a very different mood. All he wanted to do was to attack England for having stood up to Hitler. He said that our obstinacy was an insult to France, a menace to Europe and a crime against history. All this was said with passion and a certain malevolence. I realised that at this moment the French, having failed to fight the Germans, felt they must fight someone, and I listened patiently—but inwardly I was seething with rage, and after about twenty minutes diatribe I showed him the door. He said he was on his way to America, where he could pour out his far-sighted view of history into more receptive ears. If a Jew like Maurois felt so bitterly opposed to our resistance that he had to repeat it to every Englishmen he met, what, I wondered, could the other French intellectuals, many of whom had been secretly pro-German for some time, have been saying about us?

★    ★    ★    ★    ★

Inevitably Reith was sacked. He had not cleared up the chaos of the Ministry, only added to it by various impulsive and high-handed decisions. His place was taken by Churchill's friend Duff Cooper, who had the political experience that Reith so conspicuously lacked, but with his graceful intelligence had a low opinion of the 'common man' and was almost less well qualified than Reith to placate the press. Some months after his appointment I paid a call on Frank Pick, and found him pacing about his room. "Do you know what's just happened to me?" he said. "I've been sacked. The little man has sacked me. Never happened to me before." His successor, Walter Monckton, said to me "That was the nearest thing to a genius that we are likely to see here". Pick retired to his house in Hampstead which was bombed; and shortly afterwards he died. I have often wondered what happened to all those slips of paper with quotations in green ink, which he said he threw into trunks, and which would have been the legacy of a strong, original mind.

With the departure of Reith and Pick I lost interest in the Ministry of Information, and the Ministry lost interest in me. At the administrative level our lives were poisoned by a character named Colonel Scorgie, who had been introduced into the Ministry from the Stationery Office in order to enforce discipline. He gave us a short lecture to the effect that a civil servant's duty was to obey unquestioningly the orders of his superior officer. He was a strong pro-Halifax man, and greeted with open disgust the appointment of Mr Churchill as Prime Minister. Under these circumstances it was difficult for all his staff to obey him without question. He was a man with whom it was impossible to have any human relationship. He saw to that. I offered Walter Monckton my resignation. He was a friend of mine and, with his matchless powers of persuasion, he bamboozled me into staying on, which I did for another year.

As things turned out the responsibilities of the Controller of Home Publicity became more serious and more painful. After Dunkirk a great many reasonable people were frightened. Mr Churchill's wonderful rhetoric gave a temporary lift to their feelings, but when they came to think calmly about their position they could see that if the Germans chose to invade us we wouldn't stand a chance. I believe that a good many members of the Ministry, as well as Scorgie, were secretly in favour of a negotiated peace. Not a good state of mind for a propaganda Ministry.

I was instructed to set up a body called The Home Morale Emergency Committee. 'This was our finest hour.' Yes; but, as our information revealed, only just; and we had to use whatever feeble means that were at our command to reassure the doubters. We were not ourselves a very warlike body, and I remember one of our number, Harold Nicolson, who was far too civilised a man to be concerned with propaganda, saying several times "All we can do is lie on our backs with our paws in the air and hope that no one will stamp on our tummies". The government had decided to circulate to every home in the country a document entitled *If the Invader Comes*. I thought it was an unwise decision, since it could contain nothing but the most obvious advice, 'Keep clear of the roads', etc., and its very existence would put into people's heads the idea that the invader *was* coming. I wrote this useless document* and it was duly circulated to many millions of homes. There was no evidence that anyone read it, so after all it did no harm.

A more hopeful attempt to keep up people's spirits illustrates the character of Colonel Scorgie. I was worried by reports of low morale (and no wonder) in the air-raid shelters of the East

---

* I see in Harold Nicolson's diary that he says he wrote it. It is not an honour that I would keenly contest. But as a matter of fact, I did.

End, and had arranged for films to be shown in some of the largest shelters. The exhibitors, with whom I was on good terms, asked only a trifling fee. The decision fell under my competence as Controller of Home Publicity, but had to be referred to Scorgie: 'Certainly not. A criminal waste of the tax-payers' money. I absolutely forbid it.' No wonder I felt discouraged, and that the whole of the winter of 1940–41 is a blank to me.

What my insignificant Committee could not do for morale was achieved by the RAF. We were close friends with the Air Chief Marshal, Sir Cyril Newall, and heard from him day by day the story of the Battle of Britain. It was a miracle of courage and endurance that can never be overstated, and often we were down to our last weary crew. Cyril was a calm and cheerful man, but I could sometimes see in his face that he thought it was touch and go.

After September 7th, my chief memory of the Ministry of Information was of the air-raids. It was, as I have said, a solid building and I felt fairly safe in the cellar. The Senate House was hit three or four times and I never felt a tremor. I was fortunate in that my cellar companion was one of the men I admired most in England, Arthur Waley. From his works one can deduce his scholarship and his sensitive use of language. But only in these midnight conversations did I come to realise his immense range of knowledge. The tiresome part was not fear of death, but dragging one's mattress up and down every day (one couldn't leave it, as it would immediately have been stolen by the messenger boys).* Then it was miserable to go out in search of breakfast

---

* Apropos of the messenger boys: one of them stole a gilt bronze gothic figure of St. John which I loved so much that I had taken it to the Ministry and locked it in my book case. I supposed that it had been melted down; but to my astonishment found it thirty years later in the Museum of Nuremberg. What fence was clever enough to sell it to Germany in those years? I never told the director, as I thought it would give him a bad conscience.

The Manod caves in Wales

K.C. and Mr W. A. Holder cleaning a de Koninck

with the smell of burning in the air, and the clink of broken glass under one's feet. We were hungry, as the alerts sounded before dinner, the canteen ran out of food and most of the local restaurants had closed. But I must recall one exception, because it led to a long-standing friendship. The Eiffel Tower, which, under an easy-going proprietor called Stulik, had become a tourist attraction for those who wished to stare at the drunks and lechers of London's upper Bohemia from Augustus John downwards, had been taken over by a Greek Cypriot named Jani Stais, who purified it, and changed its name to the White Tower. He loved young artists and helped my friends of the so-called Euston Road School. During the war he lost his whole staff. He used to shout orders down the lift shaft, run down to the kitchen to cook the meal himself, put it on the lift and shout for it to be sent up. He had very few customers; but he survived to make the White Tower one of the best and most fashionable restaurants in London; and Mr Stais is still there, as friendly and unpretentious as ever.

Can I say that the Ministry was a sort of education to me? Certainly I learnt to deal with unimaginable situations, and I managed to accommodate myself to the infinite variety of egotisms that is comprehended under the term 'ordinary men'. In the press bar I learnt to make the appropriate noises, but I never lost my feeling of isolation and knew that I was wasting my time. My most lasting achievement happened in this way. I was coming downstairs from the canteen when I met John Betjeman, whom I had persuaded the personnel director to let me engage as a temporary advisor. Knowing that he shared my tastes I said "John, you must go up to the canteen. A most ravishing girl has just appeared there—clear brown complexion, dark eyes, wearing a white overall—she's called Miss Joan Hunter Dunn." John didn't need telling twice, and the result will probably be familiar to most of my readers.

Finally, my introduction into the film world led to real friendships which lasted as long as those friends lived (and too many of them died). They will appear in this book later on. It might have been worse but I was glad when it was over. Brendan Bracken had become Minister, and Cyril Radcliffe Director-General. They were an ideal combination and succeeded at last in giving the Ministry some point. I belonged to the old, amateurish, ineffective, music-hall-joke Ministry, and had long been an unnecessary member of even that ramshackle body. Cyril was a friend of mine, for whom I had a great admiration. He told me to leave in the kindest possible manner.

★ ★ ★ ★ ★

During the first year of the war my life was not entirely unproductive, and I will record three activities which I look back on without shame. A few weeks after the outbreak of war I set in motion a plan by which artists should be commissioned to make a record of the war. I was no doubt thinking of the Canadian war artists scheme in the 1914–18 war. In *Another Part of the Wood* I describe how deeply I was influenced by the exhibition of these artists' work at the Royal Academy in 1917. However, I was not so naïve as to suppose that we should secure many masterpieces, or even a record of the war that could not be better achieved by photography. My aim, which of course I did not disclose, was simply to keep artists at work on any pretext, and, as far as possible, to prevent them from being killed.* There were many technical difficulties in setting up such a body. Money was easily obtained, as it always was in those days, but the problems of security were daunting. We solved them having on our committee representatives of the armed forces and of the Home Office, who obtained from their departments the necessary permits. I could never have done this on my own, but fortunately I

---

* In this I was not altogether successful, as two distinguished artists, Eric Ravilious and Thomas Hennell, were killed while carrying out artist's commissions.

had discovered a perfect secretary to the committee, a civil servant, who had begun life as a serious painter, named E. M. O'R. Dickey. He knew all the ins and outs, and was devoted and resourceful beyond measure. As this was the first time the government had patronised modern artists on a large scale (incredible as it now seems, the Tate Gallery had no purchase grant of its own), it was important to form a committee that would be more or less acceptable to conservatives and yet be in sympathy with the left. In Royal Academy circles I was then considered a dangerous revolutionary, and Gerald Kelly had been deputed to call on me at the National Gallery to ask me if I would stop buying the work of young artists. I pointed out to him that two of my young friends had recently calculated that if they shared a studio they could live on £85 a year. His own income in the preceding year was nearer £80,000, and his only problem was whether to lay down Château Lafitte or buy Château Batailly that was ready for drinking. To tell the truth, I lost my temper, which I have done only three times in my life. But he forgave me, and we became friends.

The story of this interview will show the reader how careful I had to be in the choice of my committee. I was fortunate in that the professors of painting at the Royal College of Art and the Slade were modest and liberal minded men, and nobody could object to them. Nor could the conservatives object to my old friend Muirhead Bone, although he had always been a champion of modern painting. The Academy itself sent a most improbable representative, Russell Flint, who turned out to be a charming and open-minded man. We had over one hundred meetings, and never a harsh word spoken. I have said that I did not suppose that the war artists scheme would produce many outstanding works of art. In fact it did. Paul Nash, who was seconded to the Royal Air Force, painted two or three beautiful and moving pictures, *The Dead Sea of German Aeroplanes*, and the splendid, tonic *Battle of Britain*, which more than any photograph records our feelings at that time. John Piper was the ideal recorder of bomb damage, and Graham Sutherland transferred his feelings for the menacing forms of roots and trees to twisted girders and burnt out bales of paper. Above all the tube shelters gave Henry Moore a subject that humanised his classical feeling for the recumbent figure, and led to a series of drawings which will, I am certain, always be considered the greatest works of art inspired by the war. Of course we commissioned a great number of portraits, and I hoped to discover some painter who would give new life to this declining form of art. But, alas, the only portraits that rose above mediocrity were Epstein's bronze busts.

At the end of the war we found that we had on our hands over 10,000 items, and the problem of distributing them occupied us for months. The Tate had a pick of the works of art; the Imperial War Museum of the most important records. The rest went to galleries all over the country and the Commonwealth. As a result I have found in the gallery of a small provincial town in Australia a very fair representation of contemporary British art.

In order to give employment to as many painters as possible we stretched the word 'war artists' far beyond the limit. Nevertheless there remained a number of respectable artists, mainly landscape painters, who could not possibly be concerned with a record of the war, and who were going through bad times. It occurred to me that they might be employed in making a record of parts of the countryside that were likely to be engulfed in urban development, or of good buildings that would almost certainly be destroyed.\* This seemed to be the kind of project that might appeal to the Pilgrim Trust and, while visiting my two picture depots in North Wales, I broke my journey at Harlech to call on Tom Jones, the original organiser of the Pilgrim Trust and then its secretary. He was (with Horace Wilson) the perfect type of the

---

\* This idea, thanks to the support of Reith, was realised under the title of The National Buildings Record.

*éminence grise*. He had a considerable influence on many aspects of public life, which he said he owed to his 'passion for anonymity'. He was intelligent, persuasive, intensely interested in human beings, and utterly incorruptible. He wished to use his position solely for the public good. Lord Hugh Cecil once said to me "I am a very good man, but my friends are very wicked"; and, leaving aside his fellow social workers in Wales, rather the same could be said of Tom Jones. From 1916 onwards he had been Lloyd George's closest confidant. He had not merely touched pitch; he had been up to his neck in it, and had not been defiled. I delighted in his company and was glad to see him in the setting of Coleg Harlech, his best loved creation. As he looked at it he quoted the saying of the Welsh giant Bendigeidran who, when he was attacking a castle, threw himself across the moat so that his army could walk over him, saying "Avo penn bid pont" (Not a conqueror but a bridge). I put my plan to him, and after a moment's pause he said "We are already committed to a similar scheme. It is still a secret, but I will ask Buck de la Warr (then Minister of Education) to see you about it." I went next week, and was told that Buck, having already secured a promise of £25,000 from the Pilgrim Trust, was going to ask the government for a grant of £25,000 to "do something to help the arts". He knew what the Treasury answer would be "We will give £25,000 if you can get an equal sum from other sources". After a decent interval he told the Treasury he had raised the necessary money; and so there came into existence the body known as the Council for the Encouragement of Music and the Arts. I remember a good deal of confusion in the early stages. Who was going to be chairman? The Treasury were anxious to find a place for Lord Macmillan, whose position as Minister of Information was obviously insecure. I believe he remained chairman for three years, but took little part in our activities.

From the beginning the Secretary of CEMA was an inspector of schools, named Miss Glasgow. The Board of Education believed that she would be that favourite Civil Service animal, a watchdog, but in fact she became the most ardent and active supporter of the new venture. The founder members, beside Lord Macmillan, were Tom Jones, Walford Davies, that irresistible populariser of music, myself, and a protege of T. J.'s named William Emrys Williams. He was a Secretary of a body named the British Institute of Adult Education (we were not ashamed of long titles until Mr Churchill changed the Local Defence Volunteers into the Home Guard), and had started a series of exhibitions under the more manageable title of Art for the People. I had opened one of these exhibitions in the first weeks of the war, and been much impressed by Williams's enthusiasm and intelligence. Under his guidance the new CEMA virtually continued the Art for the People scheme on a wider field. Such were our first faltering steps towards state support of the arts.

No doubt the Treasury thought that CEMA would end with the war. It had been persuaded to give its contribution towards 'the encouragement of Music and the Arts' by the argument that this would be a social service. At the end of 1939 people were still grumbling at the black-out (little knowing what was in store for them later), and it was urged that a few concerts and amateur theatricals would give them something to do in the evenings. I doubt if Tom Jones himself had thought of CEMA as the beginning of state patronage; it was not a subject that interested him. But naturally it interested me, and I belonged to that section of the Council who wanted to see Miss Glasgow's 'music-makers roaming the country' turned into national orchestras. The difference of view was resolved in 1942, when Macmillan retired and his place was taken by John Maynard Keynes. He was not the man for wandering minstrels and amateur theatricals. He believed in excellence. In four years he transformed CEMA, the social service, into a universal provider of the arts known by the title, which I am said to have invented, of the Arts Council. Keynes was every bit as clever and charming as he is reported to have been, but, although I was on good terms with him, we never became friends. One reason may have been that by this time he was too tired and busy to make new friends. Another that, although I admired his brilliance, I thought he displayed it too unsparingly. I would not like to define the word arrogant, but at least I can say, in a well-worn phrase, that he never dimmed his headlights. Although a kind man, I have seen him humiliate people in a cruel way. However, we owe him the Arts Council, and it would amuse his ghost if it could perceive that the body which was started with £25,000 of Treasury money now has a government grant of close on forty million.

The third activity of these early war-years to which I can look back with pleasure was the institution of the National Gallery concerts. As I have said, fear of immediate air-raids, followed by a kind of gloomy self-immolation, had put a stop to all theatres and concerts. English people did not mind being deprived of pictures, but they were hungry for music. For some mysterious patriotic reason the BBC provided no serious music, but endless programmes of 'Sandy Macpherson at the Organ'. During this doleful period Myra Hess, accompanied by her friend Denise Lassimonne, called on me to ask if I would allow her to give a concert in the Gallery once a week. I greatly admired her playing, but I had never met her and was immediately captivated by her enthusiasm and complete absence of affectation. She had a jolly, rolling walk, and a strong element of the old trouper. But where music was concerned she was intensely serious and made no concessions to fashion or to any other form of pressure. Bach, Beethoven and Brahms for her. She once made to me the very revealing confession that Mozart made her feel uneasy—"He changes so terribly". And she rightly decided against putting experimental music into the programmes, because "What people need is reassurance".

I said she must not give a single concert in the Gallery. She must give one every day. She recovered rapidly from the shock, and said it could be done. She knew most of the leading performers, and would have no difficulty in persuading them to appear for trifling fees. We decided that the concerts should take place between 1 and 2 o'clock, and that the admission fee should be 1s. Thanks to the ingenuity of our head attendant, Mr Smith (who should have been a Field Marshal), we were able to rig up a makeshift platform under the dome. I suppose that we put a notice in the papers, but there was no other form of publicity. We had no idea whether or not people would come. On the day there were queues all along the north side of Trafalgar Square, and our concert area was packed with tired and anxious people, standing or sitting on the floor. Myra gave the first concert, and played Beethoven's *Appassionata* and her own arrangement of Bach's *Jesu joy of man's desiring*. I confess that, in common with half the audience, I was in tears. This was what we had all been waiting for—an assertion of eternal values.

I can claim no credit for the National Gallery concerts, except that I said "every day", and negotiated the obstacles formally put in our way by government departments. There was a Home Office ruling that not more than 200 people should be gathered together in one place. The Office of Works had already 'earmarked' the National Gallery for government use. Both these departments in their strange, stiff way behaved well, and the Home Office never raised an eyebrow when our audiences rose to over 1,000. H.M. Customs and Excise exempted us from entertainment tax. But these were routine matters to which at that date I was accustomed. The real heroine of the whole occasion was Myra. She gave up a very lucrative tour in America (which she loved), she attended every concert and played herself twice a week. She worked late into the night, with a kind and competent friend, a musician named Howard Ferguson, arranging all the programmes and cajoling all the performers. She must have been worn out; but it never showed; she was sustained by the romantic ardour of someone who sees a dream coming true. We had some minor troubles. The bells of St. Martin's rang every day for five minutes at 1.25. Regimental bands played *Soldiers of the Queen* in Trafalgar Square. I had to use a little diplomacy to moderate these rival sonorities. When the bombing began, and the Gallery was hit several times, the glass of the dome was broken, and the rooms downstairs were too small for a proper audience. Anyone but Myra would have given up in despair.

We had intended to limit ourselves to piano and chamber music, but quite soon we had an orchestral concert, conducted (this shows where Myra belonged) by Sir Henry Wood. We became musically very ambitious and, in spite of Myra's misgivings, played all Mozart's piano concertos in chronological order. I believe that many Londoners who remember the first year of the war will agree that the National Gallery concerts were amongst the few rewarding intervals in their daily lives.

My only direct participation in the concerts was when, on January 1st, 1940, I conducted Haydn's *Toy Symphony*. People who have never conducted an orchestra imagine that it must be fun to stand up and wave a baton, while the players do the work. In fact it is extremely difficult. I happened to be lunching in the company of Sir Thomas Beecham a few days before the event, and told him what I had undertaken. Beecham, so irresponsible in other respects, was deadly serious about conducting, and made me produce a score of this modest, familiar work, which he went through with me in detail; so that, when the event took place, I was equally serious, and was angry with Myra and Elena Gerhardt for playing the fool. We owed it to our devoted audience to give the best possible performance. It sounds absurd, but this experience gave me an insight into the art of conducting which I have valued ever since.

Myra and I became firm friends, and we used to spend happy evenings at her house in Hampstead, often in the company of Sir Stafford Cripps, listening to her playing the piano. How she loved to play—nothing could stop her. Her room was furnished in a style identical with the rooms of Mr Bernard Shaw and Miss Popham, headmistress of Cheltenham Ladies' College: a heterogeneous collection of chintzes, many photographs, much modern brass of vaguely Indian character, although no doubt made in Birmingham, a procession of elephants carved in black wood, with white tusks. This was the standard decor of the virtuous English intellectuals of the early 20th century. One might call it the Fabian style; and I have no doubt that the sittingrooms of H. G. Wells and Mr Attlee would have been just the same. Why the English of this generation lacked all response to the visual harmony of their surroundings it is hard to say. I suppose they had reacted against the comfortable clutter of Victorian interiors, and there was not as yet a modern style to put in its place. However, we were not there to look, but to listen, which we did, supported by a glass of milk or lemonade, far into the night, while Myra played on inexorably. After the war, when I left the Gallery, the concerts came to an end, and Myra spent most of her time in America. Alas, we never met again.

★    ★    ★    ★    ★

I see that I have already crossed the border between public and private life, and it is time for me to say something about my ordinary human existence. We had had the sense to sell our large house in Portland Place, and take a set of chambers in Gray's Inn Square, looking out over the garden and the mulberry tree planted by Sir Walter Raleigh. Jane, with the help of Marion Dorn, made it into one of the prettiest places we have ever lived in. The diningroom held only six people. We lived there contentedly until it was bombed.

When war was imminent I decided, with great sorrow, that we must leave our house at Lympne. It overlooked Romney Marsh, which was obviously the only place in England where an invading army could be deployed. Napoleon's great flotilla had aimed at this spot, and I had no doubt that Hitler's would do the same. A copy of the German plan for the invasion of England is in the Museum at Greenwich, and shows that I was correct. With fruitless German thoroughness the plan even shows our house. We rented a house called Upton, near Tetbury in Gloucestershire, thinking that if there was no invasion we should get back to Lympne after the war; but it was damaged by a bomb and the beautiful barn completely destroyed. We never had the heart to go back there. The Tetbury house had a distinguished façade in the style of John Wood, enough rooms for the children, for my mother and for several evacuated friends. How Jane coped with the move, which involved the usual discovery of dry rot, and with the installation of my library on the top floor, I cannot imagine.

The early months of 1940 were fantastically cold. Icicles hung from every twig, and tinkled as the wind disturbed them. Jane went heroically on, replacing the children's governess when she joined the WAAF, listening to my mother's complaints, and preparing to receive two more refugees, the Graham Sutherlands. I must add that the mood of heroism never left her throughout the year, and after Dunkirk she was one of the very few people of any intelligence who genuinely believed that we should win the war, supporting her belief by the story that when she was captain of the second hockey eleven at Malvern Ladies' College, they had beaten the first eleven by sheer will power. I visited Upton when I could, and took a great liking to Tetbury and the surrounding countryside. Sitting peacefully outside a pub called The Cock, where nothing, including the inn sign, had changed for well over a century, I did not like the thought of the Germans taking it all over, impoverishing and reforming us. I could not have foreseen that we would do this more thoroughly for ourselves.

We had a few neighbours; Lord Lee of Fareham (Uncle Arthur in *Another Part of the Wood*), and his adorable wife, were about four miles away; and further on in the village of Woodchester lived a character who did much to cheer us up, for he himself

was always cheerful, named Hiram Winterbotham. I do not think
I shall be accused of 'name dropping' if I mention him, because,
in spite of his gifts, he has remained completely unknown. He is
a man of infinite zest and curiosity, with a scientific knowledge
of gardening, and a passionate interest in architecture. During the
war he lived in a modest and somewhat austere Cotswold house,
and when I wanted to concentrate on a piece of writing I used to
go down there to stay. As a rule Hiram was away, occupied
in running aircraft factories in the company of his friend Alan
Jarves, who was Stafford Cripp's personal assistant. Alan was the
handsomest man I have ever seen, a good sculptor, with a wide
knowledge of art. He later became Director of the National
Gallery of Canada; but his face was his misfortune, and the last
years of his life were a tragedy. So when I went to Woodchester
I was alone, completely alone, because Hiram's cook usually
retired to bed, with some fancied illness, leaving me to fend for
myself. On one occasion she left a cold goose, which I ate through
steadily for five days, accompanied by a few potatoes, blackened
in the Aga cooker. Eggs and cheese were rationed and unobtain-
able; looking back on it I don't know how I survived. I went for
long walks in the snow, and I remember on one desolate Cotswold
hillside suddenly finding myself surrounded by about thirty little
children, all the same size and dressed in red, who hopped round
me crying out "Who's your name? Who's your name?" I
thought that hunger and solitude had brought on this rather
charming hallucination. It turned out afterwards that they came
from an orphanage and had escaped from their teacher.

The work on which I was engaged was a last desperate effort to
produce a piece of scholarship. While still writing about Leonardo
da Vinci I had turned my attention to the 'universal man' who
preceded him, Leon Battista Alberti. I had read all his works, and
made a vast quantity of notes, and it seemed a pity not to use this
material, especially as no adequate book on Alberti then existed.
I had laid the project aside when I went to the National Gallery,

but Alberti seemed an agreeable contrast to the Ministry of Information, and after I had been sacked I turned to him once more. Why has this immensely gifted and admirable man always proved so difficult a subject? Partly, I suppose, because no single scholar can know enough about both the social and moral codes of the higher bourgeoisie in the Renaissance, which is the chief subject of his voluminous *Opere Volgari*, and also about his architecture, which is his most durable claim to immortality. But there is another reason: that in spite of his beautiful appearance, there remains something unsympathetic about Alberti. He was altogether too good to be true, and lacked the engaging crankiness of Thomas Jefferson, whom in many respects he so closely resembled. Cold and hungry in my Cotswold retreat, I made hundreds more notes, but I never wrote the book, only a few lectures, one of which on his *della Pittura* will bear re-reading. Soon afterwards I was saved from further trouble by the discovery of a book on Alberti by a French scholar named Paul-Henry Michel which contains, in a rather more pedantic manner, practically all that I had intended to say about Alberti. The years spent on the subject were not entirely wasted as I learnt a great deal about the ethics of fifteenth-century Florence; I had also learned that this kind of plodding scholarship was not in my line, and I never returned to it.

Although most of my week-ends were spent in Gloucestershire Jane was frequently in 5 Gray's Inn Square during the summer of 1940. On September 7th we were coming back from opening an exhibition in Brighton when our train was held up. We took a car and, crossing Battersea Bridge, saw dense clouds of smoke rising from the Docks and the City. The raids had begun. At first we took them lightly and walked out to see what a raid was like, as if it were an exhibition of fireworks. Then a number of bombs fell in and around Gray's Inn Square, and finally we were blown out of bed (we had got bored with sleeping in the cellar) and landed, unhurt, on the other side of the room. We found that a bomb had blown out the two first floors, leaving our apartment hanging rather precariously over the void (I forget how we got downstairs). It was obviously time for Jane to return to Upton. Before the war Jane and I had seldom been separated from one another by more than a day or two. Now I was cut off from her for weeks at a time. Naturally I got into trouble of a kind which I need neither specify nor describe. But I would like to put on record that I am the least Strindbergian of men. Throughout my life women have shown me nothing but kindness, sweetness and forgiveness. The hell-hounds described by Strindberg, Ibsen, and even Henry James, and depicted by Munch, must exist, but they have never come my way.

When the raids grew less frequent Jane came up to stay at a large, cheerless hotel, across the Square from the Ministry, called the Russell. One evening when she had gone back to Upton, a bomb fell on the hotel, which went up in flames. I was contemplating it gloomily, considering whether one got extra coupons with which to replace clothes destroyed by enemy action, when Walter Monckton appeared. "Good God", he said, "is Jane in there?" He over-estimated my sang-froid.

★   ★   ★   ★   ★

The year 1941 has faded almost entirely from my mind and, as Jane does not seem to have kept a diary for that year, and I cannot find my engagement book, I cannot remember the most obvious dates. I do not even know when I was sacked from the Ministry of Information—spring, summer or autumn! I remember only two expeditions to visit what may be called *monuments historiques*. One of them, undertaken at the instigation of Mr Churchill, was to President de Valera, in order to discuss the Atlantic ports. Jane's aunt had been a friend of his, and her cousin was a prominent figure (afterwards Permanent Under-Secretary) in the Irish Foreign Office, so we had a domestic pretext for the flight. Moreover, John Betjeman had become English press attaché in Dublin, and had adopted the local colour so thoroughly that he signed his letters Sean O'Betjeman. In his company we visited Jane's birthplace in Merrion Square, the house in the suburbs in which she was brought up, and the beautiful Rococo Rotunda of which her mother, the first woman in Ireland to be a member of the College of Surgeons, had been the Master. Incidentally, while I was there London had one of its worst air raids, the only one I missed; so it must have been in the spring. De Valera treated us kindly, and, incredible as it sounds, I found him sympathetic. He was above all a dialectician, who loved to argue the opposite point of view. I discovered that if I put the case *against* Ireland granting us the use of the treaty ports, he would argue, with great skill, the case in favour. Naturally he did not intend to follow this pro-English policy, but he was fully aware of its advantages, and even its moral justification, and all this I could report to Mr Churchill. I believe that de Valera's reputation is now under a cloud, especially with his own adopted countrymen, who criticise his ideal of a pure and isolated Ireland. He was like a priest for whom the idea of progress has no meaning. No doubt that is why I liked him.

With my early admiration of Yeats, Synge and Lady Gregory I asked Sean O'Betjeman to take me out to Coole, but there were no wild swans; the whole place was derelict and was shortly afterwards pulled down. What a disgrace to Ireland! We also broke into the Abbey Theatre, which was a sordid building not much bigger than a village hall. The rooms seemed to be empty and, as we trod the half-lighted stage where *The Playboy of the Western World* had been hissed and booed, we felt suddenly inspired to perform an Abbey Theatre play of our own. We kept it up for quite a long time. Then the lights were suddenly put on, and we saw, sitting at the back of the auditorium, three rows of spectators. We left hurriedly by the stage door.

Our other visit to a *monument historique* was to Lloyd George, and it had been arranged by Uncle Arthur, who, in spite of a hundred betrayals, had never lost his loyalty to his old chief. We went down to Churt, and lunched with him alone. At first we were sadly disillusioned. Our host was querulous and confused. He made no secret of his belief that we should lose the war. In the middle of lunch he was called away to a telephone call. He came back with his eyes shining. "We are saved", he said, in the accents of a Welsh preacher. He had been told the news that Hitler had attacked Russia, so the date of our visit must have been the 22nd June, 1941. For a few minutes he talked brilliantly of what this megalomaniac decision could mean to us, "If only Winston will embrace the Russians". Then he grew tired, and we left him rambling on about far away things. A few days later we went to a cocktail party in the garden of No. 10 Downing Street, in the course of which Mr Churchill said to Jane "I'm thinking of asking Ll.G. into the Cabinet". To which Jane, with her usual impulsiveness, said "You can't: he's gaga". Mr Churchill grunted. He was fond of Jane, and had a regard for her intelligence, but whether this forthright statement had any effect on him I cannot say.

The bombing must have stopped gradually, because at some point in the spring we began to spend much more time in London, staying, surprisingly enough, at Claridges. The hotel was practically empty, and our magnificent suite cost us eight pounds a night. A few waiters were still on duty in the front part of the restaurant, and the string quartet still played every evening in the foyer. The leader was a serious musician, a cellist named Geiger, and as we were usually his only audience, he was delighted to play the quartettes of Haydn and Mozart. Our friends were mainly connected with music, ballet and 'show biz' generally. This was partly due to the National Gallery concerts, and partly to our friendship with William Walton. We had known him for over ten years, but in 1940, when I was so much occupied by the Ministry of Information, he became for Jane a wonderful standby. I see from her diaries how much she depended on him for the

Picnic in the train: Graham Sutherland,
Henry Moore and Myfanwy Piper

Jane in Upper Terrace garden

companionship I could not give her. Willie's irreverent and mocking manner (his coté *Scapino*), which he has long ago abandoned, never concealed a north-country good sense and kindness of heart and the warmth of feeling that permeates his music. In 1940 he was writing the music for Gabriel Pascal's film of *Major Barbara*, and I believe it was partly through him that we made the acquaintance of that extraordinary character.

Just before the war Pascal had made an excellent film out of Bernard Shaw's *Pygmalion* (directed by Anthony Asquith), which had been a success at every level. People spoke of him as a rival to Korda, but he was completely lacking in Korda's *souplesse* and diplomacy. His entry into my life was characteristic. He came to see me in the Ministry without an appointment, and walked past the two dumbfounded janitors in the front hall, simply raising his hand and pronouncing in solemn, commanding tones, the word PASCAL. I was frenziedly looking through files and dictating minutes. He sat down on the only available chair, indicated that my secretary should leave the room, and began to speak in a low voice, with a strong central-European accent, of the films he would make for me. He said he had acquired the sole rights of all Bernard Shaw's plays. I asked him how he had succeeded where so many others had failed. "I tell you the story. I come to England und go straight to see the old man. I tell him how his plays will become the greatest films ever made. He listen for two hours; then he say 'Mr Pascal, this will require a lot of money. How much capital have you got?' I put my hand in my pocket and say 'When I landed I have 17/6d., but I have a shave und take the train here, so now I have only 3/6d. left'." To say that Pascal was a liar would be an absurd under-statement. He was a sort of Baron Munchausen, who never opened his mouth without telling some obviously untrue story. But in this instance Mr Shaw told me the same story, so I suppose it must be true. Why did Mr Shaw allow himself to be conned by this impostor? One answer is that Gaby's sheer impudence amused him. He was a change from the smooth businessmen, obsequiously boastful, who had hitherto tried to secure the precious rights. But another reason is that Gaby Pascal had really persuaded Mr Shaw to believe in him. As Gaby is an almost forgotten figure, I may be excused for quoting from a letter that Mr Shaw wrote me on June 11th, 1941: 'Hollywood is courting him and even courting me. He has put up British film reputation to such a pitch that United Artists rank him economically with Chaplin. I cannot do without him; there is no one else in the field whom I can trust artistically: even his extravagance is an asset.' That Gaby should have 'sold' all this nonsense to such an intelligent and sceptical man as Mr Shaw was almost an act of genius, and encourages me to describe him in greater detail.

He was short, thick and swarthy, but he grinned like a naughty boy, and one couldn't help liking him. Behind all his bluff there was a genuine feeling for quality, and this made him a great talent-spotter. All the actors and actresses that took leading roles in his films became stars. When he first visited me, I had to tell him that *Major Barbara* could hardly be considered good propaganda and we could do nothing to help him. To tell the truth, I couldn't think of a single Shaw play that would be effective English propaganda—quite the contrary. He was not at all put out, and said that we should meet again which we did a week later, lunching with Jane at the Ivy. In those years the Ivy restaurant was like a sort of club for all theatrical and film people, and I see from Jane's diary that we lunched there almost every day.

My children often tell me that I like monsters, and this may be true as they are a sort of complement to my own timid and conventional character. Gaby was the most complete monster I have ever known, and I liked him. He was perfectly shameless, and would pee in a crowded street, which embarrassed me. But I delighted in his Baron Munchausen stories, and I wish I had made tape recordings of them, for print doesn't do justice to his low solemn tones, and the words 'you onderstand' repeated when an

*Inglorious War*

obviously glaring lie was about to emerge. Almost the only one I can remember is how he became the lover of Duse: "was with my little troupe going down to bathe in Arno und a beautiful voman, you onderstand, put her head out of a vindow und say to me 'Come ti chiami', und I say 'Gabriele', und she beckon me up". I doubt if Gaby had ever been in Italy as a young man. When I met him in Venice I found that he could hardly speak a word of Italian.

We saw a lot of Gaby in the 1940's. He was said to be penniless, but this did not prevent him from buying and doing up with considerable taste a house just off the London-Oxford road, about two miles from Denham, where we occasionally stayed. He said that he intended to marry. "I give up the old hobo life, and marry a sveet Californian girl." It didn't turn out like this, and ultimately he married a very beautiful Hungarian girl, with a watchful mother, which suited him far better.

*Major Barbara* was a good film, with excellent performances by Wendy Hiller, Bob Newton and Robert Morley. It was directed by David Lean. Gaby then took the suicidal step of saying that he would produce *Caesar and Cleopatra* and direct it himself. It turned out that he had never directed a film except a sort of travelogue to the music of Respighi's *Fontane di Roma*. This was immediately apparent to the very experienced professionals whom he had persuaded to join the cast, including Claude Rains as Caesar and Vivien Leigh as Cleopatra. The result was chaos, and involved an infinite number of retakes. We often went down to see it being shot, and became almost hysterical when Ernest Thesiger had said the same sentence over fifty times. Added to this, Gaby could not resist building enormous sets of Alexandria in the current Hollywood manner. Where all the extra money came from I cannot imagine; I suppose from the savings of poor people which had been entrusted to an insurance company. After delays which seemed interminable the film was finished, and we were invited down to Denham to see it. We sat in a large film studio, alone with Gaby and Mr Shaw. It was a cold morning, and the old gentleman's false teeth clicked and chattered. Mr Shaw was the most courteous of men, but in the sequence in which Caesar discovers Cleopatra lying on the paws of a sphinx, he could contain himself no longer. "Oh, she's ruining it. That was a delightful piece of comedy. It goes for nothing now." He kept up these comments on Vivien Leigh throughout the whole film (he could not complain about Claude Rains, who was excellent), and at the end said "Gaby, you've ruined it". This, alas, was true, for, in-so-far as the play has any point, it lies in Caesar's education of Cleopatra, and the development of her character. This was over-shadowed by a poor imitation of Cecil B. de Mille. We went back to lunch with Gaby, and for the first and only time in my life I saw him crestfallen. We were joined by one of the children, who saved the situation by admiring a sword that hung on the dining-room wall, "Is my old Hongarian cavalry sword", said Gaby, and then, having sipped the necessary stimulant, began to tell stories of his exploits in the Hungarian cavalry, in one of which he described in great detail ("you onderstand") how he had captured a whole detachment of the Allied Army single-handed. Meanwhile, Colin, who was inspecting the sword, silently observed that it was marked 'Wilkinson, London'. We drove home, and had no sooner entered the house when the telephone rang "Darling, what did Mr Shaw think of my performance?" There was nothing for it but a complete and total lie "He thought it marvellous, darling. He thought you had exactly caught the spirit of his Cleopatra." I am a bad liar at the best of times, and I may have laid it on too thick. But Vivien swallowed it, and, since I doubt if any of her other friends knew Mr Shaw, she may never have heard the truth.

The film was a failure; indeed I doubt if the critics stayed to the end of the first showing, because when we went to the buffet afterwards every scrap of food had been eaten, and nothing was left except some bedraggled leaves of lettuce. The drink was also exhausted. Every day or two Gaby rang up to say "Is doing fantastic business". But this deceived nobody, least of all his backers, and he was never able to make a film in England again. He unostentatiously left the country. I imagine he went to Hollywood, and lived on royalties from the various stars he had signed on, Deborah Kerr, Stewart Grainger and Jean Simmons. Many years later I received a letter from Gaby on the paper of the Racquet Club of New York, of which I very much doubt if he was a member. He said that *Pygmalion* had been made into a 'fantastic' musical. He had kept his rights, and had stipulated that it should be first produced at Sadler's Wells Theatre, in which he knew we were both much interested. We thought "Poor old Gaby, still looking back to his only genuine success", and I wrote him a temporising letter saying that I didn't think the Trustees of Sadler's Wells would take on a musical, however fantastic. In this way I deprived Sadler's Wells from some share in the great avalanche of gold that was precipitated by *My Fair Lady*. Gaby himself died before the avalanche began to fall, and left a legacy for his heirs as complicated as anything in his life. We were at the first night of *My Fair Lady* in New York, when its success was assured, and were sad that Gaby was not there to enjoy it. Or would he have enjoyed it? Bluffing, cheating, living from hand to mouth, had become so much a part of his life that genuine riches would have changed his style. I am told that after his death his pockets were found to be stuffed with hundred-dollar bills that he could not be bothered putting into the bank. Probably he was going to give them as tips.

# II

## *Inglorious War Continued*

M Y SHORT and unsuccessful effort to make myself useful in the Ministry of Information had consumed a lot of time and kept me away from my family; but it did not prevent us from seeing the artists who had become our friends before the war. I have described most of them in my first volume, and have little more to add. We continued to stay with the Pipers, and I was invited to become Godfather to their younger daughter. My fellow Godmother was Janet Stone, wife of the wood-engraver, Reynolds Stone who, in an old-fashioned style and a limited medium, has produced work to which the word perfect can be applied without overstatement. I had not met the Stones. Myfanwy Piper described Mrs Stone as looking like a beauty in the Court of Queen Elizabeth, and added "I think you will get on". This turned out to be an understatement. Henry Moore had become a fixture in our lives; no man can have had a more loyal and affectionate friend. We watched with infinite admiration how the abstract-looking style of the 1930's was modified, without any loss of completeness, by his observation of sleepers in the tube shelters. The process can be followed in one of the two small sketch books upon which all his own shelter drawings are based. He gave one of them to Jane, and it remained her most treasured possession. Graham Sutherland and his captivating wife stayed with us at Upton for two years. One day in 1940 Graham said to me "You know, when the war is over, I should like to paint portraits". I was dumbfounded. Memories of the portrait painters

I had known, from Sir John Lavery, who had painted my portrait at the age of six, to Simon Elwes, raced through my mind, and did not at all fit in with the character of Graham's art. At that time he was known almost entirely by his landscapes of an estuary in South Wales, inhabited by twisted trees and somewhat sinister roots. Occasionally these roots took the stage alone and looked positively evil. They were the nearest he had got to a portrait. I said "I somehow don't see you as a professional portrait painter; technically you can do anything [which is true]—but just think of how some of your sitters would bore you". "Of course I would make my own selection. The human head is only an *objet trouvé*—and a most interesting one." Even then I didn't recognise the strength of Graham's confidence and replied, kindly but tactlessly, that during the period in which he was learning the craft of portrait painting, he could count on my help. He said he didn't think it would be necessary. When I saw his portrait of Mr Somerset Maugham, to whom I had introduced him, I realised how foolish I had been.

In another instance my intervention was more useful. I greatly admire the work of Victor Pasmore, whom I believe to have been one of the two or three most talented English painters of this century. I knew that, in spite of conscientious objection, he had joined up as a protest against Nazism. He went to Sandhurst, which he loved, and was reckoned 'first class officer material'. I was therefore surprised when he called on me in my rooms in the National Gallery. I said "Victor, are you on leave?" He replied "Yes, in a sort of way; but as a matter of fact I've walked out". I knew just enough to realise that there was a difference between overstaying leave and deserting. If you overstayed leave you were in serious trouble, but if you deserted you were shot. I said "How long have you been away?" He said "Oh, about three weeks". Strangely enough, I knew that 'overstaying leave' was limited to 21 days, and said "Think carefully. Is it 20 days or 21 days?" After some cogitation he said "20 days". "Victor, you must give yourself up immediately. There's not a minute to be lost. We must go to the nearest police station." We went, and were treated with great consideration. Of course Victor had to go to prison, but he soon got permission to fresco the walls of the prison corridors, and was perfectly happy. He then had a formal examination. His mental processes are sometimes too complicated for the ordinary mind. He said he didn't mind joining the Army—rather liked it—but he was not going to kill anyone. He was sent back to prison, not so happily, and finally discharged.

In 1941 Philip Hendy, Director of the Galleries at Leeds, organised an exhibition in Temple Newsom of Moore, Sutherland and Piper. I was thought of as the spokesman of the 'new romantic movement' (not that they needed a spokesman), and was invited to open the exhibition. We travelled up to Leeds with the three artists and their wives, and Colin and Morna Anderson, and we took possession of two adjacent third class compartments. We still had a dozen half-bottles of Orvieto Secco left over from before the war, and we hung them in their raffia jackets over each seat; we also prepared a supper as magnificent as rationing would allow. It was a hot evening, and the men took their coats off. Jane had found in a shop in the Burlington Arcade named Noble Jones some braces decorated with very seductive mermaids, and had given them to all her friends. What with the heat and the Orvieto and the general feeling of escape, our faces shone and we all talked at the same time. Morna, who is an excellent photographer, took our photographs. The ticket collector was slightly shocked. "You be careful", he said, looking at the empty bottles and the mermaid braces, "or you won't be able to do your act this evening". We were still very jolly when we arrived in Leeds and were soberly greeted by Philip Hendy.

A less agreeable expedition to an opening was when we went down to unveil (not that it was veiled) Henry Moore's *Madonna* in St. Matthew's Church, Northampton, commissioned by that admirable patron of the arts, Walter Hussey. It was a cold day, the train was unheated and had no lavatories. After about half an hour it stopped, and went into a siding as the line had been bombed. We stayed there, in extreme physical discomfort, for two hours, and finally arrived at the ceremony over an hour late. Nobody sympathised with us—in fact they felt in an obscure way that we were responsible for the bomb. To fill in time Benjamin Britten's Anthem specially written for the occasion had been performed three times. I have never faced a more hostile audience. As I walked up the aisle my coat was taken from my shivering shoulders, and the Bishop said in a furious voice "Sir Kenneth Clark will speak to the people". God was on my side, and I made an inspiring speech on art and the church, in which I spoke of the iconoclastic controversy, Gregory the Great, the Incarnation, and other serious and relevant topics. When I came back to my seat beside the Sutherlands (who are Roman Catholics) they congratulated me. "All right", I said, "but not C. of E. You wait". The Bishop then ascended the pulpit, and opened his address with these words: "A few days ago I was reading that delightful book by E. V. Lucas *Over Bemertons*, and in it there is a description of a match of Gentlemen versus Players". "There you are", I whispered, "that's the real thing". I wondered how he was going to relate this social event to religious art, but of course he made no attempt to do so. He did not mention art or refer to the Henry Moore *Madonna*. He simply gave the kind of jolly sermon which had gained him the love of his parishioners and a seat on the Episcopal bench. The service was brought rapidly to a close, fortunately as we were all in desperate physical need. There was, however, only one lavatory on the premises, and it was occupied. After what seemed like an eternity the verger emerged, and I cannot say that we looked on him with favour. We were also very hungry, as lunch was to have been before the service, and in our absence everything had been eaten up except for some disgusting bread and margarine. The journey back was not much better. The train stopped frequently, and finally came to a complete halt at Willesden. There was of course no means of getting from Willesden to Hampstead except on foot. Nearly all the pubs were shut. With relief we saw lights coming out of the door of one of them, but it too had run out of drink except for half a bottle of cherry brandy.

Already before the war we had become friends with the Sadler's Wells ballet. In the creation of what is now a world famous company Ninette de Valois provided the drive and discipline, Constant Lambert the musicianship, Freddie Ashton the inventive genius. They were a perfect combination, and received the benefice of a great star, Margot Fonteyn. All of them became our friends. We saw almost every one of Freddie Ashton's ballets, and watched the emergence of Margot with delight. In fact we made the mistake of asking her out to dinner when she was only sixteen, and was too embarrassed to speak. As she said when I reminded her of it "I've made up for it since". At the beginning of the war the Governors of Sadler's Wells decided that it would be a patriotic gesture to close the Ballet down. The sum involved was small enough for Willie Walton and me to provide it; so the ballet remained in being and toured the country, performing new works by Freddie to music chosen and played on the piano by Constant Lambert.

If statistics mean anything, exercise prolongs life. Nearly all conductors are still on the rostrum in their eighties, and dancers live to incredible ages. Many members of Diaghilev's company, including Karsavina, Lopokova and Idzikovsky, are still alive, and I am glad to think that my ballet friends will outlive me. The one we saw most of in the 1940s was Freddie Ashton. He is a most difficult man to describe. Everyone agrees that he is charming, but no one quite knows why, because although he is remarkably truthful, he is also a master of evasion. I have never known another man who contributed so much to public enjoyment and led so completely a private life. The various resolute ladies who have tried to winkle him out of his shell have failed; but to the few friends whom he has chosen for himself he is talkative, funny and alarmingly observant. Most of the time he seems to be dreaming, and is, I suppose, inventing those wonderful interlacings of arms and legs with which he embodies musical ideas. Ninette is a totally different character. On the job she is merciless; off it she giggles a great deal, and has a vein of Irish fantasy. She is also an artist of an unexpected kind. The best parts of her ballets are concerned with trulls and hoydens, to whom she gives very realistic movements. I once asked her under what circumstances she had the opportunity to observe them so closely; she answered, "My dear, I've danced on every pier in England".

I seem to have done a lot of talking in those years, opening, shutting, lecturing and speaking on the radio; and this facility won me a place on an institution which was for a time a form of popular entertainment second only to the incomparable Tommy Handley; a radio programme known as The Brains Trust. It owed its popularity to the dramatic contrast of the three principal performers. Cyril Joad (always known as Professor Joad, although he never occupied a chair) was a quick-witted, bumptious disciple of Bertrand Russell, who treated The Brains Trust as a competitive sport and a chance for showing off. Julian Huxley took the whole thing seriously, and was irritated to the point of peevishness by foolish answers, especially if they were propounded by the third member of the group, known as Commander Campbell. Julian could not see that some kind of Sancho Panza was a necessary contrast to himself and Joad. Campbell was a genial impostor, who had in fact been to sea and was said to have been a purser. He had been co-opted at the last minute because the man the BBC had invited couldn't be found, and it was said that Campbell was a man who could talk about anything. It turned out to be a stroke of genius. When we were asked to define the word 'allergy', he got in before Huxley and said "I suffer from an allergy. If I eat marmalade my head steams." Huxley and Joad were furious, but next week Commander Campbell said "I've had 200 letters from people whose heads steam when they eat marmalade". The team included two other members, who were often varied; but for a long time they consisted of a charming and intelligent woman named Mary Agnes Hamilton and myself. I was the most inarticulate of the group. My end came when we were asked "What is the best form of government?" My four colleagues answered dutifully, and without qualification, "Democracy". I was flabbergasted, not only because I didn't agree, but because the answer was so incredibly unhistorical. When our genial chairman pointed ominously at me, I could only mutter "No comment".

Being on The Brains Trust was like a form of gambling. One sat round the table waiting for the question to come up like a number at roulette. Joad usually got in first, and sometimes left us with nothing to say. His answers were treated with contempt by intellectuals, but they were humane and reasonable, and did more good than harm. Millions of people listened to him who had not previously been aware of the process of thought, and he became an intellectual folk-hero. He showed me a room in his house in Hampstead where people who wanted him to read their manuscripts could leave them at their own risk. It was piled to the ceiling. I have been told, but have never checked the story, that in 1942 there were more Toby jugs made of Dr Joad than of Mr Churchill. In appearance Joad was like a rather scruffy hedgehog, but he had a round face which would have made a good jug. Then it was discovered that he was in the habit of travelling up to London with an inadequate railway ticket. The BBC still under the shadow of Reith, would no longer employ him, and one of the most famous men in England vanished into obscurity.

I suppose it was partly my performance on The Brains Trust and other public utterances, that induced the Foreign Office to send me to Sweden as a sort of advertisement for English culture. The Ambassador, Sir Victor Mallet, was a friend since Oxford days, and probably suggested my name; but the Foreign Office would certainly have sent someone more illustrious if they had not thought I could make some of the hundreds of short speeches that a visit to Scandinavia entails. I was the first British visitor to Sweden since the outbreak of war, and in 1942 it looked as if our brave defiance of 1940 was going to end badly. The King of Sweden, under the influence of his friend Count Wallenberg, was known to be pro-German. The Crown Prince was pro-British. The Swedes clung to their neutrality, but were terrified of the Russians, and no wonder after the Russian attack on Finland two years earlier, and therefore inclined towards the Germans as the less alarming threat of the two. Sweden was important to us on account of the ball-bearings made in Gothenberg. But I was told nothing of this: mine was to be purely a cultural visit.

Before going to Sweden we decided to leave Upton and buy a house in London. I still had to be in London most of the time, and there was the further reason that Uncle Arthur had become too possessive, and, when I was away, drove Jane mad. Someone told us about a charming little house on the summit of Hampstead Heath called Capo di Monte. We fell in love with it, and bought it without having it surveyed. It turned out to be even smaller than it looked, and very damp. Our larger guests, like Oliver Lyttelton, entirely filled the dining-room, the children's blankets were wringing wet, and I had no room for books. A house is like a husband; you have to live with it, and charm is not enough. Poor Jane had to furnish this little deceiver while I was away in Sweden, and we continued to love it for some time, although the children hated it, and tell me that Capo di Monte was the lowest point in their young lives.

After long delays the weather for a flight to Sweden seemed favourable, and I went up to St. Andrews to await a 'plane. I set off in a fighter piloted by a very reassuring looking Norwegian. He lost the way—no doubt there were many directional interferences to mislead him—and at one point we were over Hamburg;

but I was not worried. I could think only of the cold. I had on my father's old sealskin coat and fur boots, but I felt as if I were freezing to death.

Being an official guest can never be unalloyed pleasure. A programme is drawn up filling every hour of every day, and by the time one has admired everything and everybody one's stock of effusiveness begins to run low. Fortunately there was no native dancing in Sweden, so I was saved that terrible infliction on Royalty which the Television invariably portrays. The Swedish alternative is more agreeable, a concert of songs by a lyric poet called Bellman, whom the Swedes think is like Burns, but who is in fact almost identical with Tom Moore. My trouble was that everyone who wished to do me honour arranged for a Bellman recital, and I had to treat each occasion as an agreeable surprise. Another slight embarrassment was the convention that after a meal one has to make a speech to one's hostess thanking her for her hospitality and complimenting her on the food and drink. These speeches were taken seriously, and too much levity was resented. Then the Swedes are a very hearty people, and my best friend could not describe me as hearty. I find it almost impossible to shake hands and laugh simultaneously when I meet a man for the first time. Worst of all, the Foreign Office, which had insisted on sending out the slides for my nine lectures, lost them, and when they did arrive a week later they were all broken; so I had to re-write my lectures on the basis of slides of English painting such as were available in the University of Uppsala. No wonder they were a little thin. My host and hostess did their best to secure for me some freedom; but, after all, I was there to be victimised.

There was a great difference of feeling between Northern Sweden and the South. I was given an uproarious evening in Uppsala, and even sang student songs, which is not in my character. But in Lund I was regarded with some reserve, and in the neighbouring town of Malmö, which was in sight of German-occupied Denmark, my lecture was delivered to about twenty-five residents in the small back room of an hotel. When I returned to Malmö in 1944 I lectured in the great hall of the University to 450. My journeys to Gothenberg were made uneasy by the fact that I had to take with me various secret documents relating to the shipment of ball-bearings. This turned out to be one of the chief justifications of my visit. If one is a secret agent it is extraordinary how like a secret agent one comes to look. I could have recognised myself as one, and expected at any moment to feel the barrel of a revolver on my neck. In the end seven of the nine ships containing the ball-bearings were sunk. All I remember about Gothenberg was the Karl Milles fountain, which was out of fashion, but impressive, and my meeting with Ekwall, the compiler of the *Oxford Dictionary of English Place Names*. I had always thought this a dreary book on a fascinating subject, and when I met Ekwall I realised why. He could not speak a word of English. We conversed in German.

In Stockholm I visited the Palace and saw the King's famous collection of silver, which he would not allow to be cleaned, so that it had all gone black, and smelt. I also saw the King playing tennis in his 92nd year. With the Crown Prince I began a friendship which grew and lasted till his death. I enjoyed visiting his uncle, Prince Eugene, a charming, sunny old character, who lived in a house hung from floor to ceiling with modern paintings. I met innumerable painters, and spoke more enthusiastically about their work than would have been possible in normal circumstances. This, I think, was the most successful part of my visit, although I must confess that I got quite skilful at those speeches in praise of my hostess's food. An unexpected handicap was that so many Swedes believed that they owned paintings by Constable. They would waylay me in the streets with these miserable *croûtes*, and even jump on trams to thrust them under my nose. One picture of a stormy sky was brought to the Embassy so often that I had to look at it to save the butler trouble. I said "I'm afraid it's not even English". "Yes, yes, is English." "Why do you think so?"

"Because I read the story of a great dog." (I was defeated) "A terrible dog." Of course, *The Hound of the Baskervilles*. I have known some strange arguments advanced in favour of an attribution, but nothing as strange as that the authenticity of a Constable could be proved by a reference to *The Hound of the Baskervilles*.

In winter the Swedish landscape is very monotonous: snow on the ground, woods that look blue, and rusty-red houses— just the three colours. I can't imagine how their painters survive those long months. Flying home in a warmer 'plane we circled over St. Andrews at about 6 o'clock in the morning, and I shall never forget the enchantment of the tender greens and reddish earth after my long diet of white, blue, rust. I had made 60 speeches, given 19 lectures and 46 press interviews. I was succeeded by Mr T. S. Eliot, and could not help wondering how that scrupulous economist of words would deal with the situation. I warned him of what was in store for him, but he only smiled, and I am sure he got by far more creditably than I did.

Victor kindly invited me back in 1944, but by that time visiting Englishmen were no longer a novelty, and, although my lectures were considerably better, I did not receive much of a welcome. "Oh, that man again." I was sent to some new places, including a town in the North of Sweden called Gaevle, which had an admirable museum. My host spoke a very few carefully pre-pared English words, and thenceforward my intercourse with the people of Gaevle was restricted to bows and handshakes, and un-convincing laughter, as in Japan. I listened to an interminable lecture, of which I did not understand a word, and then gave a very short lecture, of which my audience did not understand a word but applauded its shortness. After it was over an unattrac-tive-looking lady with a strong cockney accent came up to me and said "I'm the only person in this town who knows any English. I'm from Bermondsey, you see. And I must tell you that I hate art." After that we settled down to a Bellman concert. As I walked back to my hotel about midnight I could not help wondering what purpose was served by such an evening.

The things that I enjoyed most on this second visit to Sweden were my expeditions with the Crown Prince to visit the painted Gothic churches in the region of Uppsala. 1942 had been a bitterly cold and prolonged winter, but 1944 was warm and sunny, and I could see something of the country. My host was a rigorous archaeologist. We started at 9 a.m., ate a sandwich for luncheon, drank a glass of water, and looked at each church in great detail. The 14th-century frescoes of Sweden are wild flowers compared to the great cultivated wall-paintings of Italy, but have a charming freshness and some rather surprising popular imagery, usually directed against kings, which made my companion laugh. I liked even more the runic stones, which were in almost every church-yard, and sometimes used as part of the wall of a church; best of all when they stand, solitary and mysterious, in a wood. Runic stones are the kind of abstract art that I enjoy, perhaps because I feel that, although I cannot interpret them, they have a meaning. In this they resemble certain forms of Islamic art, and, although it is a shocking suggestion, I incline to think that this combination of writing, hieroglyph and arabesque had an Islamic origin. The Vikings spent a lot of time in Islamic countries. The only other thing I can remember about this visit was that I frequently went to the Opera and fell in love (and no wonder) with a new soprano called Söderström. But after all I had not been sent to Sweden to go on archaeological picnics, or to fall in love with opera singers. I hardly know the meaning of the word guilt, but on this occasion I felt slightly guilty at having been on the spree at the public expense and done no good whatsoever. The whole expedition was what Colonel Scorgie called 'a criminal waste of the tax-payers' money'.

Looking through my engagement book for 1942 is a humiliat-ing experience. In the year of Tobruk, Singapore, the end of the British Empire, I don't seem to have done anything remotely connected with the war. Once the bombing was definitely over I brought back a picture a month for exhibition in the Gallery. In case of an alert two men were on hand to take it down to the shelter, where it spent the night, but this never happened. I also arranged some good loan exhibitions in the ground floor galleries. When in Ireland I had been much impressed by the later work of Jack Yeats, and had been to call on the old gentleman. He had none of the panache of his brother, whom he clearly considered rather absurd. But although he seemed so modest, he knew his worth. I put on an exhibition of Paul Klee, whose work was then scarcely known in England, and finally I did an exhibition of French 19th-century art, containing some great pictures from English private collections. The day after it was opened I received a letter from General de Gaulle, full of indignation that I had not asked him to open it. I replied that it was part of the routine work of the Gallery and that in any case I disliked opening ceremonies on principle. This apparently pleased the General, and he asked me to lunch at the Connaught Hotel. At this time everyone in England was against him, and by October he was hardly on speaking terms with Mr Churchill. His entourage were a poor lot, shifty and, I should imagine, disloyal, and he treated them like dirt. I was immensely impressed by him. No one had told me that he was a genuine intellectual, a pupil of Bergson, whose *tournure d'esprit* was very marked in his conversation. He invited me to come again, which I did, with increased admiration. Later his courage in the Algerian Crisis and his books, in an admirable French style, seemed to prove that I was right.

The last of my exhibitions, typically backward-looking, was of designs for Diaghilev ballets. I had made friends with Madame Karsavina, and had persuaded her to leave her Hampstead seclusion and come to the opening. I made a speech at the opening, and was punished for my inconsistency because when I came to the name of Madame Karsavina, the adored idol of my youth, I broke into loud, irrepressible sobs. So did Madame Karsavina. It would have been an embarrassing moment, but fortunately almost everyone in the audience also wept. I am very prone to tears (all that I have in common with the great soldiers of the early nineteenth century), and cannot read my favourite poems, even to myself, without weeping. For this reason I cannot quote poetry in a lecture. However, this was, I think, the only time that I have disrupted a public meeting by my tears.

How did I fill in my days? Chiefly by sitting on committees. The Mint Committee, the Post Office Advisory Committee, CEMA, The National Art-Collections Fund, the Council of Industrial Design (for which, with Francis Meynell, I had drawn up the charter), the National Gallery Concerts, and, my only worth-while activity, the War Artists Committee. I suppose I was a good committee member, for the number of my committees continued to swell, so that for twenty years they took up more than half my time. Committees often seem to be a complete waste of time; but the convention has grown up that decisions must have the backing of a committee. My dear friend David Crawford, who sat on twice as many committees as I have done, did untold good. Usually the upshot of a meeting is a foregone conclusion, fixed beforehand by the executive director; or the decision is taken by one forceful personality. Maurice Bowra used to listen to a discussion for two hours and then say "How's this for a compromise?", giving his own opinion, which was always accepted. The nicest committee I have ever sat on was the National Gallery of Scotland; the nastiest the National Theatre. But all this belongs to a later period of my life.

Meanwhile Jane was occupied in two activities of much greater value. For four or five years it was difficult for the average man to get enough to eat. The rations, which applied perfectly fairly to every section of the community, were just too small for a hungry and hardworking family. They covered everything except a cabbage. The government, I suppose through local authorities, had therefore instituted large, dismal eating houses, known as British Restaurants, where food of a kind was available for a very small sum. They were in disused parish halls, specially constructed huts, or even abandoned churches, and their interiors were not calculated to make a bad meal any more appetising. In fact they were so depressing that many people said they would rather go hungry than enter a British Restaurant. Somebody (perhaps Alix Kilroy, at the Board of Trade) had the idea that they might be more successful if they were attractively decorated, and asked Jane to undertake the task for Greater London. Whatever had been meant by 'decorated', Jane used it as a pretext for employing artists on large schemes of mural painting. I remember that Duncan Grant and Vanessa Bell did an enchanting series of 'murals' in North London telling the story of Cinderella, which was brilliantly opened by Maynard Keynes. I don't doubt that they were destroyed long ago. John Piper decorated a derelict church in South London. It was just off the road to Hampton Court, and I went to look for it a few years ago, but it had been pulled down. There were many other such schemes of mural painting, which I have forgotten. How shameful it seems, in retrospect, that we kept no record of them, and did not think of having them photographed. It is a very minor example of how difficult it was to think beyond the end of a war.

Jane's other activity was connected with the arrival of the American forces in England. Amongst them were a number of university graduates who longed for an escape from the noisy bonhomie of army life, and someone had the idea of founding a club where they could meet each other, borrow books and listen to music or lectures. It was situated in a beautiful eighteenth-century building called Ashburnham House, which had been part of Westminster School. The sponsors of the scheme were our dear friend Barbie Wallace (later Mrs Herbert Agar), and a ravishing young lady called Pamela Digby (later Mrs Randolph Churchill, and currently Mrs Avril Harriman). They asked Jane to take charge of the library and arrange for 'cultural' pro-grammes. It was an ideal job for her. On her first day a very hand-some young G.I. said to her "There are three people in England I would like to meet, William Walton, Henry Moore and Kenneth Clark". She replied "You've come to the right person". He added that, although he knew it was impossible, he would also like to meet E. M. Forster. "Yes", said Jane, "that can be managed too." The meeting was a success, and for the next year the G.I., who was called Bill Roerich, became one of the two or three chief props of Mr Forster's old age.

Barbie Wallace hated music, so could conscientiously take a night off when Jane had arranged for Clifford Curzon, Denis Matthews, or what Barbie called the Gorilla Quartet to play in the beautiful drawing room of Ashburnham House. Lectures were given (too often by me, when a more eminent performer had let us down) in a less inspiring hall at the back of the house. But on one occasion it was the scene of an unforgettable incident. I must remind the reader that by 1943 the Germans had perfected a new weapon, which was in fact a small unmanned aeroplane carrying a very large bomb, and making a noise half-way between an aeroplane and a may-bug. They were known as buzz-bombs. When the noise stopped one knew that the bomb would fall, and it was wise to take cover. This happened to me once in Water-loo Station. I was going to Hampton Court, and was at the back of a fairly long queue. I bellowed at my companions to take cover, but they simply thought that I was trying to take their places in the queue. I found what shelter I could, the bomb fell, and after the smoke and dust had subsided, I found my queue companions on the floor, two dead and the others severely injured. I broke my way in to a telephone, still miraculously intact, and rang for an ambulance. After a few grisly episodes I went out to lunch, and could not think why my hostess laughed at me as I appeared. In those days we all wore hats, and mine, which I had not removed, was entirely covered with small fragments of broken glass, so that I looked like a hedgehog. The only point of this reminiscence is to introduce the buzz-bomb.

One of the chief attractions of the Churchill Club was the reading of contemporary poets, from Mr Eliot downwards, of their own poems. At that time Edith Sitwell, now disgracefully underrated, was at the height of her reputation, and the hall was crowded for her reading. She had begun to read one of her greatest poems when the unmistakeable sound of a buzz-bomb was heard. It came nearer and nearer, and seemed to be over the house. Then it cut out. At this point a diminutive air-raid warden appeared at the door and blew what were intended to be three sharp blasts on a whistle, the sign that we should take cover. The last blast was inaudible, as he had run for the shelter himself. Edith Sitwell read on: *Still Falls the Rain*. By the time it was over we could be sure that the bomb had fallen into the nearby Thames. I have never heard more moving applause. Edith's only comment, to me afterwards, was "The great point of wearing long skirts is that people can't see when one's knees are knocking together".

Edith Sitwell was one of two new friends who entered my life in the first year of the war. The other was Vivien Leigh. It is often said that friendships with women are difficult for a man. But this has not been my experience, and I think it is what Sir Thomas Browne called a vulgar error. There have been occasions in my life where friendship has turned into love. But with these two remarkable women love, in the popular sense, was out of the question. They were not as dissimilar as might be supposed. Both were intensely proud. Looking through what has been written about their characters one finds the words 'queenly' and 'imperious' on practically every page; both loved to laugh; both were fantastically generous, both had great courage. Of the two Edith Sitwell had the more tender heart.

I first became friends with Vivien when she was playing the part of Mrs Dubedat in *The Doctor's Dilemma*. She had come back to England in 1941 from the triumph of *Gone with the Wind* and the disaster of *Romeo and Juliet*, with Larry Olivier. *The Doctor's Dilemma* was running at the Haymarket Theatre, which is round the corner from the National Gallery, and on matinée days I would go to Vivien's dressing room for tea. It became an accepted custom, and I used to make for her rather better tea than her dresser would have done. At first I went because I enjoyed looking at her. When she had taken off all her make up, put on a turban, covered her face with cream she was as beautiful as a piece of renaissance sculpture. But very soon I went because I enjoyed her company and was fascinated by her character. She was not only intelligent; she had style. Who are the outstanding exponents of style in literature? La Fontaine, Pope (another link with Edith Sitwell), Voltaire, Sterne; and I suppose I must add Oscar Wilde, because Vivien's conversation had much in common with that of Gwendoline in *The Importance of Being Earnest*; which examples imply an ear for the rhythm of words, a personal voice, and an occasional sacrifice of the whole truth in the interests of economy. These seem to me the chief characteristics of style, and Vivien had them all. Add to this her frequent silvery laugh, which was not quite insincere, and the reader will see why those who knew Vivien Leigh found her irresistible. I stayed with her first in Gerrard's Cross, when she was acting Cleopatra, and listened to descriptions of Gaby worthy of the *Dunciad*; later she and Larry bought a beautiful half-derelict gothic house called Notley Abbey, a few miles from Thame. It appealed to Larry's romanticism, and Vivien liked it because it was near running water. As it was a mile from the main road, and about four miles from Thame, the servant problem was insoluble, and solved only by employing Portuguese, who lived by stealing the visitors' jewellery.

Almost as soon as Notley was purchased, and they were beginning to settle in, Vivien had her first attack of tuberculosis. Larry was away on an ENSA tour, and she was left alone to cope with the aftermath of the move and her illness. She was sublime—calm, courageous, above all practical, as one might have guessed from her ugly surgeon's hands. As a result of the T.B. diet she became quite plump, which I loved, but of course it wouldn't have done for her 'public'. She occupied her mind with plans for the enhancement of Notley, and although I admired her ambitions, I liked Notley better in its early stages. The big drawing-room, when it was finished, was too big for me and made me feel I was staying at Petworth, a resemblance accentuated by the after-dinner games, at which Vivien excelled (she could do *The Times* crossword puzzle in ten minutes).

These were the great days of Notley, when Vivien's sense of style made her formidable. I remember walking round the garden with her, accompanied by a horrible little girl, kid-star daughter of some visiting Americans; we found some tame rabbits, and the kid-star seized one of them with an ungentle grasp. "Put that rabbit down, darling," said Vivien in honeyed tones. The kid-star continued to maul the rabbit. "PUT THAT RABBIT DOWN," said Vivien in the voice that she had developed for Antigone. The little girl turned pale, dropped the rabbit, and ran away boo-hooing. I must say it had made even me jump.

At the zenith of her good fortune Vivien had setbacks. She loved Anna Karenina, and was thrilled when she was invited to play the part in a film. But for some reason she couldn't convey the feeling of love. She could act it very skilfully, but one never felt it was really true. She was a passionate, but totally unsentimental character: that was part of her charm for me. Her Anna was bitterly attacked by the critics. We were staying at Notley on the weekend that the reviews came out; Vivien could not face her guests, and Larry asked me to take her out for a long walk. We walked for hours by the stream—the sound of running water doing her good, as it always did—and got back just in time for lunch, which she conducted with her usual good sense, but less than her usual sparkle.

All her old friends knew that she was what is now called a 'manic-depressive' (although Charcot's original name for the affliction 'folie circulaire' is far more expressive); but I never witnessed a 'black' till quite late, when I dined alone with her and Larry at Durham Cottage. He should have put me off, but I suppose she would not let him. It was terrible. The devils had got hold of her, and one could almost see them hovering round her. I left as soon as I decently could, and it took many deep breaths of the mild Chelsea air before I could feel sure of my own identity.

When she came back from her first bad breakdown in California we went down to Notley. Pale spring sunshine, just warm enough to sit out. Vivien lay wrapped up on a chaise longue, very pale and quiet. She spoke about her illness quite simply. She knew what had happened to her; but there seemed to be no way of breaking these cycles, because as soon as she got better she became confident again and impatient of interference. I remember trying to interfere when she gave me the script of *Streetcar* to read. I hated the play; also I have found that although actors can play any part and shake it off, actresses (except for Peggy Ashcroft) cannot. Their parts get into them and influence them; and I was worried at the idea of Vivien playing Blanche. I now discover that other people had felt the same way, and had told her so. "You're an impossible," she said; the nearest thing to a hard word she ever addressed to me. I don't know if my Pirandellian fears were well-founded. One of her worst periods came at the end of the run of *Streetcar*: but then she had another when playing the heroine of *Titus Andronicus* on tour in Europe—so after all her parts may have had nothing to do with it. It was simply a cycle with a diminishing rhythm.

The friends who wrote about her in Alan Dent's *Bouquet*★ attributed her breakdowns to overwork. This is not the whole truth. She wanted to be a great actress, but she also wanted to be

---

★ *Vivien Leigh, A Bouquet* compiled by Alan Dent, I am much indebted to him and to Hamish Hamilton for allowing me to quote some passages from a piece I wrote anonymously in that book.

a great social figure, and she would sit up till all hours in pursuit of that aim. That is what wore her out, and it also wore out Larry, who said to me "I just want to act well. Nothing else." It led to the great tragedy of her life. We were staying at Notley on the night that the final blow was struck, by telephone from America. It was one of the most miserable nights of my life.

As time went on I saw less of her, entirely through my own fault. The truth is that Vivien only came to herself about midnight, whereas I like to be in bed and asleep by 10.30. We are born to be either larks or owls. I am a lark, happiest between 6.0 and 8.0 a.m. It is a weakness that has cost me many friends. When we met she treated me as if nothing had happened, but I knew she thought I had neglected her. Finally she found a kind and patient protector and an enchanting house called Tickerage Mill, where she could hear the sound of water. She did it up, as always, with perfect taste (she was one of the few English people I have known with a genuine love of painting), and all seemed set for a new, less social life. But she was tired; the devils had exhausted her, and when she had another attack of tuberculosis she couldn't defeat it, as she had done the first one. Almost everyone who has written or spoken about Vivien has quoted Shakespeare 'A lass unparalleled'. I must add to their number; no other words will do.

As so often with friendships (and love affairs) I cannot remember precisely when my friendship with Edith Sitwell began. It may have been accelerated by an essay I wrote on her (my only venture into literary criticism) in *Horizon* for 1940. I find the *Selected Poems* of 1936 inscribed 'To Kenneth Clark with all best wishes'; and after 1942 her books (she sent me five copies of *The Song of the Cold*) are inscribed 'To my dear Kenneth, with deep affection', so something must have happened in the intervening six years. By 1941 we had begun to receive those enormous letters, sometimes touching, sometimes funny, and slightly embarrassing, of which several hundred were to pour in during the next twenty years. We also received hand-written copies of each new poem as she wrote it; and I say 'we' advisedly, because she always sent two copies, one for Jane and one for me. It must have been a considerable labour, and we tried to convince her that we were not going to separate; but I understood her motive. She saw that Jane had her own individual identity, in many ways very different to mine, and she wanted her to know that she recognised it.

I need not describe her appearance, for no face of the period is better known. It was irresistible to photographers and to painters, with whom the sittings often led to stormy relationships. But her body must always have been an embarrassment to her:

> Jane, Jane,
> Tall as a crane,
> The morning light creaks down again;
>
> Comb your cockscomb-ragged hair,
> Jane, Jane, come down the stair.

She said that she was thinking of herself, "although changed into the situation of a poor young country servant". Later she escaped to Paris, and fell passionately in love with the painter Pavel Tchelitchev, who painted six portraits of her. What his feelings were it is hard to say. "A very beautiful woman. She is alone. She is very positive and very emotional. She takes herself very seriously and seems to be as cold as ice. She is not so." Tchelitchev, apart from his bewildering gifts as an artist, was an extremely intelligent man who had seen a great deal of life, but I fancy that Edith's attachment to him was something beyond his experience and became unbearable to him. Both he and Edith told me a confused story of how he chased her round his studio with an axe, saying "I kill you. I kill you," a crisis prevented by the unexpected appearance of Osbert, who told me the same story. Fifteen years later, when we first became friends, she had come to terms with her demanding, but ungainly, body, and looked like a rather mischievous mother superior. But the body still haunted her imagination, and accounts for the frequent allusions to physical beauty in her later poems.

How Edith chose her enemies is obvious. They were people who did not like her kind of poetry; and she persecuted them, not only from personal motives, but for their impiety: Dr Leavis, Geoffrey Grigson, and of course the 'noisy, blustering blue-bottle', Percy Wyndham Lewis, who received endless abuse. Much of it seems to me rather childish. But she invented one device which delights me. She received, as we all do, many letters from Indians asking for praise, or money, or both. To these she would answer that she herself knew nothing about India, but there was a Dr Leavis in Cambridge who was known to love Indians and be most helpful to them. No wonder that Dr Leavis hated her, and wrote that the Sitwells were only 'part of the history of publicity'.

How she chose her friends is much more mysterious. One knew who they were because every month or two she would invite them to lunch at her Club. It was an old-fashioned institution, evidently founded by a devout Ruskinian, and called the Sesame Imperial and Pioneer Club. Most of the members were elderly people, and Edith introduced me to one old lady who had travelled back from China with General Gordon. Wearing a long dress, a small fur coat, an enormous hat, huge rings and the urim and thummim that always occupied her breast, Edith would monopolise two-thirds of the drawingroom; and, since my mania for punctuality always landed me there before anyone else, I had to spend twenty minutes fighting off indignant members of the Club who did not see why they should be kept out of their own drawingroom. Gradually the guests would arrive, Stephen and Natasha Spender, John Lehmann, Father d'Arcy S.J.—so far so good; then some really extraordinary misfits; and finally Dylan Thomas and his quarrelsome wife. Let me interject that on the many occasions when I met him I always found Dylan Thomas charming, warmhearted, and with great natural dignity. But he had clearly not been brought up to resist the assaults of American literary cocktail parties. After an eternity of fetching drinks from an improvised bar, we all filed off down a long corridor with a landscape wallpaper, going rather slowly, as our hostess was lame, and entered the crowded dining-room, where a table, holding about sixteen, had been arranged for us. There would be a hush, and every disapproving eye would be turned towards us. Edith was delighted, and took her time over the *placement*, particularly relishing the name of one of the guests called Commander King Bull, whose place was frequently changed. Curiously enough, when we were finally installed we had a very good lunch with quantities of excellent wine, which made us all a little tipsy. Somewhat to our hostess's disappointment the dining-room would be empty by the time we moved unsteadily back down the landscape corridor.

It is amazing that such a sensitive person should have enjoyed being stared at. Logan Pearsall Smith told me that he was walking down Kensington Gore when he was faced by three tall young people, a sister and two brothers, walking arm-in-arm. In common with the other pedestrians he stepped off the sidewalk and stared at the trio. As they passed they said in unison the word 'Sitwell'. I am sure that Osbert or Sachie would never have indulged in this sort of display. It was Edith who needed to compensate for the repression of her girlhood. But was she all that repressed! Those who have seen the famous group of the Sitwell family by Sargent will remember that, whereas Sachie is a baby, Osbert a little boy in a sailor suit, and Sir George and Lady Ida are ghosts, Edith, wearing a brilliant red dress, dominates the composition. In a fit of naughtiness I asked her who had chosen the dress. She knew exactly what I meant, and gave me a warning glance from her small, piercing eyes. "It was Mr Sargent", she said, not expecting to be believed.

But I have spent too long on the comical side of a great poet and a woman of the tenderest and most generous character I have ever known. The present fashion for cerebral or non-poetical poetry will pass, and Edith will once more be recognised as the author of some of the greatest poems of their time. Her early poems may seem trivial. One can enjoy their pleasant sound and texture, and sometimes their fantasy. They are the work of a true poet, but are written from within a sort of *hortus conclusus*, and are full of references to flowers and gardeners. But, when she looked over the wall, her sheltered upbringing made the cruelties and horrors of life even more intensely painful; and she did not close her eyes to them. She did, however, succeed in fusing them into a kind of mythology which she created for herself so that they seldom give us the shock of raw experiences. This mythology, based on a wide reading of the early Greek authors, the Christian mystics and many other sources, resembled that of Yeats, in that it was an imaginative and not an intellectual construction. Sometimes the debt to Yeats is evident and entirely creditable:

I see the children running out of school:
They are taught that Goodness means a blinding hood
Or is heaped by Time like the hump on an aged back,
And that evil can be cast like an old rag
And Wisdom caught like a hare and held in the golden sack
Of the heart . . . But I am one who must bring back sight
    to the blind.

But her language is usually less direct and her myth lacks the identifiable *dramatis personae* of Yeats. It was largely directed by certain qualities of light and colour which she came to think of as symbols of our human condition, and was expressed through a number of words which had a special, and almost magical, meaning for her. These are all words derived from sensory perception, either of colour, taste or feeling, and they were used almost interchangeably to denote certain moral or spiritual states. There are the golden words of life—honey, amber, wheat, corn, the lion, the fox and above all the sun; and the white words of death, dust and the bone, frost and snow. Almost all of her later poems are concerned with the conflict of life and death, and these words flash through her elaborate stanzas like warring angels carrying their heraldic blazons of colour.

It is true that in moments of weakening inspiration she felt that the mere repetition of these words was enough to produce the effect of poetry, and in her later poems certain combinations of magic-making words reappear in almost identical form. It might have been a good thing if her confessor had ordered her, as a penance, to omit the word gold from her writings for six months. Her love of euphony and texture sometimes led her too far from the purpose of the poem. Her first rebellious action was to force her governess to take her to the Isle of Wight so that she could place a wreath on Swinburne's grave. But granted all this I am convinced that *Eurydice*, *The Poet Laments the Coming of Old Age* and *The Shadow of Cain* are what we all thought when we first read them, *great* poems. *Still Falls the Rain* is an outcome of the war comparable to Henry Moore's 'Shelter Sketchbooks'.

I would not like to say at every point exactly what Edith's later poems mean, but they give me the feeling that I am on the brink of understanding some profound mystery, which, after all, is about as much as one can hope to derive from even greater writers.

In spite of her Plantagenet nose she was entirely without arrogance. She behaved to poor or humble people with the utmost sweetness and naturalness. I remember that before a lecture in Aldeburgh she asked the housemaid in the Wentworth Hotel how long she thought it ought to last. Would half an hour be too long? The housemaid, thinking that she had said an hour and a half, answered 'yes'; whereupon Edith cut it down to twenty minutes, and I, who was in the chair, had desperately to fill in time, while a volume of her poems could be found in the local bookshop, and she could complete the hour by some readings.

She had an intense and uneconomical sense of obligation towards anyone who had helped her. Once when she was staying with us we found her copying out her poems for a foreign publisher; and I therefore produced two typists who could copy them for her. She was deeply grateful, but when the typists had done their work, she made manuscript copies of the poems for each of them to show her gratitude.

At the end of her life she became depressed by the awareness of failing powers. But her sweetness of character and warmth of heart never left her. I hope the reader will forgive me if I break my self-imposed rule not to quote letters, which I believe disturb the flow of an autobiography, and print the last letter she wrote to me.

December 6th, 1964

My dear Kenneth,

What a truly wonderful book your "Ruskin To-day" is. What a writer he was, and how infinitely fortunate he is to have a great writer reconstruct his life, his work—that was his life, and every moment of his wretched, great being. Your preface is infinitely touching.

Of course his whole trouble arose from the fact that, as he said, he had no one to love. (Incidentally, what an old beast his mother must have been!)

I am so happy and so proud to have this great book from you; what you have written in it for me, makes me very proud, and I am *very* grateful to you.

The book is amongst the most living books of our time. I do not nearly know it all, yet, but find every page revivifying. It throws a light on all our present problems, as well as on that dead great man (the nib of my pen has gone wrong, so please forgive this hopelessly bad writing).

I opened the book on the sentence in the introduction "We find it hard to believe that anyone who is sincerely anxious to tell the truth will do so in long and well-contrived sentences, rather than in a series of mono-syllables and grunts."

That might have been said of poets' problems to-day.

This letter would have been written before, but I have been in really agonising pain. Not only did the hospital in which I was put with pneumonia poison my whole system, but the sheath of all the muscles in my right foot are badly inflamed, and the pain is such that I only sleep for about an hour a night.

I will write again in a day or two.

Meanwhile, all my most grateful thanks, and best love to you and Jane. When shall I hope to see you both?

Yours affectionately

Edith

This letter must have been written only a few hours before her death, and I received it next morning after I had read in the paper that she had died.

*   *   *   *   *

Opposite our small, romantic Capo di Monte was a large walled garden in which stood a modernised eighteenth-century house, called Upper Terrace House. As the inconvenience of our pretty deceiver became more apparent to us we began to cast lustful eyes on this almost too obviously 'desirable' residence. The owner had fled to Barbados, and ultimately we were able to buy it for a sum that then seemed large, but would now be considered ridiculously small. The house had been 'made over' by an architect without convictions named Oliver Hill, who practised in a 'modern' style so contrived as to put conventional people at ease. The staircase was hideous, but looked very solid, and we sat under it during the occasional air raid warning. The garden was charming, and became Jane's chief delight. We thought that we should live there for ever. Our first act was to bring our pictures from Upton. Renoir's *Baigneuse Blonde* hung over the chimney piece in the sitting-room, and was the tutulary goddess of the house. We brought her up in 1943 to greet our new friend, René Massigli, the first French Ambassador to England under the de Gaulle régime. He was, (and, as I write still is) a perfect type of Frenchman, intelligent, warm-hearted and universally beloved. What a stroke of luck that he should have been with us during these years of difficult relationship between France and England.

Jane was a born hostess, and in addition to our friends from the ballet and visitors from America, who suffered tortures of cold in those fuelless days, she filled the house with G.I.s from the Churchill Club, who looked at the pictures (which, of course, no English person ever does) and listened to Denis Matthews playing the piano. By this time it was clear that we were winning the war, and we suddenly realised that under our apparent indifference there had been a latent anxiety. Even the V2s, the silent successor to the buzz-bombs did not greatly worry us.

We had one disaster, a fire that broke out in the cellar under my library. My mother was sitting there, and thought she smelt burning, so put her knitting in her bag and moved into the next room. A few minutes later the library floor fell in. Considering that all the pictures and most of the books fell into the flames our losses were comparatively slight. I was away in Cheltenham giving a lecture to the Ladies College, of which I was an inefficient governor. Jane was staying with Hiram. So we could not be found, and I never discovered who alerted the fire brigade. Their hoses, as usual, did more damage than the flames. The only irreplaceable loss was a collection of letters that we had stored in the cellar, including dozens from Cyril Connolly, together with his brilliant diary of a visit to the Balkans, of which the only other copy was also burnt; also all Logan Pearsall Smith's letters teaching me how to write English prose. But I lost many books that I valued, and must record the generosity of Stephen Spender and Cyril Connolly, both of whom gave rare and splendid volumes to console me.

A few days after the Germans left Paris I persuaded the Treasury to let me go over there to see if I could buy anything for the National Gallery. John Rothenstein came with me, hoping to do the same for the Tate. I suppose we imagined that French collectors would be impoverished and anxious to sell their pictures. How little we knew about conditions in Europe! Instead I found a sense of prosperity and social gaiety, which made London seem very drab. The only difficulty was a shortage of fuel. This meant that the skies were clear of smoke and that the streets were empty of traffic, except for a few Army jeeps. Never again will Paris look so beautiful. The sun shone, so that I did not suffer from the absence of central heating. I went to call on my old friend, Charles de Noailles, who lives in a large house in the Place des États-Unis, and, as I was about to enter, a crowd of young people streamed out. I said to Charles (thinking of England) "I see you have a lot of people billeted on you". "Billeted", he said. "What *do* you mean, billeted—Oh, those are friends of my daughter's." He thought the idea of having people billeted on him very amusing. His gifted wife, Marie-Laure, turned out to have been an arch *collaboratrice* and, in spite of being née Bischofsheim, had become a close friend of the German general commanding Paris: so perhaps Maurois was right after all.

During the four years of our isolation artists had often said to me "What do you suppose Picasso is doing?" and I had to bring them back a report. I met him at lunch with a splendid character named Madame Cuttoli, who had made the paintings of Rouault and Léger into tapestries. I brought for her to look at the first book ever published on Henry Moore, which contained photographs of his work. Picasso seized it in a mood of derision. At first he was satisfied: "C'est bien. Il fait le Picasso. C'est très bien." (In fact some of Moore's early drawings are slightly influenced by Picasso.) But after a few pages he became much worried. He left the table and took the book with him to a far corner of the room. There he sat for the rest of the meal, turning the pages like an old monkey that had got hold of a tin he can't open. He handed back the book to Madame Cuttoli without a word. Next day I went to call on him. His house in the Rue Buonaparte was stratified. On the ground floor there were G.I.'s and American journalists; then came communist deputies and prominent party members, who showed signs of impatience; then came old acquaintances; and finally one came to Picasso. He lived in a large, empty studio, furnished only by two green park benches. Around the walls were (literally) hundreds of canvasses, neatly stacked and all dated on the back. Among them was a number of the worst landscapes I have ever seen. Nature, in the Claudian sense, had no appeal to Picasso whatsoever. He was extremely perceptive, and saw at once what I thought of them. He then produced a large portfolio of drawings of a Cupid and Psyche motive—in most of them the man asleep and the girl looking down at him, which were amongst his most beautiful drawings. What on earth has happened to them! He did not show me the hideous, but power-ful, pictures of children with distorted faces, which were exhibited in England a few years later, and were supposed to express his mental anguish at the thought of the German occupation. This is the kind of nonsense that makes a critic 'feel good'. In fact great artists seldom take any interest in the events of the outside world. They are occupied in realising their own images and achieving formal necessities. As is well known, the images that are the basis of Guernica occur in drawings that antedate by over a year the bombing of the Basque town. Rodin had the right instinct when he used to ask a group of his literary friends to think of titles for his works.

In Paris we were put up at an hotel near the Étoile which had been taken over the British Army for visiting officers and govern-ment officials, Ardizzone characters in high spirits and drinking quantities of champagne, for which no one seemed to pay. I asked my old friend Dunoyer de Segonzac to lunch with me there. Time passed and he did not appear. I looked out of the window and saw him pacing up and down with bowed head. I went out to greet him, and he immediately began to pour out a confused apology for France's part in the war. He was a high-minded, patriotic Frenchman, and was particularly troubled by the fact that he had gone to Germany during the war, to plead, as he said, for French artists who had been interned. I tried to calm him. I told him that to have spent the war doing his etchings for Vergil's *Georgiques* was more important than any exercise of patriotism. But he was inconsolable; he was the only Frenchman I met who realised what England had done, and France had not. On the other hand, I found, to my delight, that my friend Georges Salles, who was half Jewish, being the grandson of M. Eiffel, had been made Directeur des Musées de France. I never enquired how he had spent the war, but clearly he cannot have shown open hostility to the authorities. During the years that followed we became even closer friends; in fact I can say that, with the exception of David Crawford and Maurice Bowra, he is the man whom I most miss in my life. The conclusion is that what people do under wartime conditions should not influence personal relationships.

Needless to say, the pretext under which John Rothenstein and I had gone to Paris, the purchase of pictures from impoverished Frenchmen, turned out to be a ludicrous error of judgement. The art-market was booming. The occupying Germans were the best customers the dealers had ever had. When I visited the dealers I knew, including Jews, I was laughed at. The only place where I had a friendly welcome was the Hotel Crillon. We had stayed there for over fifteen years; during the war it had been the headquarters of the German High Command. I visited it out of sentiment; I was kissed by every member of the staff, including the old head porter, and the hideous old maids from the fifth floor were brought down to join in the orgy. I took away quantities of notepaper, bearing the stamp and insignia of the German High Command, which I gave to my children to write letters to their friends at school. This was the only tangible thing I got out of my visit to Paris in 1944.

The end of the war was delayed long after the outcome was certain. When I was in Sweden, in March of 1944, I was shown (very indiscreetly) the letters in which Himmler (the faithful Heinrich) was putting forward his sensible terms for peace, which would, I think, have been acted upon, had it not been for the Russians. They were bent on revenge for some of the most appalling atrocities in the whole abominable war, and I have no doubt that Himmler foresaw this. The unfortunate Germans still worshipped their madman of genius, and believed him when he said he would find a way of saving them. In all history there has never been so strange a tragedy on such a colossal scale.

The end came suddenly, and I remember very little of the same hysterical rejoicing that marked the end of the 1914–18 war. We were lunching with Mr Bevin that day, and the subject was hardly mentioned. Jane had been feeling exhausted, and thought that she could regain her energies by injections, a medical practice then much in vogue. The doctor (the celebrated Plesch) had broken the needle in her behind, and after lunch he brought a German surgeon up to Hampstead to try to extract it, which he failed to do. Such faint cries of jubilation as might have been heard were rendered inaudible by a noisy altercation in German between Plesch and the surgeon.

I suppose that we all were glad that the actual fighting was over. But for me this feeling was soon overcast by the horror of the immediate sequel. The brutal Russian occupation of Berlin, the discovery and visible documentation of the German extermination camps, these and a dozen other ghastly revelations filled my mind. I felt that European civilisation could never again recover its confidence and equilibrium. Finally the dropping of the atom bomb on Hiroshima filled me with a despair about the future of mankind from which I have never wholly recovered. I knew just enough about physics to realise that something had happened which upset the whole structure of human life. I remember that I was staying in Gloucestershire when the event was reported, and I wandered about with a misery far more profound than anything I had felt five years earlier, when I had supposed that we should be invaded, and probably conquered by the Germans. Wars are horrible, but they are part of a natural human process. They are an inevitable element in history. But the discovery of nuclear fission was unnatural. Sooner or later, it seemed to me, the human race would be exterminated. I seem to have been mistaken—so far. The skill with which technicians have developed these weapons of destruction has produced an unexpected result. International peace, which could not be achieved by love or reason, has been achieved by fear.

# III

## Writing and Lecturing

THE WEST SIDE of the National Gallery had been badly damaged by bombs, but three rooms on the east side, where the War Artists exhibitions had been held, were intact. When the war in Europe was over I persuaded the Ministry of Works to redecorate them, and immediately brought back from the caves enough pictures to fill them. They were relatively small (to have moved the bigger pictures would have taken months), but they were all masterpieces; and the sight of these survivors hanging together in amity was extremely moving. One had the illusion that genius was indestructible. This should have been my 'finest hour'; but already I was worrying about my future. I had been Director of the Gallery for nearly thirteen years, and my renewal for another fifteen would soon be under consideration. Thirty years in a single job is too long. One loses impetus and grows blind to obvious mistakes. I do not like institutions and would have been sorry to become one of them myself. Moreover it seemed to me that whoever brought the pictures back from Wales should have the chance of installing them and rearranging the Gallery in his own way. I suggested to my Trustees and to the Treasury that I should resign, giving these as my reasons, and they made no attempt to dissuade me. This may have been because my Trustees did not wish to embarrass me; or it may have been that they saw I was not really cut out for an administrative post; and if the second was their reason they were perfectly right. I had come to the same conclusion.

## Writing and Lecturing

My overwhelming need was to communicate my feelings about works of art in words. I wanted to write, occasionally to lecture, indirectly to teach. This I have done, with many interruptions, for the last thirty years, and thus my resignation from the Gallery was the turning point in my life.

Had I been a good Director? The answer is, not very, but better than my predecessors in this century. I made a number of good purchases for incredibly small sums. I installed a scientific department with all the latest apparatus, and had used it in carrying out a programme of cleaning which, restricted and amateurish as it was compared to the achievement of the last thirty years, was on a different scale from anything that had preceded it. Personally I do not believe very much in the application of science to the problems of cleaning. Everything depends on the experience and sensibility of the restorer. But until quite recently the cleaning of pictures used to arouse extraordinary public indignation, and it was therefore advisable to have in the background what purported to be scientific evidence to 'prove' that every precaution had been taken. In fact the rare occasions when a picture has suffered from restoration are usually due to the restorer having been carried away by his own skill, which, of course, no amount of science can forestall. The only safeguard is to keep a restorer constantly under observation. I used to visit the conservative Holder twice daily; but I persuaded the brilliant Ruhemann to work in my own room in the Gallery, on the pretext that it had a better light. He complied because he did not want to work, in alternate shifts, in the same studio as Holder. The two were even unwilling to pass each other in the passage; the jealousy which eminent restorers feel for one another goes far beyond that of actors and actresses, which strongly suggests that they have something to hide. A cleaned picture often looks very bright when first it is finished, but it loses its shine after a year or two, and I was fortunate in that the pictures I brought back for the reopening of the Gallery, all of which had been cleaned, had had time to 'settle down'. No one complained about them.

I also set up a publications department which made a handsome profit, little foreseeing that this harmless activity would grow until it took over Gallery I, where, in my time, hung the paintings of Uccello, Masaccio, and Piero della Francesca. Finally I spent a lot of time visiting provincial galleries, in an attempt to persuade them to borrow pictures from our reference section. This was very seldom successful, because at that date provincial galleries were generally controlled by their committees who did not like 'old masters', either because they represented religious themes, which might have lost them some nonconformist votes, or because they were too dark. One must remember that the provincial eye had been conditioned by the bright, banal colours of contemporary academic art. We had at the time nine landscapes by Ruysdael in the reference section, and I never succeeded in lending one of them. However, these well-meant expeditions gave me an insight into industrial England which I would never have achieved otherwise, and Jane, who always accompanied me, dressed in exquisite Lanvin clothes, gave immense pleasure to the local mayors.

During the war the National Gallery, by means of the concerts, the War Artists exhibitions and the exhibition in the basement, had 'kept going' when other museums and galleries were completely out of action. It was frequently said that I had 'put the National Gallery on the map'. So when I resigned there might therefore have been some embarrassing comment. But, by a piece of good fortune, the news appeared on the same day as the result of the 1945 election and my disappearance passed unnoticed in the general astonishment that the country had rejected Mr Churchill.

I will not describe the events that accompanied my leaving the Gallery, except to say that my successor, who had been appointed solely on my recommendation, refused to come and see me. I suppose he wanted to take over the job with an 'open mind'; but in fact it meant that many things which I could have said to him in conversation were never said, and he thus made a lot of unnecessary trouble for himself.

By a fortunate coincidence, a few months after I had left the Gallery I was offered the job of Slade Professor in Oxford. I said something about this curious institution in *Another Part of the Wood*. The professor was supposed to give twelve lectures a year but no one counted the number, because practically no one came to them, and he usually got away with five or six. By tradition he did not live in Oxford, but came down just in time to speak and left by the next train. There was no professor of art-history at the time, and so the understanding of art as a part of education, on which Ruskin had set so much store, played absolutely no part in the University's curriculum.

The Slade Professorship had been founded at the instigation of Ruskin, and he himself had been the first Professor. This connection with Ruskin meant a great deal to me. In *Another Part of the Wood* I describe the deep influence that *Unto This Last* had on me as an undergraduate. My economics tutor, Freddie Ogilvie, who was to become Reith's successor at the BBC, was trying gently to persuade me of the reasonableness of classical economic theory. Ruskin made me entirely unresponsive. At that time Ruskin's writing on art was so totally at variance with anything I heard in Bloomsbury that I could not take them in. But when I began work on *The Gothic Revival* I had to read them seriously, and from then on, for many years, Ruskin became the greatest single influence on my mind. My chapter on Ruskin in *The Gothic Revival* must have been the first attempt to do him justice since his obituaries, and I am glad to find that I refer to the chapter in *Stones of Venice* called 'On the Nature of Gothic', as 'one of the noblest things written in the nineteenth century'. Much later I tried to repay my debt to him in a book called *Ruskin To-day*. I spent fifteen years, off and on, in putting it together, and I believe it to be one of the best things I have done. But one cannot swim against the tide of fashion, and in the U.S.A., where almost a million copies of *Civilisation* have been sold, the far more valuable *Ruskin To-day* has been remaindered.

The Slade Professorship not only gave me the pretext to put together some of my ideas on art, but also encouraged in me the notion that, in art history at least, I might to some very small extent be carrying out Ruskin's intentions. I decided that, in addition to my courses of lectures, I would spend an hour or two talking informally to any undergraduates who would care to ask questions about the history and theory of art, and at first my old College, Trinity, lent me for the purpose a room called the Old Bursary which, by its sympathetic character, positively generates conversation. We stayed in Oxford for the night with Maurice Bowra, which greatly added to my pleasure in the whole assignment.

My inaugural lecture was entitled *Ruskin in Oxford*. This was perhaps inevitable, but it had the disadvantage that Ruskin's Oxford lectures were given when he had lost his powers of concentration, and in the later ones there are signs of a complete mental breakdown. Even in his Inaugural he allowed himself a piece of Imperialist rhetoric which had a profound influence on Cecil Rhodes, but which is far from our way of thinking to-day. Moreover, Ruskin had already announced that he was no longer interested in the history of art, and this is painfully apparent in the bewildering confusion of historical fantasies of which his lectures chiefly consist. I had to admit all this, and still present Ruskin as inspired and inspiring. I think I succeeded, if only by calculated digressions.

*　　*　　*　　*　　*

I write all my lectures in long hand as carefully as I can. I know that a quasi-impromptu lecture can have greater freshness and vitality; but I am afraid of either drying up or becoming too garrulous. Moreover, I am very fond of writing. It has given me as much satisfaction as anything else in my life; and even now, when my faculties have declined, a well-turned sentence or a well-constructed paragraph gives me back some of the happiness that I used to take for granted in the past. My first series of lectures at Oxford was about man's response to landscape, a subject which had come into my mind when we were living in Italy in 1928. I may add that all my books have had an equally long period of gestation, and I see from Jane's diary that I first outlined to her a book on the nude in 1940, although it was not written till 1951.

The Landscape lectures were a success. My audiences increased from 25 to about 500, and my 'pupils', who had almost all been serving in the forces, were bright and eager to learn. Almost unconsciously I seem to have discovered an approach to the subject which, although it was basically historical, allowed me to consider works of art as expressions of human needs. I said exactly what I felt about each particular painter, and finally about the place of landscape in contemporary art—this, like all my speculative writing, was less successful than my interpretation of individual artists, and when I came to prepare a new edition of *Landscape into Art* it was the only part of the book in which there was a lot to cross out. My judgements were not at all 'original'. My natural inclination is to believe that, if any painter has been accepted as a great artist for a fairly long period, he probably *is* a great artist, and I must go on looking at his work till I know (as far as possible) the reason why. Ruskin's total dismissal of Claude or of Palladio is a symptom of genius to which I cannot aspire. The only one of my judgements to arouse criticism was my admiration for Turner. He had been the *bête noire* of the Bloomsburies, and my few pages of praise, mild enough by modern standards, were considered a terrible 'give away'. Clive Bell, who reviewed the book in the *Times Literary Supplement* wrote: 'Sir Kenneth Clark is supposed to be a man of taste, yet he can find something to say in favour of that old vulgarian Turner'. Perhaps this was one of the last battle cries in his war on behalf of Cézanne,* more probably it meant that Clive had never looked at a Turner except for the few overworked ones in the National Gallery, and disliked the idea of Ruskin.

After drastic rewriting, the lectures were published under the title *Landscape into Art*, with a beautiful dust-jacket by Graham Sutherland. The book was well received, and I found myself involved in the routine of a popular author, signing copies, attending literary luncheons, and giving little talks. Genuinely successful authors are said to hate these accompaniments of their popularity, but I was not successful enough for that. On the contrary, I much enjoyed such praise as I received, and signed copies of my book with enthusiasm. This is still my natural instinct although, as I describe in a later chapter, some of my experiences in America have been embarrassing.

My next course was on Rembrandt. I had loved his work since I was a child, and copied his etchings in my schooldays. There was little enough of any significance to read about him; the big, heavy books, like that of Muntz, were obviously out of date. But I must record my debt to a book which I had read at school by one of my predecessors at the National Gallery, C. J. Holmes, called *Rembrandt as Self-Educator*. It at least showed Rembrandt as an artist trying to deal with the kind of problems that beset all artists, however great their genius. I believe that this modest and completely forgotten book may well have been a determining factor in my own attempts to write art-history.

What a joy it is to work on Rembrandt! I doubt if anything else in my life has given me so much pleasure. To begin with there are relatively few documents, so little time is wasted in the·

---

* It must be remembered that as late as 1935 D. S. MacColl, who had long been the most intelligent and respected art critic in what might be called Athenaeum circles, never concealed his contempt for Cézanne. 'Butcher', 'Bungler', were his favourite words. That was at least as peculiar as Clive Bell's comment on Turner.

virtuous scrutiny of archives. All the evidence (as with Shakespeare) is in the works themselves, and, as the most revealing are drawings and etchings, one can study them in reproduction without feeling that one is losing nine-tenths of the message. (As a matter of fact the study of Rembrandt's etchings through reproduction is a kind of visual corruption, and one must return to the originals as often as possible). But of course the real reason for one's joy is being in the company of such a marvellous human being. When one first looks at Rembrandt he seems like the supreme Mr Everyman, with all the normal human instincts, emotions and appetites. But, looking more attentively, one becomes aware of a greatness of mind, an understanding of every allusion and an intense seriousness for which the Mr Everyman of the self-portraits is a misleading embodiment.

My lectures on Rembrandt were on the whole the best things I did as Slade Professor, and I had the pleasure of seeing young people leaving the hall in a state of genuine excitement. I then gave a series on the conflict between Classic and Romantic art in the early nineteenth century, and this too I greatly enjoyed writing. When asked which I loved most, Ingres or Delacroix, I could not reply. There is no doubt at all as to which was the more interesting person: Delacroix, who through his journals and his letters reveals himself as one of the most fascinating characters of his time. Ingres was almost totally uncommunicative, and evenings in the Villa Medici, when he was director, are said to have sunk to an unfathomable abyss of boredom. But then his whole mind was concentrated on one thing: the perfect realisation of certain forms that obsessed him, in particular the female body; and he achieved it. To say that one cannot like both Ingres and Delacroix equally is to admit that one cannot follow two different approaches to form and imagery. It is to admit an impoverishment. I will allow that one's mood changes: one may have Ingres days and Delacroix days. Most of the time one turns from one to the other with equal delight.

# Writing and Lecturing

Mr Berenson used to say that we all have only a very few pennies to rattle about in our tins, and I have found this to be profoundly true. Although my enjoyment of art covers a very wide field—Egyptian, Byzantine, Indian, Chinese, Japanese—these are not pennies that I can rattle in my tin. I used my thoughts on Rembrandt as the basis of a book thirty years after the Slade lectures; I made my lectures on Ingres, Delacroix and David the centre-pieces of a book twenty-five years after they were given. I can rattle a few more pennies: Blake, Turner, and the artists of the school on which I was brought up, the Italian Renaissance. What is it that prevents me from writing about the other schools of painting that I love? Fear of making a gaffe? Fear of writing hot air? Or simply the feeling that I am looking at them as an amateur and not from within. I have an uneasy feeling that, unless I know the language of a particular country, I ought not to write about its art; but this is nonsense, because Arthur Waley's translations of Chinese poetry are so obviously truthful that they should give me all the literary background I need for writing about Chinese art. But I also know that to do so without being able to practise calligraphy, or to recognise instinctively that certain natural objects—trees, rocks, tigers or sparrows—also have a symbolic meaning, would be mere dilettantism, and so have resisted what has been since my youth a very strong temptation.

Even before my five year term as Slade Professor was over, I had begun a book on Piero della Francesca. The choice of this subject was largely accidental. I had written a somewhat offensive review of a book on Donatello, published by the Phaidon Press. The morning it appeared the director of the Press, Dr Horowitz, came to see me in the National Gallery (so it must have been in 1945). He was a born diplomat and, instead of upbraiding me for my review, he simply said "You must write a book in the same series to show how it should be done". This was a fair proposition, and I undertook to write a book on Piero della Francesca, not only because I loved him, but because at that time no reputable

Bernard Berenson with Nicky Mariano
at the Villino, Corbignano

K.C. with student audience in Wellesley College

book on the subject existed except for Longhi's brilliant but eccentric masterpiece, which had not then been translated into English. As I afterwards discovered, Dr Horowitz did not know who Piero della Francesca was, but he agreed with enthusiasm. Of course the work could not begin till after the war, when I could revisit Arezzo. Meanwhile, he arranged for scaffolding to be erected in S. Francesco in order to take fresh details of the frescoes. As soon as possible I went out to Florence and drove over to Arezzo with Dr Horowitz. He had never been there before, and was suitably impressed. On the way back he offered to take me to my hotel. I said I was staying at i Tatti with Mr Berenson. He said "Who is Mr Berenson?" (No one will believe this story but I swear that it is true.) I described Mr Berenson's standing in the world of art history. I told him that Mr Berenson's best works were his four prefaces to his lists of authentic pictures. Dr Horo- witz listened attentively. Next day he rang up i Tatti, and asked if he could visit Mr Berenson to put to him a business proposition. Mrs Berenson must have been at home, and with her love of 'business propositions' she asked Dr Horowitz up immediately. Within half an hour he had obtained Mr Berenson's consent to buy the rights of the four prefaces from The Oxford University Press, and print them with illustrations as an introduction to Italian art. It seemed that The Oxford University Press, which had published the prefaces in a very dismal style, had sold only seven copies in the last few years. Dr Horowitz's illustrated edition, within a few weeks of its appearance, sold 60,000. This is an ex- ample of flair which Duveen himself could not have surpassed— in fact the two men were not dissimilar. That Dr Horowitz, with all his enthusiasm and geniality, should have died in middle age was a disaster for writers of books on art.

Writing about Piero was the ideal complement to writing about Rembrandt. Instead of total involvement with a human being who, whatever his skill and unique powers of sympathy, remains one of us, the writer on Piero is faced with a detachment from ordinary life so great as to seem at first out of reach. Yet this remoteness is more a matter of form than of content. At first we feel that we shall never know anything about him as a man. His two books, on perspective and on regular bodies, tell us even less than his paintings. But if one looks carefully at his frescoes in Arezzo, and tries to describe in detail both the incidents and the shapes, a character gradually emerges, who lifts one up to his own high level. I will not deny that there is a good deal in Piero that is inexplicable, notably the Urbino *Flagellation*, which will keep art historians busy far into the foreseeable future. But I found that daily contact gradually produced a certain confidence which did not involve geometrical analysis: only a complete surrender to an imagination far beyond our normal experience.

I stayed in Arezzo and became an accepted local figure. My work was done in the morning, when the Church was empty; and by 4.30, when smart people began arriving from Florence, I was seated at the café overlooking the Piazza di S. Francesco, and could witness the short visits paid by social figures, many of whom I knew. I did the same in Borgo San Sepolcro, which was not as comfortable, nor as amusing, since visitors seldom got so far. When I started to write my mind was full, and the book went well. It has a quiet tempo that seems to be in keeping with the subject.

*The Nude* was written in 1951, in response to an invitation to give the Mellon Lectures in Washington. As the subject had been in my head for over ten years, I did not need to make a plan of it, but sat down at the round table in Barbie Agar's summer dining-room and wrote the first sentence of the first chapter. I continued to write uninterrupted till the end, when I suddenly ran out of steam, and wrote on the last galley of Chapter IX 'Can't think up another word'. It needs another sentence, and I still can't think of one.

I had had trouble in turning the lecture style of *Landscape into Art* into a literary style, and had therefore decided that *The Nude* should be written as a book, and 'colloquialised' for the lectures.

The printed text is almost exactly as it was when first written. It is without question my best book, full of ideas and information, simplifying its complex subject without deformation, and in places eloquent. Much of it was written in Aldeburgh, which ever since my childhood has had the effect of sharpening my mind; and once or twice an idea or phrase came to me which surprised me. Where had it come from? I remember that after writing the passage on Rubens I began to tremble, and had to leave my hotel bedroom and walk along the sea front. I make no claim to be an inspired writer but I know what inspiration feels like, which makes it easier for me, as a critic, to recognise it in others. *The Nude* is a full book; in fact it is too full, and Lawrence Gowing, who has the best critical mind in my subject, wrote to tell me that I had put too much in. I had left myself nothing more to say in the future. I scoffed at this suggestion, because at the time I felt I could go on for ever. For some unknown reason my mind worked better from 1945 to 1955 than it had ever done before, and very much better than it has ever done since. As things have turned out there was a lot of truth in what Gowing said.

I gave the lectures in Washington in the spring of 1953, one a week for six weeks. We had many friends there, and were much fêted, which we enjoyed enormously. When I first entered the Washington Gallery I was surprised to see my lectures announced without a title. Simply 'Sir Kenneth Clark will give six lectures'. My old friend David Finley, a man of much practical wisdom and political experience, had foreseen that if a congressman from New England or the Bible Belt had heard that lectures on the nude were being given in the National Gallery he might have made a fuss and had the lectures stopped. To-day this sounds almost incredible but in support of David Finley's decision I must admit that my dear lantern operator, who had been a sergeant in the Marines, and came along to find me in my room before each lecture, shouting "Where's my boy?", said at the end of the lecture on Venus "My that was swell, better than a Vaudeville show".

We enjoyed everything in Washington—or, rather, I did. Jane had a bad experience when we went to visit Ezra Pound in his lunatic asylum. I think she might have survived if, as had been promised, we had met him on the lawn; but in fact we had to go through a small door, which was locked after us, and up a twisting staircase. Jane, who suffered from claustrophobia, was in a state of panic, and when we met on the stairs three burly men carrying clubs she became almost hysterical. She thought that they had been belabouring the inmates. Actually they were only three of the wardens going out to enjoy a game of baseball. When at last we reached the lunatics' hall even I became slightly uneasy, because it was full of *bona fide* lunatics behaving exactly like those in Hogarth's *Rake's Progress*. The great man was in an alcove, separated from them by a thin red curtain which he did not bother to draw. He showed no obvious signs of madness, and was kept in the asylum only to prevent his being shot as a traitor; but the fact that he did not seem to mind the company of madmen suggests that he was not perfectly sane. While his daughter did her best to revive Jane I had a conversation with him. I had met him once or twice before, but had never liked him so well. He talked about Alberti, Rimini, and finally about Chinese ideograms. The mind that had fascinated Yeats and brilliantly revised *The Waste Land* was still there. After an hour, when he was growing tired, a little nonsense slipped out. But I am convinced that in his disorderly way he was a genius, and I was proud when I received postcards* from him praising my work.

The visit to Ezra Pound was exceptional. In general our social activities in Washington were decorous; but this does not mean that they were dull. On the contrary, the social life of Washington, or rather of Georgetown, its pretty eighteenth-century suburb, was in some ways the most agreeable I have ever ex-

* Ezra Pound was one of three men whom I have known who would correspond only on postcards, in order that one should not sell their letters. The other two were T. E. Lawrence and George Bernard Shaw.

perienced. Living within a stone's throw of each other were a number of very intelligent men, Walter Lippmann, Felix Frankfurter, Dean Acheson, Joe Alsop, who were in the thick of affairs at a vital moment in the world's history. With one exception they were all friends, and we met them almost every day in each other's houses. Then two of our friends had beautiful collections within walking distance. If ever the unfortunate word 'civilised' could be accurately applied it would be to Georgetown in the 1950's.

On the non-political side the queen of Georgetown was Mrs Robert Woods Bliss. We had met her with Edith Wharton before the war, and, although she had seemed to us rather a goose, we had gladly accepted an invitation to stay with her in Dumbarton Oaks, the most famous house and garden in Georgetown. She had a lovable, good-natured husband, who, although he was no fool, had realised that the only hope for a peaceful life was to let his wife 'make the running', and had developed the, to me, sympathetic habit of falling fast asleep after dinner. Mildred Bliss was no fool either. She would say something asinine, and follow it up with something very perceptive. For some reason she always seemed more intelligent in French, which she spoke and wrote to perfection, than in English. There is a tradition of silliness amongst Englishwomen that does not exist in France. After the war Dumbarton Oaks became famous as the site of an economic conference and the title of one of Stravinsky's most obscure pieces of music. Finally, the Blisses gave it to Harvard as a centre of Byzantine and early Christian studies, and built an exquisite gallery to display their collection, while they lived in an almost equally agreeable house a few blocks away.

The other great Washington collectors, Duncan and Marjorie Philips, did not live in the family house, but used it entirely to house their collection of nineteenth-century and modern pictures, in which the learning of Duncan and the painter's eye of Marjorie were perfectly combined. It was open to the public free. Duncan's devotion to art was such that his conversation consisted almost entirely of short lectures on his favourite painters, delivered with an air of finality. In fact he was the most diffident of men. When we first stayed with them in their house just outside Washington he asked me at 6.30 if I would like a drink. When I said 'Yes', he was somewhat dismayed, as he did not like to disturb the English butler, but after a short conference with Marjorie he rang the bell. The butler appeared, resentfully, majestically. "Sir Kenneth would like a whisky and soda." "You have one, Duncan", I said. "I, no, no." "Yes, go on." "I'll have a whisky too," said Duncan, with unusual firmness. The enormity of this decision left the butler speechless, but the whiskies appeared.

It was while staying with the Philips's that Jane brought off her greatest diplomatic triumph. Duncan worshipped Walter Lippmann, and always had him to lunch on Sunday. He asked if there was anyone we would like invited as well. Jane answered "Felix Frankfurter", not knowing that he and Walter had had some mysterious estrangement and were not on speaking terms. When this was explained to her she said "It's too sad that such good men, both on the right side, should have quarrelled. Do try." Duncan agreed with great misgivings. When the two met there was a moment's shock, then relief, and finally a return of friendly feelings, which must, I think, have been of advantage to American polity.

I have allowed myself this digression because I want to modify the caricature of rich Americans that English people may derive from the newspapers. Flamboyant and aggressive millionaires undoubtedly exist, but I have known only one, Chester Dale, and he was redeemed by his passion for painting. All the rich Americans I have known, and I have probably known a good many more than the average journalist, have been quiet and intelligent people with a respect for the arts that is extremely rare among their equivalents in England. They are incredibly generous. They found and endow trusts, and form magnificent collections of works of art which they give away. There are no 'national treasures' lurking unseen in American private collections: they will all have been given to public galleries.

The happy days when Felix Frankfurter and Dean Acheson walked down to their work every morning, and Walter Lippmann lunched with Duncan Philips every Sunday, survived into the Kennedy régime. But Georgetown became a backwater and, under Lyndon Johnson that charming society vanished altogether. I am glad that, on one pretext or another, we managed to spend a certain amount of time in Washington every year. But I doubt if I should have enjoyed living there; it was too much like a very superior cathedral close. No one could say that of New York.

★   ★   ★   ★   ★

*The Nude* was favourably received, the only objection to it being my statement that our enjoyment of the nude in art had something to do with sex. I had rather mischievously quoted a sentence from a leading aesthetic philosopher, Professor Alexander, 'If the nude is so treated that it raises in the spectator ideas or desires appropriate to the material subject, it is false art and bad morals', and had not imagined that anyone would take this preposterous statement seriously. But they did. That was in 1956. One could not have believed that Victorian humbug would have lasted so long.

After *The Nude* there followed a period of public activities, which will be the subject of a later chapter; most of my writings were short and topical. But I began to turn over in my mind a possible subject for a long book, which I hoped would be a worthy successor to *The Nude*, and would indirectly expound my aesthetic philosophy. I realised that, in the visual arts, the central problem of aesthetics is the relationship between form and content, and believed that I might go some way towards elucidating this problem by studying certain motives where form and content are so closely connected that they have a recurring fascination for artists, and are used in the illustration of quite different subjects. I first thought of this theme when looking at one of my favourite works of art, the two pairs of porphyry Emperors outside the corner of St. Mark's in Venice, who lay their hands on each other's shoulders. I could remember many other works in which the encounter of two human beings, related to one another in such a way as to achieve a new unity, had been the motive of a moving work of art—Giotto's meeting of Joachim and Anna in the Arena Chapel, Luca della Robbia's *Virgin and St. Elizabeth* in Pistoia, many versions of the Annunciation, Rembrandt's *Jewish Bride*, ending with Brancusi's confronted figures in Philadelphia. Two into one. And with this clue in my mind I went on to discover several other motives that had a powerful effect, in particular that of one beast devouring another. Motives became an obsession to me. When I was reappointed for a year as Slade Professor in 1961, I gave nine lectures on the subject. By this time I had become a 'draw', and my lectures were held in the Oxford Theatre. Only undergraduates were admitted, and the north Oxford ladies who had, for half a century, provided the Slade Professor's audience, were justly indignant. At the door of the theatre were two burly men in bowler hats, known to undergraduates as 'bulldogs'. That my lectures should have demanded the presence of these dreaded instruments of law-enforcement seemed to me the summit of glory. The theatre was packed, but the lectures were not a success. No one could make out what I was trying to say. I gave three of the lectures later to the University of Los Angeles, and they were met by equally polite incomprehension. People expected them to be about the fashionable subject of iconography, and were baffled when they turned out to be exactly the reverse. Finally I gave up in despair. Either the subject was not as rewarding as I had expected it to be, or my intellectual powers were not up to it. But it still haunts me, and, if I live to collect my speculative writings on art history, I shall include one or two of my 'motives' for readers to judge.

## *Writing and Lecturing*

However, one of my Oxford lectures went well. Maurice Bowra, when he was Vice-Chancellor, very loyally invited me to give the Romanes lecture, which is the greatest honour that the University can bestow on a lecturer. I already had in mind what seemed to me a promising subject, those moments of heightened perception which the artist can occasionally embody in his work. What arouses them? How do we recognise them? I wrote the lecture in the solitude of Mr Berenson's *villino* at Settignano, and it shows evidence of a more sustained contemplation than my daily life in London allowed. I could not resist borrowing the title of one of Thomas Hardy's collection of poems, *Moments of Vision*. It remains, on the whole, my best lecture.

In 1958, when I was still threshing around among my 'Motives', I was invited by *The Sunday Times* to do a series of articles on single pictures. This has now become common practice, indeed whole books are devoted to single pictures; but at the time it was a novelty, and I gladly accepted because it would give me the opportunity of describing the very various means by which a great picture conveys its message. I wanted to attack, by implication, the fallacy of one cause. I tried to make the articles easy to read, and evidently succeeded, as dozens of headmistresses of girls' schools wrote to say that they had pinned them up on their school notice boards. Looking through these essays again, I find many passages of keen observation, and very little to be ashamed of. The style was referred to as graceful, which is often only a polite word for facile. In fact they were very difficult to write and are a good deal better written than anything I can do to-day. The subject suited me because it dealt with concrete things. I have gradually learnt that I can be myself only when I have an actual picture before my eyes or an individual artist in my mind. For years I felt it my duty to struggle with general topics, and churned out lectures with titles like 'Art and Society', 'The Value of Art in an Expanding World'. The offprints of these pieces are thick on my shelves. I cannot say that they are bad. They are reasonable, unpretentious and lively. But they suffer from my basic incapacity for abstract thought. Philosophy has for me the fascination of the unattainable. How much Plato, how much Hegel, Schopenhauer, and even Plotinus, have I read, plunging into their depths in a sort of trance of boundless admiration. But when I try to do the same thing only commonplaces come to the surface, and I read my old notebooks on aesthetics with a kind of compassion.

An autobiography must be to some extent a form of showing off. Anyone who describes his character, or records the events in his life, evidently believes them to be of some interest. I must therefore record the fact that I was thought to be a good lecturer. I cannot see any particular reason for this. My voice is not at all sonorous and I do not attempt any flights of oratory. But I feel enthusiasm for my subject, and do a lot of work on it before I begin to write. I assume that what interests me will interest other people. I am never conscious of an audience when I speak, but I enjoy the acting of communication, whether to the few or to the many. This is something I never intended to do but, looking back on the last thirty years of my life, I see that it was what fate had in store for me.

I have been asked to give the chief lectures in Oxford and Cambridge, New York and Washington, Berlin and Copenhagen, Montreal (where all my slides went up in smoke) and Venice (where I lost my voice), so the notion that I was good at lecturing seems to have been widely spread. Two of these invitations gave me particular pleasure. One was to speak in the Rijksmuseum in 1969 on the three-hundredth anniversary of Rembrandt's death. Imagine the British Academy inviting a Dutch scholar to make the official oration on the four-hundredth anniversary of the birth of Shakespeare! The other invitation was similar. It came from the Florentine Academy of Fine Art, of which Michelangelo was the first member, and I am a member myself. I was asked to speak in the Palazzo Vecchio to commemorate the four-hundredth

anniversary of his death. I did so in Italian. These are two of the
events in my life of which I am most proud, and it would falsify
my autobiography if I did not mention them.

Most of my recent lectures have been given on television;
*Civilisation*, which was in the nature of a performance, will be
described in a later chapter; but my last television programmes,
*The Romantic Rebellion* and *Rembrandt*, have been straight lectures,
with the enormous advantage that the camera can focus on a detail. This transforms one's whole mode of presentation. Now on
the rare occasions that I give a lecture with slides I feel frustrated.

If the reader will forgive me for taking myself seriously for
once I will end this chapter by considering what effect lecturing
has had on my way of writing. At first sight it seems to have done
harm. *Piero della Francesca*, which is the only one of my books on
art not to have been given as a lecture, is, on the whole, the best
written. I set out, under the guidance of Logan Pearsall Smith, to
write in a polished style, with occasional purple patches, of which
I was proud. Traces of this can still be found in *Landscape into Art*.
But literary polish is not appropriate to a lecture, which must have
some of the character of the spoken word, and so gradually my
style has grown freer and more colloquial. I do not think this is
all loss. The directness and vividness of speech has advantages
over the intricacies of too self-conscious a style. 'Fine writing', as
it used to be called, has gone completely out of fashion, and to
write in a style that is no longer acceptable can lead to artificiality.
But I still feel a hankering after a fine phrase, and a nostalgia for
those hours spent in what Logan called 'the labour of the file'.
Style is a form of craftsmanship, and, just as I would look with
suspicion on an artist who took no interest in his tools, so I find
myself out of sympathy with the writer who is not interested in
the sounds and overtones of words and in the rhythm of a sentence.

# IV

## *In Europe*

ONE MORNING in the middle of the war the telephone rang, and I heard to my surprise the familiar voice of Mr Gulbenkian. "Never too old to have a new experience, my friend. Where do you think I spent last night? In prison!" When France was occupied Mr Gulbenkian had made his way to Lisbon, and lived in a small, but luxurious, hotel called the Aviz. The Germans did nothing about him or his collection. I cannot imagine how he got through to me on this occasion; but with enough money one can do anything. It seemed that his rivals in the oil world, who had for long been trying to deprive him of his famous five per cent, thought they could discredit him by proving that he was trading with the enemy. They had therefore bribed the Portuguese authorities to put him in prison while they searched his rooms in the Aviz for evidence. With the help of the Turkish ambassador Mr Gulbenkian got back sooner than anticipated. The investigators only just had time to escape, and left his rooms in disorder. Needless to say, they found no incriminating evidence whatsoever. I know who was responsible for this plot, but will not reveal it. I will only say that it did not sweeten Mr Gulbenkian's feelings towards the British Government.

As soon as it was possible to do so I went out to Portugal to see him. It was like a prolonged dream. Lisbon was even more untouched by the war than Sweden, and, in spite of the fact that for four years it had been full of spies, speaking every conceivable language, no one in the shops learned to speak a word of anything but Portuguese. The foyer of the Hotel Aviz led into a square hall round which ran a gallery. In the middle of this gallery facing the front door there was a small protuberance. It was opposite Mr Gulbenkian's room, and the moment anyone entered the hall he would dart out of his room on to the protuberance and scrutinise the newcomer. "Always on the bridge, my friend", he used to say to me. At the same moment his secretary would emerge from a corner room and look down into the hall. The Aviz had relatively few visitors; it probably belonged to Mr Gulbenkian, and it closed down after his death. I was shown to a room of inconceivable luxury, decorated like a rather tawdry and inconsistent illustration to *The Arabian Nights*. After a decent interval I was summoned by my host. His room was quite small and in a green penumbra. It contained a large desk and a number of small tables. On desk and tables were piles of papers, very neatly arranged and kept in place by green glass paperweights. "Always on the bridge". One realised how hard he had to work to defend his enormous fortune. If he had neglected to look through any of those files of papers almost every day, they would have got him. The room contained no easy chair, and rather to my surprise (for he really loved them) he had brought from Paris none of his beautiful objects, not even the Northwick Dechadram nor the Macgregor head, which would have looked at home in this austere setting. We began immediately to talk of the future of his collection: whether or not the Germans won the war was incidental; indeed he never even mentioned the war, which did not surprise me. Next morning Mr Gulbenkian very thoughtfully arranged for his secretary, named Madame Theis, to take me shopping. The reader may have forgotten that clothes as well as food were rationed in England, and we had all grown very shabby. The sight of shops full of beautiful shirts made my mouth water almost as much as those full of beautiful cheeses. Madame Theis was a large, pleasant looking lady, in early middle age, who led, I should imagine, a very restricted life. She was glad of a new companion, and we had a successful morning; but on the following afternoon she made a mistake. She arranged to take me for a drive in the hills above Cintra. This is one of the most beautiful pieces of landscape in Europe, and she knew all the finest views. We returned with our eyes shining with pleasure. This was not lost on Mr Gulbenkian and I was never allowed to see her again, except in his presence. No amount of Westernisation had deprived Mr Gulbenkian of his near-Eastern instincts.

In the evenings we sat on the terrace in the warm darkness (so it must have been September) discussing future plans. The National Gallery extension was not so often mentioned (Mr Gulbenkian had not forgotten his night in prison), but his dreams had become vaster and more comprehensive. His institute was not simply to be an art gallery, but a source of revenue for every kind of cultural activity. Rich as he was, he foresaw that he would become incomparably richer. More than ever the world was going to depend on oil. His first aim was to see that no one took his holdings away from him, and this involved continual hard work. He would delegate nothing—and quite right, too. Where such enormous sums and such complicated manoeuvres were involved no delegate could have been trusted. I described in *Another Part of the Wood* how, during our walks in the Parc de Saint-Cloud, he had given me some notion of the oil industry. During these long warm evenings in Lisbon he went into the subject in much greater detail. Why on earth did he do so? He must have known that I could not grasp it in all its complexity, and would never have occasion to make use of my knowledge. I believe that, like Madame Theis, he was simply lonely. He wanted someone to talk to, so, to that extent, was human, after all. On the following days Mr Gulbenkian took me for expeditions himself. He loved the rocks beyond Cascais, where the Atlantic breaks into vast pillars of spray. On the other hand, he did not approve of the Palace of Queluz. My friends in England had told me that it was the most 'charming' thing in Portugal, and its pink provincial rococo is indeed very seductive; but Mr Gulbenkian, with an eye trained on Versailles and the Invalides, could analyse all its faults. Mansard or Gabriel could not have been more destructive. I used to tease him by saying that he did not like wild flowers. "Ha! Wild flowers, my friend! No, this is simply incompetent."

In spite of my misdemeanours Mr Gulbenkian continued to treat me with great kindness, and invited me to bring out Jane and the children to stay in Portugal during the spring holidays. As the limit of exportable currency was then £20 (or was it £50?) this offer was a godsend. I had noticed in Cintra a modest hotel in the village square, called the Hotel Central and Madam Theis had told me that it was kept by an English lady, who had been Lady Cook's maid in the splendid villa of Monserrat. This seemed the place for us. In fact it was a fraction too uncomfortable (beds too hard, water never hot, food only just bearable), but there was a welcoming atmosphere, and it was a pleasure to walk out on to the main square, with its assortment of Rembrandtesque beggars. I found a number of quiet places with beautiful views in which I could sit and write, and the children were enchanted by shops in which one was allowed to buy things that were rationed in England. They had not seen a banana for six years, and ate so many that they made themselves ill. We were all blissfully happy. Mr Gulbenkian, who had a strong sense of propriety, thought it wrong of me not to stay in the large, fashionable hotel in Estoril; but by this time he had grown resigned to my dislike of grandeur. He rang me up every morning except two, after which he began by saying "You see, my friend, I respect your holiday". By 1945 I had resigned from the National Gallery, which I fear weakened Mr Gulbenkian's resolve to build his institute in Trafalgar Square. My successor never bothered to meet him, and spoke disparagingly of him, so that when John Walker turned his matchless charm on to him his pictures were removed from London to Washington. One very hot day when I was driving with Mr Gulbenkian through the tumbled down suburbs of Lisbon, he began to speak sympathetically about the Portuguese. They were lazy, and unable to seize a main chance, but he liked them. This emboldened me to say something which had long been in my mind: that his great institute should be built in Lisbon. The Portuguese were a poor and deprived people, and all his schemes for human betterment would be of more value in Portugal than elsewhere. Moreover, his collection would be the artistic centre of Lisbon, and would bring visitors to that comparatively neglected town. I must have been the first man he had met who voluntarily renounced a great donation. He emitted the curious sound, somewhere between a grunt and an 'ah', which was always the sign that he was disturbed, and let the subject drop. I do not pretend that I am responsible for the Gulbenkian Institute being in Lisbon. That was achieved by a very remarkable man named Dr Perdigao, who got over all the legal difficulties.

Mr Gulbenkian invited us all to Portugal several times more. On one occasion Jane was ill, and the four of us came out alone. Without her restraining presence we became very unruly. As we were usually alone in the Hotel Central it did not matter, but one evening a couple of serious looking English people, with two children, came to dinner, and even I was a little ashamed at the noise we made. The English couple never spoke. Some years later I met the father—he was a professor in Bristol—and apologised. He said drily "We thought you were a very united family".

Mr Gulbenkian was very kind to the children, and on Alan's eighteenth birthday asked us all to luncheon with him in the Aviz. As we went in he looked searchingly at Alan, and said to me "I can see that he is a fighter". He sat on his raised chair in the corner of the empty dining-room (he always lunched at 3 p.m.) talking to the children like a wise old vizier. The near-Eastern tradition, chiefly Islamic, of a teacher, or chairman as he is called, for he alone may sit on a chair, has been scoffed out of existence in the West, and any father who propounded words of wisdom to his

Saltwood Castle

The library and K.C.'s study
Roman tower and Yevele towers

Jane, K.C. and Emma in front of the towers,
Saltwood Castle

children would be considered a joke. But Mr Gulbenkian did so with such natural benevolence, and, I must add, so much wisdom, that the children were impressed. As I looked at him I pondered on the widely held view that he was one of the wickedest men alive.

The end of my good relations with him came about as the result of an extraordinary piece of bad luck. We had set up Covent Garden as a National Opera and, although we had been promised a government grant, we had been urged by the Treasury to do anything we could to secure outside aid. Our friend Francis Queensberry said he had a partner named Ansbacher who was immensely rich (Francis's eyes were like magnifying glasses), and who would certainly give a huge sum to Covent Garden if we paid him some attention. We therefore asked him to dinner. He turned out to have no interest in opera and ballet, only a natural interest in ballerinas; and he never suggested giving us a penny. Socially the evening was not a success, and we never saw him again. This was soon after the time when Mr Gulbenkian's son, Nubar, was bringing an action against his father for not giving him enough money—only a million pounds. A number of City firms put up the capital for this action, hoping to draw a handsome dividend as a result. Amongst them was the firm of Ansbacher. Needless to say I was perfectly ignorant of these matters. I knew that Nubar had brought a lawsuit, but thought he could have paid for it out of his million pounds. Mr Gulbenkian often talked to me about him with affection "He is a good boy, but weak. He makes the wrong friends". He certainly did, and I suppose it was they who drove him into this action. Nubar's lawsuit naturally failed, and the judge congratulated Mr Gulbenkian on his parental generosity. Father and son resumed (for a time) friendly relations, and Nubar evidently told his father, perhaps out of malice, that Mr Ansbacher had dined with us, and immediately the old gentleman's suspicions were aroused. I was playing a double game, I was in league with his enemies. He wrote me a blistering letter in his own hand. I wrote back explaining why Mr Ansbacher had visited us; but I was deeply hurt by the lack of trust, and did not disguise my feelings. We must have made peace, as I continued to write to him, and even went out to see him in Portugal; and I remember meeting Nubar, who was then on excellent terms with his father, in the Aviz bar. But the episode had repercussions. I fancy that Mr Gulbenkian had thought of me as a possible director of his institute, but further acquaintance showed him that I was not sufficiently thorough. I, on my side, recognised that I was not competent to enter into the recesses of the near-Eastern mind.

Mr Gulbenkian's parents had lived to be well over ninety, and he himself, with his excellent health and careful régime, expected to do the same; but at the age of eighty six he had a stroke, what he described to me as a 'smart alert', from which he never fully recovered. He died at the age of eighty nine. The result is that his final wishes were not given his usual careful consideration, and the Institute in its present form is largely the work of Dr Perdigao. I was asked to speak at the opening, and it was curious to find that each of the three speakers on this occasion spoke of this famous ogre with affection.

Mr Gulbenkian would have recoiled with horror at the sight of the building in which his great collection is housed.\* Inevitably it is in a 'modern' style, and this works well for the Islamic section; but the great pictures and furniture of the seventeenth and eighteenth century look very unhappy in this bleak modern setting, and I wish the architect could have swallowed his pride, or suppressed his moral scruples, and bought some eighteenth-century rooms with fine *boiséries* to give these sumptuous objects an equally sumptuous setting. The Institute also contains an archive which was of interest to me, because it showed the

---

\* And what he would have thought of the activities now carried out by his Trust, and recorded in their annual reports, I do not know. *Il voyait grand*, and I find it hard to believe that he would have sympathised with all the small sociological schemes on which so much of his grant in England is dispersed.

immense pains Mr Gulbenkian had taken to form his judgement on works of art. He took notes on them wherever he went, and bought hundreds of postcards on which he wrote his criticism of the works illustrated. So his collection was not at all the by-product of a rich man's whim.

Portugal was a treat, but of course our first aim was to return to Italy. We had been there in 1939, staying at i Tatti, and never before had Mr Berenson seemed to me so sympathetic. He had quarrelled with Duveen over the authorship of the Allendale Nativity. Duveen wanted him to say that it was by Giorgione; Mr Berenson, partly I believe out of sheer perversity, said it was a Titian. There is some evidence that it was a joint work, and it is ironical that, having done so much to please Duveen, he should have taken this final step away from him over such a doubtful case. It can only have been a symptom of his desire to get out of the whole business of authentication once and for all. In face of the impending war, which he had foreseen for years, Mr Berenson was quiet, gentle and resigned. Curiously enough he did not believe that his old bugbear, Mussolini, would go in with Hitler—he would have nothing to gain and everything to lose. With all his wisdom Mr Berenson could not adjust himself to the crudity of human motives. This was one reason why he would not leave i Tatti in 1939; the other was simply that he could not bring himself to leave his beloved library and his walks in the hills. He loved Italy and loved the Italians, and knew that he would have been unhappy in the U.S.A., and bored in Switzerland. In that last pre-war visit I began to feel that affection for him which, with a little more humility, I might have felt ten years earlier.

When Italy entered the war things began to go badly for him. People who wanted to curry favour with the Fascists said that he was a dangerous alien, even a spy, and it took all Nicky's persuasive gifts to prevent him from being deported. Fortunately he had a letter of recommendation from Ciano. After Pearl Harbour he became technically an enemy alien, and took refuge with a friend who, on the flimsiest pretext (Ambassador from San Marino to the Holy See), enjoyed diplomatic immunity. Mrs Berenson remained in bed in i Tatti too ill and too heavy to move, and the house was taken over by the Germans, who used it to billet all kinds of displaced persons. Confined in a villa with a small garden, unable to see friends or take walks, Mr Berenson would have spent an unhappy year had it not been for his lifelong passion for reading. Anyone who doubts the range and alertness of his mind should look at a book called *One Year's Reading for Fun*, written in his eightieth year, and printed with an introduction written when he was nearly ninety.

I was naturally much worried about him. Friends assured me that he was safely in Switzerland, but, judging by what he had said to me in 1939, this did not seem probable. However, in October 1944 I heard he was back in i Tatti, that the worst damage had been put right, and that, as soon as light and fuel were available, he hoped that we would visit them. Mrs Berenson died in March 1945, so I never saw her again. I owed her a great debt, and would have been glad to tell her so: not that it would have meant anything to her, for in her last years she was 'beyond good and evil'. We returned to i Tatti in 1946, and it was very moving to find that it had not changed at all since we had been there in 1939. But if the building had not changed, and the servants had not changed, the atmosphere had. Vituperation had become very rare, explosions practically unknown. This may have been partly due to the disappearance of Mrs Berenson, who had a positive genius for enraging her husband, whereas Miss Mariano had an equal genius for mollifying him. But it was due even more to a change in Mr Berenson. 'And then he came to himself'. These words were constantly in my mind, because although in the material sense Mr Berenson's career had not been at all like that of the Prodigal Son, he had regained in solitude the unclouded love of beauty which shines out of his early letters; and he had 'come to himself' quite literally, by writing his *Sketch for a*

*Self-Portrait.* Thenceforward practically all his writings were more or less autobiographical.

In the next ten years Mr Berenson behaved to me with the utmost sweetness and generosity. He lent me his villino three times, and allowed me to stay at i Tatti twice, when he was in his sunless mountain retreat at Vallombrosa. He even allowed me to work in his study, and I wrote looking at his Madonna by Domenico Veneziano, one of the most beautiful pictures in private possession. In fact I was treated like a son of the house, and was recognised as such by the servants. If I wanted company there was Nicky's adorable sister, Alda Anrep, who had made herself into a very competent librarian; and between us we planned a redistribution of the books (the library now numbered 50,000 volumes), which was an improvement.

Alda deserves a paragraph to herself. Of all the inhabitants of the little court of i Tatti she was to me the most sympathetic. I remember the first time I met her, saying that I was a little frightened of Mr Berenson. "Aren't you?", I said. "What me be afraid of old BB. How ridiculous." The thought made her laugh uproariously. She had inherited the Russian characteristics of her Baltic forebears, and her sitting-room was exactly like a room in St. Petersburg, decorated with prints and pictures of old Russia. She loved scandal, and sentences beginning "They tell me . . ." usually contained the most appalling revelations. "Oh, no, Alda. It's not possible." "Well, that is what they tell me." But she was also the most affectionate friend, and, surprisingly enough, extremely efficient. It was she more than anyone who was responsible for saving the library during the war by having all the books boarded up, and also for getting the whole place straight in record time. I once did a film about Mr Berenson in which I had a hilarious conversation with Alda: it 'stole the show'. Her part was cut out of the American version.

During two of my visits to i Tatti I was at work on *The Nude* and was trying to look at antique sculpture with an eye unprejudiced by the almost groundless traditions of antiquarianism. Greek art had been Mr Berenson's first love, and he was glad to have someone to talk to about it. We spent a few weeks in Rome together, and gazed at the Hellenistic copies of Greek bronzes in an effort to find the original qualities hidden behind their lifeless execution.

But of course the great experiences were the walks in the garden and the hills. 'Nature I loved, and, next to Nature, Art'; this line of Landor's famous epigram was more true of Mr Berenson than anyone could have suspected who knew him only through his books. He was astonishingly observant of detail, the lines of growth in a plant or tree and its relationship to earth. These things came as a fresh revelation to him every time he saw them. "Where were my eyes yesterday?" he used to say. There was one old tree which he visited as a kind of pilgrimage almost once a month. He said that its roots were a better illustration of his theory of tactile values than anything in art. There should be a photograph of this tree in any book on Mr Berenson, but it is very hard to find; indeed I have never been able to find it since his death, and cannot even say what kind of tree it was. I remember only that it was some miles north of Fiesole, and that the valley behind it led to the Convent of the Camaldoli. We were driven up to the daily walk in the hills by old Parry, his chauffeur since 1900, in a small and very badly sprung car: the days of the panting Lancia were long over. I have never been so biffed about in a car, but Mr Berenson seemed impervious to it. He was thinking only of the prospects that would unfold themselves before him when we arrived at our destination. When we came to the climax of the walk Mr Berenson would stand silent for many minutes, enraptured by the relationship of falling ground and swelling hills, by the placing of every beautiful farmhouse and the dark accent of every cypress. In between these moments of ecstasy he talked, talked, talked about ideas, history and people, but practically never about art. Up to the age of ninety his memory was amazingly retentive and he could cite parallels between the Macedonian cavalry and the Viking ships, or some even more recondite episodes, in a manner that made me feel very humble. He was practically never malicious about people. The extraordinary thing was that, in spite of all his disillusioning experiences and his knowledge of history, with all the ground for pessimism which history provides, he never became a pessimist. He was incurably hopeful, and was always prepared to think that a goose was a swan—and, my goodness, he saw enough geese to put a strain on his credulity. The fact is that he loved life. When he was very old, almost 90, he said "I would willingly stand at street corners, hat in hand, asking passers-by to drop their unused minutes into it". He came to spend more and more time in a small, uncomfortable house called the Casa al Dono, near Vallombrosa. Trees pressed round it, and creepers hung over the windows so that no ray of sunshine ever entered it. Perhaps he thought this would save him from pilgrims, but they came nevertheless, up the long twisty road, and, after losing the way several times, found him, seated in a little summerhouse of fir-cones, like some wise man of the woods of Nordic legend, or a Chinese statesman in retirement. And there was another reason why he liked the Casa al Dono. As one grows older one wants to recapture one's childhood. He had been brought up in Lithuania in a landscape of birch and pine trees, and at Vallombrosa it was on his doorstep.

During his last two years his zest for life began to fade, and gradually he lost the power of speech. Instead of his dapper London suits he was dressed in a sort of black soutane, and wore a black biretta and dark glasses. He seemed to have stepped directly out of a play by Beckett. We went out to see him in i Tatti, and the first impression was painful, but somehow we got on to the subject of the German romantics and, in describing the absurdities of Carolina Schlegel, I made him laugh. Yes, I heard him laugh. Few things in my life have given me more satisfaction.

The villino, where I spent so many fruitful weeks, is a small house on the side of a hill overlooking the garden of i Tatti. It sounds idyllic, and many eminent people have stayed there, including Igor Markevich and Yehudi Menuhin; but it is in fact uncomfortable, and terribly cold in winter. It was presided over by an old lady of Sibylline beauty named Giulia, who lived in the neighbouring hamlet of Corbignano and had never been into Florence. Her husband, who was a worthless character, had somehow acquired a motor bicycle, of which Giulia was very proud. "He is always on the wing" she would say "like a seagull".

I lived in solitude, surrounded by books on the history of religion, which have always been my favourite reading. This may help to account for a curious episode that took place on one of my stays in the villino. I had a religious experience. It took place in the Church of San Lorenzo, but did not seem to be connected with the harmonious beauty of the architecture. I can only say that for a few minutes my whole being was irradiated by a kind of heavenly joy, far more intense than anything I had known before. This state of mind lasted for several months, and, wonderful though it was, it posed an awkward problem in terms of action. My life was far from blameless: I would have to reform. My family would think I was going mad, and perhaps after all, it *was* a delusion, for I was in every way unworthy of receiving such a flood of grace. Gradually the effect wore off, and I made no effort to retain it. I think I was right; I was too deeply embedded in the world to change course. But that I had 'felt the finger of God' I am quite sure, and, although the memory of this experience has faded, it still helps me to understand the joys of the saints.

\* \* \* \* \*

We brought the children out to i Tatti in order that they might see a place which had played so great a part in my life, and Mr Berenson took a great liking to Alan. But for our holidays we went year after year to Venice. It had every advantage: no traffic, inexhaustible delight to the eye, and for the children the Lido, which, in a puritanical spirit, we had never visited before the war. I went out with them once or twice, and dutifully lay in the sun doing nothing; but this is not at all in my character. How people can pass whole weeks in this manner I cannot conceive. I soon became restless and invented some excuse for returning to Venice.

Sometimes in a back canal I can feel the deathly character of Venice, so much insisted on by sensitive spirits like Thomas Mann, and by many Italians. But in general it is a source of end-less happiness, not only on account of its churches and palaces, but because of the untidy intimacy of its narrow *calle*, where one trots along with the crowd and never sees a tourist. Package tours confine themselves to San Marco and the Ducal Palace, and the sacristans of other great churches all tell me that they see fewer visitors than before the war.

To describe the light of Venice is unnecessary. Few great prose writers, from Ruskin and Turgenev downwards, have been able to resist doing so. But I might add a warning that the Venetian light is not always benign. In June the sun is often too strong and the colour becomes as garish as a picture postcard. This changes in autumn. It usually rains from the 12th to the 15th of September, and the Lido closes down. Then comes a month when almost im-perceptible mists filter the sunlight and give a magical bloom to the white stone. The façade of San Giorgio and the Redentore turn a delicate pink, and sensuous pleasure is added to Palladio's intellectual power. All the pleasures of Venice are intensified. In the morning one sits in the Piazzetta and looks past the two columns to the Ducal Palace; in the afternoon one changes from the shady to the sunny side of the Piazza, and can watch the shoppers bustling up the Merceria, the children sliding inter-minably down the pink marble lions, and contemplate the loot-encrusted corner of San Marco. I once had the curious experience of making a film inside San Marco after it was closed. It was full of cats, which had appeared from nowhere. One could not record sound, because the band in the Piazza played till 2 a.m.

and seemed to make a deafening noise in the basilica. One's pleasure in having this holy junk shop to oneself was somewhat disturbed by the strains of the 'Merry Widow'.

One of the lovable things about Venice is its informality; apart from the Piazza anything may happen anywhere. There is hardly a single frontal approach in Venice, except for San Moise. Every walk has in it an element of adventure and surprise, and if one takes an unfamiliar *calle* one suddenly finds oneself in a familiar, but unexpected, *campo*. The perfect time in Venice is the early morning, immediately before or after 8 o'clock Mass, when all the churches are open. After this there are many frustrations for the diligent sightseer, although, Heaven knows, there is always plenty to see. Jane was not an early riser, and it was sometimes difficult to get her under way in time for a little stroll before all the churches close at 12.0. For me the best year in Venice was 1949, the year of the Giovanni Bellini exhibition. I went every day for three weeks, and felt, in all humility, that I had been in the company of a dear and kind friend, who at every point restored one's faith in mankind. Almost alone among supremely great artists Bellini is optimistic. He had known tragedy in his youth, but in middle age he came to look for those things in life that are calm and life-giving. Men, landscapes, buildings, all take on this feeling of natural goodness.

Walking back to the Hotel Monaco, at the corner of the Piazza, I could see through the open doors of an exhibition gallery, large canvasses covered with scrawls of aggressive paint. They screamed and shouted at one from the back of the banal modern gallery. No greater contrast to the quiet and comforting voice of Bellini can be imagined. At first I was horrified, but in the end I went in before visiting the Bellinis, and recognised that these explosions of energy were the work of a genuine artist. It was the first European exhibition of Jackson Pollock. Now that an enormous painting by Jackson Pollock has been made the culminating point in the Metropolitan Museum's exhibition of its masterpieces it may seem that I have no cause to congratulate myself on recognising his greatness; and indeed in his native land there is no difficulty in doing so. He is the archetypal American painter, as Whitman is the archetypal American poet. But in Venice, in the year of the Bellini exhibition, it was less easy.

Venice has given me more happiness than anywhere else in the world; but I have never felt that it is my true centre. I suppose that a residue of my Quaker ancestry has inwardly and unconsciously rebelled against so much self-indulgence. I know that as the train emerges from its tunnel into the Val d'Arno, and I see once more the grey olive trees of Tuscany, I think of the grey-eyed Goddess of Wisdom and feel that I have come home.

Would I have enjoyed living in Florence, as so many of my friends expected us to do? A small house in the Chianti hills is a great temptation; but Florence itself is too circumscribed; everyone knows everyone else too well. The conversation is largely devoted to gossip and scandal. I have always wanted to live somewhere where I could lead several separate lives. This is easily done in London and New York, and a few people have managed it in Paris, but it would not have been possible in Florence.

Florence is a town of essences. The parts are greater than the whole. One cannot saunter in Florence with delight. One passes from one marvellous experience to another, say from Santa Croce to the Baptistry, through uninviting streets, with façades intended to keep people out; and somehow one never seems to participate, as one does in Venice, with the life around one. To this there is one exception, Or San Michele, which is the complete, unravaged child of the Renaissance. There more than anywhere one can feel the continuity of the Florentine spirit, with all its seriousness, its humanity and its unexpected love of beauty. I like it best on a market day, when farmers from the surrounding countryside push round it shouting and bargaining with a Tuscan accent so strong that one can scarcely understand them, and Or San Michele rises above them as the City Guilds intended that it should, to remind them that brute vitality can be humanised and transcended. The Florentines were too serious to accept the baroque; their grim, narrow streets were never opened out. And they were too serious to admit colour: black and white marble and grey *pietra serena* was their limit. When I was young I enjoyed the bracing severity of Florence; now that I am old I find it too restrictive, and go more frequently to Rome.

Rome is the great compost heap of civilisation, one layer lying beside the other, so that at every step one is reminded of some great human achievement. For the time-traveller it offers every day a choice to satisfy his mood—antiquity, primitive Christianity, the glorious early days of the Church Triumphant, the quattrocento, the High Renaissance at its summit, and finally the Baroque in unsurpassed splendour and variety. In contrast to the restriction of Florence, Rome is ample, opening out in unexpected places and revealing a colour of rich, dark greenery contrasting with the pinkish bricks of antiquity and the golden stone of the seventeenth century, which is almost as beautiful as that of Venice. Of course it has been much more damaged than Florence by modern developments. When we first went there, fifty years ago, we could take a car out to the deserted Appian Way, and walk for miles without seeing a modern building or a human being, except for the shepherds, who still wore the huge hats and cloaks that one sees in Pinelli's engravings; walking down from the Lateran to San Stefano Rotondo one could look over vineyards to the Campagna; and, best of all, one could walk round St. Peter's without being rudely prevented by one of the odious Swiss guards and climb a hill behind it on which was one small farmhouse. Sitting on the step, one could see the great dome on a level, and the City behind it. All over now! Greed and bureaucracy have destroyed all these wonderful experiences, which could have been preserved at a very small cost. But in Rome one can always shift one's ground, and if the Vatican Stanze are so full of people that one cannot move, one can find solitude in the mysterious emptiness of the Quattro Coronati, and stimulus in the baroque churches that surround the Piazza Navona. They are not absolutely empty, since they always contain a few ladies in black who feel, as I do, that they bring one to one's knees. When I first fell in love with Borromini his name was almost forgotten (although Roger Fry singled him out for special abuse); now he is beloved by a few amateurs, but his churches are still empty, which shows the huge gap that exists between informed and popular taste. God forbid that it should ever be narrowed! But the day when Pietro da Cortona becomes a travel-agent's talisman, and bus loads of tourists draw up in front of Santa Maria della Pace, is still a long way off.

The reader may ask what these Roman churches have to do with my autobiography. If I had climbed Kanchenjunga, or sailed to Australia in a dinghy, mountaineering and the sea would have been the essential elements in my life. As it is, great works of architecture, seen in their setting, have been my dominant experiences, and have shaped my character and my beliefs. Seeing things in their setting has become more and more important to me. I love individual pictures as much as ever, but to take them away from the places for which they were painted and hang them in galleries is a relatively new convention, and I do not accept it as easily as I used to do. The worst instances are the gold-back paintings of the fourteenth and early fifteenth centuries which were taken out of their churches and hung in rows in the 'Academies' of Florence and Siena. Many of them are mediocre works which lose all their meaning, either as decoration or as objects of devotion, when removed from their altars. If all old paintings were put back into their original positions one would see them less clearly and less often; but one would see them as their original patrons intended; in fact one would see them rather better, because in most churches one can now illuminate the altarpiece in a dark chapel by putting a coin into a slot-machine. Now that the Italians keep half of their galleries shut owing to *mancanza di personale*, in other words a refusal to pay for an adequate staff, they might try putting a few pictures back in their original positions—if the churches would accept them. The reason for this change in my point of view is that, without forgetting the unique character of individual genius, I think of a picture rather less as an isolated 'work of art', and rather more as a response to various human needs. For years I was the dupe of what the Russians call 'western formalism', and I still believe that ultimately a work of art must exist in its own right. But, instead of asking "Who did it?", I tend to ask "In what circumstances was it done?" Having tried to answer that question I begin the process of analysing my own responses and, as far as I dare, interpreting the artist's motives. Finally I come to "Who did it?", the question which occupied so much of my youth. I have said already that the careful scrutiny and application of visual memory, is a good discipline to the eye. The claim that it is a science is unfounded, as so much of the evidence can only be interpreted subjectively; let anyone who uses that word consider the problem of Giorgione and Titian. But I don't suppose that anyone still does. Connoisseurship has passed completely out of fashion, and it is sad to think that a man as gifted as Berenson, and as diligent as Richard Offner, should have wasted their lives on it.

We went frequently to France, for two different and unconnected reasons. One of them was that we had made friends (if that word be applicable in such a curious context) with Mr Somerset Maugham, and he asked us every year to stay for a week or two at his villa at Cap Ferrat. He said he asked us to stay because we were the only people who put the lights out when they went to bed. We were invited in March (in summer there were more lively guests), and it took the place of Edith Wharton's Sainte Claire le Château in Hyères. It is a curious fact that, although I am almost incapable of reading a novel, some of my closest friends in the past have been novelists; perhaps they welcome the company of someone who does not talk to them about their books. Mr

Maugham's villa had been built by a bishop in a moorish style, hence its name, the Villa Mauresque. The excrescences, which might have given it some character, had been pared away, and it had become a large, featureless house, very different from the cosy intimacy of Mrs Wharton's Sainte Claire. It too was surrounded by a well-kept garden but, unlike Sainte Claire, where the garden gradually lost itself in the *maquis*, and one could take limitless walks in the country, the Villa Mauresque was surrounded by equally featureless villas, and I suffered from a feeling of imprisonment. I have never lost my love of taking long walks, I feel that a day without one is almost as incomplete as it would be without a meal; and if I do not take them so often now, this is not because my legs have grown too feeble, but because my thoughts on a solitary walk are now so melancholy that I cannot face them.

We were grateful to Mr Maugham for his hospitality, but staying there was rather a strain. He expected to be entertained, but not too much, as he enjoyed talking himself. More than once he spoke ironically of my flow of conversation. He told his stories with all the skill and economy that distinguish his writings, but sometimes digressed to express his contempt for the Bloomsburies, and his low opinion of Max Beerbohm and E. M. Forster. When Jean Cocteau (who called him 'Somerset') came to call on him, and talked, as I thought, brilliantly, but non-stop, Mr Maugham became extremely restive, and after a time showed him politely to the door.

There have been many descriptions of this strange being, and I will add only a few footnotes. He was very vulnerable, and his well-known cynicism was largely defensive. No doubt he had plenty of grounds for it, as much of his early life had been spent in the world of the theatre, and later he moved into the sort of society where money is the chief objective. It was quite unnecessary for him to see such people who were not even amusing, but I think he enjoyed the confirmation of his cynicism.

He had not seen much of ordinary life since he ceased to be a medical student at St. Thomas's Hospital, and the stories in his books, especially his books on the East, were nearly all collected for him by his extraordinary secretary, Gerald Haxton, who could sit up late drinking with the locals and repeat what he heard to Mr Maugham next day. Of course the narrative skill with which they are retold was entirely Mr Maugham's own, but it is notable that after Gerald Haxton's death Mr Maugham wrote only two more novels, and confined himself to reminiscences and criticism. Every morning he retired to a large room at the top of the house and wrote at a table in a firm, clear hand. His MSS are almost entirely free from corrections. I can guarantee this as several times he showed them to me to consult me, very flatteringly, about an epithet, or even a critical judgement. He was remarkably perceptive of excellence in all the arts. I remember once when we were staying there, Desmond MacCarthy came for the night, and spoke indignantly about the current praise of Dylan Thomas's poetry. He read a piece, very badly (very badly, as he didn't care for poetry) and said "Did you ever hear such nonsense?". "Give me the book", said Mr Maugham, and read the same poem. It sounded sublime. The same was true of painting. In the big sitting-room were pictures by Renoir and Monet in richly carved frames; on the staircase pictures by Matisse; but if one showed him reproductions of work by a painter unknown to him, like Paul Klee, his response was surprisingly quick and just. I once tried him to the limit with a Mondrian. To my astonishment he said "Yes, it is very fine".

The evenings were a problem. We had exhausted our conversation by the end of dinner, and the sitting-room was too big for comfortable talk. There was an ancient phonograph, but fortunately our host did not care for music, so we never heard it murdering the classics. He had one or two songs from musicals that he enjoyed, in particular 'Diamonds are a Girl's Best Friend' but one couldn't play it every night. What he really liked was a game of bridge, but Jane cannot play, and I pretend that I cannot. We were always relieved when he was invited out to play bridge, but it happened too seldom. Sometimes he took us to call on his neighbours, who lived in large houses of unspeakable vulgarity. One of them was called Princess Ottobuoni, who had insulted Mr Maugham's daughter, and been put into an extremely offensive short story under the thin disguise of the Princess Novemali; but they seemed to be on excellent terms. People in small societies can't afford to quarrel for too long. One evening, Mr Maugham said we must go up to Roquebrune to see the Good Friday procession. For some mysterious reason the village of Roquebrune, situated in the middle of the poison belt between Monte Carlo and Mentone, has preserved its original character. All around it are the villas of the rich; Roquebrune itself remains squalid and poor. We left the car outside and went on foot to the pitiful little area outside the church. The procession had not yet begun, but a group of people from Monte Carlo and the surrounding villas was huddled together in a corner of this humble place. It was a chilly night, and the Princess Ottobuoni's nose poked out of her mink coat. Then the church doors opened and a number of pious old women in black, carrying candles and chanting discordantly, walked across the square and up the hill. The group of rich people grew impatient and melted away, agreeing that the performance had not been worth seeing. Only an extremity of boredom would have induced them to make such an expedition.

Mr Maugham was exceedingly kind to us, and we grew to have a genuine affection for him, so it sounds ungrateful to say that we always left the Villa Mauresque with feelings of relief. He was no doubt equally relieved to see us go. We drove to an old-fashioned hotel in Menton-Garavan which belonged to the grand-daughter of *le bon père Desboutins*, who plays such a sympathetic part in all books on the Impressionists, and his gentle imitations of Degas hung around our sitting-room. Our bedroom was a pure Matisse of 1926.

For about twenty-five years before the 1914 war Mentone had been taken over by respectable middle-class English people. At one corner of the *jardins publiques* was the English church; at the other the English tea room. In the main back street was the Scottish Presbyterian church, with a very eloquent Minister. Smart people considered it the most boring town on the Riviera, and it inspired two lines in a song by A. P. Herbert 'People who think that Mentone is dull/Come over and try a wet Sunday in Hull', which gave offence to the people of Hull. But for some reason this English 'take over' stopped short of the old town: I suppose it was considered dirty, and when we took refuge in Garavan its beautiful silhouette, which we could see from our hotel window, was unchanged.

As a child the old town had been almost out of bounds (fear of infection?), but I had persuaded my governess to take me there; and returning to it after forty years whiffs of memory used often to envelop and delight me. I even went out to the villa at Cap Martin which my father had built, and which still belonged to the same formidable lady who had bought it from him. She, too, was unchanged. She had decorated the villa in much better taste, but for some inexplicable reason she had not altered my own room, which was quite commonplace and aroused in me no emotions whatsoever. The Graham Sutherlands lived in the hills behind Mentone; and what hills they are. It sounds like blasphemy, but I believe they are as majestic as the approach to Delphi. And across the Italian border was the marvellous garden of La Mortella, the most coveted expedition of my childhood. We loved it all, and, like so much that we loved, it is all gone. Madame Desboutin's hotel has been pulled down and almost all the other hotels have been taken over by industrialists to provide holiday rooms for their workers. It has become a capitalist Kuibychev. The Presbyterian church is a dance hall; I don't know what has been done with the more substantial gothic of the Church of England.

# In Europe

I have described in my second chapter how my friend Georges Salles had been made Director of the Musées Nationaux, which means Director of the Louvre and all its provincial dependencies. In 1946 he invited me to become a member of the Grand Conseil. Honours usually embarrass me, but this honour gave me great pleasure. It also gave me an excuse for coming to Paris six or seven times a year. The Louvre is not only the greatest collection of works of art in the world, but its very imperfections are lovable. The ordinary gaping tourist, who feels out of his depth in any art gallery, must feel completely lost in the Louvre. But when one grows familiar with the extraordinary juxtapositions of the Louvre (French nineteenth-century painting up a twisty staircase leading from the early Egyptians) they become the object of affection. To adopt a French usage, one might say that the Louvre is a very feminine institution—complex, unpredictable, sometimes maddening, and always enchanting. However, there was nothing feminine about the Grand Conseil. It was made up of about twenty gentlemen (there are now three lady members), a few of them amateurs, a few genuine scholars; the other members of the Conseil d'État, the Finances and other public bodies. I was at first the only non-French member and, as most of my colleagues were unaware of my existence, I was able to observe what the French are really like. The first thing that struck me was that they were very much more disorderly than a similar body would have been in England. They came very late, gossiped with each other, interrupted, got up and wandered about in a manner unthinkable among the Trustees of the British Museum, who sit round as solemn as owls. The reason was that they were easily bored, and didn't mind showing it; and they were bored because it was the practice in the Louvre for the head of a department to 'present' to the Conseil anything he wanted to purchase. This gave him a splendid opportunity for showing off. He introduced his would-be purchase with a mixture of rhetoric and irrelevant erudition that sometimes lasted for twenty minutes. The members of the Conseil grew very restive, but the speaker's face shone with complacency, even when it must have been apparent to him that no one was listening, except our President, M. David David-Weil, the most patient of men. The meetings often seemed interminable, but in fact were over before 12.30, which allowed time for me to walk upstairs with Georges Salles and to discuss any changes that he was considering. Then came lunch in Georges' rooms overlooking the Quai des Tuilleries.

What is civilisation? I have often refused to answer that question, but will answer it now. It was lunching with Georges Salles. The greenish light coming up from the Seine, filtered through the leaves of the Quai, and gave to everything and everyone in his rooms a unity of tone. The walls of his sitting-room were lined with books to the ceilings. The pictures as is usual with French amateurs, were on easels—examples of Matisse and Picasso chosen with perfect discrimination, and a superb late Renoir. On the tables were Maya carvings and Islamic pots, and there was a splendid mask from the Torres Straits, which had been given to Georges by Guillaume Apollinaire, and had been the inspiration of Picasso's *tête nègre* period. (Georges bequeathed this mask to me). In the dining-room were two Vitrines filled with rustic French pottery, genial, fanciful, decorative—nothing could have been further from the good taste rooms in coloured supplements. The food was worthy of this idyllic setting, and so on the whole was the company. Georges had been a great ladies-man in his youth, but the few ladies who came to his luncheons were disappointed and resigned. Instead he used to invite eminent artists and men of letters whom he thought would interest us; I will not 'drop' their names. Eminent men are not always willing to make an effort, even in France, and things went better when there were only a few old friends. My favourite was Francis Poulenc; one felt, under his joyous participation in all that was amusing, the deep seriousness that is expressed in his religious music. He was a passionate lover of painting, and I have never known a man with whom I had rather visit a picture gallery. He had in the highest degree the gift of self-identification with each artist, without which no critic should open his mouth.

Those who saw Georges Salles only at his luncheons might have thought of him as an aesthete and a dandy, and would not have realised how efficiently he carried out his duties. We witnessed a striking instance of this. In 1945 the French, very reluctantly, agreed to hold an exhibition of work by Henry Moore. It was to take place in the recently opened Musée de l'Art Moderne, of which the Curator was a man named Cassou, very intelligent but, since he was almost blind, interested in art chiefly as a subject for dialectics. We arrived in Paris two days before the opening, and found Henry at the exhibition looking as dejected as it is possible for him to look. His work depends very much on how it is placed, and in the Museum, either through malice or indifference, his sculpture was so badly arranged that it made no impression. I asked M. Cassou if we could make a few changes, but he said he had no staff to move these heavy pieces, which was obviously untrue, as he had only just installed them. In despair I rang up Georges Salles. He replied "I will send you the equipe from the Louvre". They arrived in about an hour (including several old friends from 1938), and within the afternoon Henry and I had rearranged the whole exhibition, so that it looked stunning. Georges Salles had only a loose jurisdiction over the Musée de l'Art Moderne, and it was an act of considerable courage to override his colleagues in this way. M. Cassou did not attend the opening, which had a modified success. The School of Paris had been the undisputed centre of art for over a century, and the fact that Henry Moore and Jackson Pollock, to say nothing of Paul Klee and Max Ernst, had become the chief modern artists, was hard for the French to swallow.

In 1961 Georges Salles succeeded David-Weil as President of the Conseil, and so escaped from the drudgery of administration. But soon afterwards his health began to fail. His voice became so faint that his pronouncements as President were inaudible, and he suffered from Parkinson's disease, which he would not admit; but I had grown to recognise it all too well from Maurice Baring and Osbert Sitwell. Those trembling hands are the saddest things a friend can witness. He had had to give up his beautiful rooms in the Louvre, and lived in an apartment overlooking the Luxembourg Gardens, which was arranged with his usual perfect taste; but, without the magical penumbra of the Quai des Tuilleries, nothing looked the same, and when we lunched with him it was usually in a small restaurant in Les Halles. Finally, he would not go out. "Je ne suis pas presentable". When I last lunched with him he was in bed, but he had a view over the whole of Paris, which comforted him.

When Georges Salles died I felt that my close tie with Paris was severed. It is true that he was succeeded at the Conseil by one of the most charming and intelligent of men, René Huyghe. I enjoy every minute I spend in his company; we neither of us stop talking for a minute. It is also true that we had another old friend in Paris, Julien Cain, the great Librarian who transformed the Bibliothèque Nationale from one of the worst to one of the best run libraries in the world. We had travelled out to Russia with him in 1936, and had known him ever since. This good, wise man, who gave hope and confidence to the prisoners in Auschwitz, is often in my mind when I hear people speak critically of the Jews, and I am glad to think that I had the chance of giving him an honorary degree at York University. He lived in the Bibliothèque Mazarin, in rooms full of books and engraved portraits of his favourite authors, presided over by his bizarre and lovable wife. She had been a close friend of Paul Valèry, looked like a very animated Pekingese dog, and talked non-stop in a squeaky, but not unpleasant, voice. She had clear ideas about the English; they liked sweet-peas, strawberry jam and whisky, and all these were provided at her tea parties.

France has been very kind to me in my old age. I have been

made a member of the Académie des Beaux-Arts and of the Institut de France. I have been given the gold medal of the Académie itself. Sitting under the cupola of the Institut, that perfect creation of the great Mansard, I have had plenty of time to reflect on the difference between our two cultures. I doubt if Matthew Arnold was right in saying that England needed an Academy. We have several, even a Royal Society of Literature, where one is given a cup of tea in the basement of a house in Bayswater. To give an academy dignity and splendour, as the French have done, one must have a ruler and a ruling class that genuinely believe in the value of culture. In the nineteenth century the only man who had this belief was a foreigner, the Prince Consort, and the upper classes considered him ridiculous. Power was in the hands of men like Palmerston, who thought learning and the arts were an absurd interruption to the pursuit of politics. Even Lord Salisbury declined to give a grant to the South Kensington Museum on the grounds that Her Majesty's government saw no reason to provide people with luxuries. The English are a philistine people, and I will not deny that I am proud to have been received into the long tradition of French culture. But I can no longer enjoy this honour as I should; and I think wistfully of green light and happy talk at Georges Salles's luncheons, and of the strawberry jam, whisky and sweet-peas of Madame Cain's tea parties.

# V

## *Private Life and Public Works*

W HEN WE GAVE UP our house in Gloucestershire my
mother, who had been living with us, retired to a
small, sunny bedsitter in an hotel in Cheltenham.
She had come a long way from the splendours of Sudbourne, and
it suited her far better. She became once more the frugal, orderly,
Quakerish lady that she had been when my father picked her out
of her home in Haslemere. She could make her tea in the morning,
walk for half an hour in the garden, observe, with her clear and
critical eye, the other guests in the hotel, and take a strong tot of
gin before going back to bed. As far as I know she did absolutely
nothing else, but she never complained of boredom, or even of
indigestion. Self-pity and hypocrisy gave place to a peaceful
acceptance of life. Our son Colin was at Cheltenham junior school,
and used to pop in to see her practically every day during term
time. He had already developed that gift of sympathy which has
distinguished him ever since, and I believe his visits gave my
mother as much happiness as anything she had known since her
girlhood. But she remained remarkably reticent. She would not
talk about the past, and showed very little interest in my activities; she gave me the feeling that she thought my busy public life
was a waste of time (which it probably was), and she never read
one of my books or articles. However, it was a blessing to have
her so benign, and a certain unspoken intimacy grew up between
us.

Returning from our second happy holiday in Portugal we were

met at the airport with the news that she had had an accident. We went to Cheltenham immediately, and found that, as usual, the accident had been more serious than anyone had liked to say. She had fallen downstairs, broken her hip and banged her head. She was barely alive and her mind was very confused; I could not tell whether or not she recognised me.

A complicating factor was that Mr Bevin had persuaded me to go out to Chicago to open the first important exhibition of English painting to be sent overseas since 1938. It had to be rather a long assignment, starting with a visit to Washington to pick up our Ambassador and take him on, silent and indifferent, to Chicago. Altogether I should be away at least ten days. I hate breaking engagements, and at this date England was very unpopular in Chicago. Every day we were attacked in the McCormick press, and the mayor threatened to come over to England and 'punch George V (who had died ten years earlier) on the snout'. Any change of plan could have been interpreted unfavourably. I knew slightly Lord Horder, then the most eminent English doctor (we had both been asked by the Foreign Office to sign a polite letter to Hitler from 'men of good will', asking him to be nice to us), and in despair I asked him to visit my mother in Cheltenham and advise me. Most doctors funk giving a diagnosis. Horder was always prepared to do so, and it was usually correct. He said "Your mother will live for three weeks. She will not notice that you have gone away, but will recognise you on your return". I therefore went to Chicago and Jane stayed behind with my mother.

In spite of the many beautiful pictures in the Art Institute my week in Chicago was one of the most miserable of my life. The only thing I enjoyed was the banquet, in which I sat next to the famous Robert McCormick, the arch-enemy of England. He admitted that his hatred of England was due solely to the unhappy years he had spent at an English private school, and after dinner he made a speech 'off the cuff', which was pro-British.

Our Ambassador replied, reading a prepared speech, and never taking advantage of McCormick's change of tone. Was it simply that he could not be bothered using his mind, or was it Foreign Office practice? I must also confess to a certain exhilaration at the opening, when I had to address an audience of four or five thousand, stretching out of the Art Institute and along Lake Shore Drive. I realised how dictators become intoxicated by such experiences.

On my return I went straight to Cheltenham, and Lord Horder's prediction was exactly fulfilled. My mother recognised me, and the next day it was apparent that she was dying. I sat silently in her darkened room, and suddenly her mind cleared. She spoke to me with a love and understanding she had never shown before. What mysterious inhibition had prevented her from talking to me like this before? And what Heaven-sent intervention had allowed her to do so in the last half-hour of her life?

My mother's death had a ridiculous sequel. She had been looked after by an exceptionally stupid doctor, who reported that her death was due to her having fallen downstairs. The result was a coroner's inquest, and I had the interesting experience of witnessing the relish with which a small-minded man conducts this operation. The coroner seemed anxious to prove that I had pushed my mother downstairs. I pointed out that I was in Portugal at the time of the accident, and could produce my passport to prove it. "Well, we shall see." Temporarily foiled, he started on a new line of attack, and said that I had done nothing to help her on my return. I said that I had persuaded Lord Horder to come down to see her. In Cheltenham in 1946 a peer was an object of respect and not, as nowadays, of derision. "Ah, Lord Horder", said the coroner, in a different tone of voice, "then you may go." The whole episode taught me what defenceless people must suffer from local officials anxious to justify their positions.

We continued to live in Upper Terrace House, and are said

to have given 'glamorous' parties, but I do not remember any of them, except for one luncheon when we heard, as our guests were arriving, that our daughter had won the top scholarship at Oxford. This made us both weep with joy, and when we met the Queen Mother at the door she was astonished to see tears pouring down our cheeks.

Our children were always a joy to me. When I read of people who have been hated by their children, and even been betrayed by them, I realise how lucky we were, and still are. Alan was at Oxford, where he was later joined by Colette. They are both people with good minds, but at Oxford they decided to live for pleasure, and were, I suppose, a disappointment to their tutors. They have made up for it since. Colin, after doing his military service in the R.A.F., and becoming a jet pilot, also went to Oxford. He seemed to be getting a lot out of it but, like many ex-service men, he found the disciplines of the university life a step backwards. He therefore left Oxford and became personal assistant to Lawrence Olivier, a job for which his naturally sympathetic character suited him perfectly. He had daunting allocations, like waking Marilyn Monroe in the morning and telling her that she was already three hours late on set. (Olivier was acting in a film with her called *The Prince and the Showgirl*.) And he had to look after Vivien Leigh during the tour of *Titus Andronicus*, when she passed through one of her bad phases and almost had to be taken home. He was to have been in charge of the second unit in the Olivier film of *Macbeth*; but, even after the success of *Henry V* and *Richard III*, money could not be found to make it, and so posterity was deprived of seeing what I believe was Olivier's greatest performance.

Meanwhile, Jane had become president of the Incorporated Society of London Fashion Designers, partly because she was always so well dressed, and partly because they knew she could be trusted to do the job conscientiously and without pushing herself forward. This involved grand fashion shows at Upper

Terrace, which, as a lover of feminine beauty, I ought to have enjoyed; but for some reason I have never found fashion models at all attractive, and so the occasions have vanished from my memory.

Although I can remember very few of our own parties, I do remember one dinner party at No. 10 Downing Street, which I may describe, as it has a certain historical interest. As I hold an Italian honour, and am known to speak Italian, I am on the Government hospitality roster as someone who can be invited when an eminent Italian is being entertained. We were therefore invited to No. 10 Downing Street for a dinner given for the Italian prime minister, di Gaspari. Madame di Gaspari sat on Mr Churchill's right, but, as she spoke no English and he spoke no Italian, conversation in a rather rudimentary French was rapidly exhausted. I was sitting opposite, and heard Madame di Gaspari say to Field Marshal Alexander, very slowly, "Do you know Italy?" He replied "Yes, Ma'am, I do, a bit." "Where have you been?" she went on inexorably. "Oh, up and down, don't you know", he replied, "up and down." I wonder if she ever discovered who he was. I had been looking across at Mr Churchill somewhat apprehensively, but when the time came he made an excellent speech about Italy, and one could feel a wave of relief passing over the guests. The men left the table immediately after the ladies, and we got as far as the door of the drawingroom when Mr Churchill slumped into the first chair. I saw Jane standing nearby, and told her to sit beside him. He took her hand and said "I want the hand of a friend. They put too much on me. Foreign affairs . . .", and his voice drifted away. I discovered Mary. There was no doubt of what had happened. Mary and Christopher got him to bed. This took place in 1953, and Mr Churchill never recovered the full use of his faculties.* It is unforgiveable that the Tories should have persuaded him to stand

---

* Lord Moran, whose memoirs of Churchill are so vivid and convincing, was not present on this occasion, and his account of the episode is not quite correct.

again as Prime Minister. They might have pleaded that they had no one to put in his place except Anthony Eden, but in fact they thought that the name of Churchill would allow them another term of office.

★   ★   ★   ★   ★

During one of our visits to Portugal Maynard Keynes had died, and most people imagined that I would succeed him as chairman of the Arts Council. I confess that I expected to do so, and rather looked forward to the prospect. I still thought of myself as a 'public servant', and enjoyed having to make decisions. I was not so foolish as to imagine that such positions give one what is known as power. Even a cabinet minister has very little power. It is something confined to those in very humble occupations: the ladies in white coats who carry a sign saying 'children crossing' have power, and enjoy using it. But the Treasury have a principle that a volatile chairman, and in Keynes's case a brilliant one, should be succeeded by what the eighteenth century used to call 'a man of bottom'; and they discovered an amiable example in Sir Ernest Pooley, who was Warden of the Drapers' Company. Having no interest in the arts he could be relied on not to press their claims too strongly. After a moment's disappointment I felt relieved at not having on my hands the tricky juggling with human relationships which I saw would be inevitable.

A year later I asked leave to retire from the Arts Council for a year or two. I had been chairman of the Art Panel for almost ten years, and thought that the Panel would benefit from a change. I was lucky to be away at that time, because Pooley came to the conclusion that there should also be a change in the general direction, and set himself to get rid of Miss Glasgow. How this was achieved I never asked; it must have been a painful process, as the Arts Council was her whole life and, although sometimes a little governessy, she seemed to me to carry out her duties in an exemplary manner. She was succeeded by W. E. Williams.

*129*

Meanwhile I had become involved in something far better worthwhile. In *Another Part of the Wood* I describe our love of opera, which had led us every year to the Scala, Berlin and Vienna. Thanks to the generosity of Sir Thomas Beecham (who, it should be remembered, had spent all his own money before he began to spend other people's), and the persuasive powers of Lady Cunard, Covent Garden offered a season of three months every year, and we went as often as we could. But our real education in opera took place later at Sadler's Wells. The Director, Norman Tucker, had a love and knowledge of opera that I have never known equalled, and he had the courage to put on a series of works which are prominent in all books on the subject, but are seldom performed. What an astonishing list it is! *Werther, Russalka, The Cunning Little Vixen, Count d'Ory, Bluebeard's Castle, The Pearl Fishers, Mahogonny*—I mention only a few of the less obscure. We went to them all, and had an education in opera that we could not have achieved anywhere else.

The finances of opera are very peculiar. The moment you move into a grand opera house a production costs not twice as much but ten times as much as in a more modest theatre. Norman Tucker's productions were perfectly adequate. In some cases (e.g. John Piper's *Simone Boccanegra*) they were positively better than subsequent productions of the same work at Covent Garden. But the theatre itself is off the beaten track, had effectively no boxes, and only a small, crowded bar. Sadler's Wells lacked the 'panache' that persuades society people to go to opera and could not afford stars.

During the war the Covent Garden Opera House had been occupied by Mecca Cafés, which provided the kind of entertainment that is always supposed to be more suitable in a national emergency. But after the war it evidently ceased to make money, and the lease was taken over by Messrs Boosey & Hawkes. They asked for an interview with the Arts Council. Keynes was away in the U.S., either at Bretton Woods or Dumbarton Oaks, and I, as vice-chairman, received the deputation. Mr Boosey explained what they had done, and suggested that the Arts Council might be willing to put on a short season of opera, say in August. As with Myra Hess and the National Gallery concerts, I said "No; we will take on Covent Garden altogether, giving your firm full representation on the Board". I had long dreamed of seeing Covent Garden established as a national opera, and the moment had come. I immediately wired to Maynard Keynes at his arboreal conference, and received his enthusiastic assent. I then referred the project to the Treasury. I told them frankly that I had no idea what it would cost, but that state operas on the continent were known to be very expensive. My enthusiasm must have melted their hearts, and they agreed. I may add, in parenthesis, that when Keynes returned he said to me "How much will it cost? About £25,000 I suppose," which showed a kind of *légèreté* that I often observed in him. I said "Add a couple of noughts", but he thought I was joking. Messrs Boosey & Hawkes behaved with great public spirit and made the take over as easy as possible.

There remained the crucial problem of finding a director-general. The obvious choice, Rudolph Bing, was ruled out because he was connected with Glyndebourne, and Keynes had an ancient, implacable hatred for John Christie, which Christie returned with interest. A year or two earlier we had been to Liverpool to hear a performance by the Liverpool Philharmonic of William Walton's *Belshazzar's Feast*, and had met the chairman of the orchestra, David Webster. He loved opera, knew it well, and was an experienced administrator. As we went home after dining with him we said "That is a man who might run Covent Garden, if ever it became a National Opera". So when Boosey & Hawkes asked me to suggest a possible administrator for what was still their project, I pronounced, rather hesitantly, the name of David Webster. Apparently someone else had already mentioned his name to Mr Hawkes, and so he was appointed in August 1944, some months before the setting up of the

Covent Garden Trust. It was a shot in the dark, and I must confess that for some years I thought it had been a bad shot. David Webster did well in putting the house back into its former condition. This was still the age of rationing, and every member of the Covent Garden staff gave up some clothing coupons so that the seats might be covered in their original red stripes. He built up a good orchestra and an excellent chorus. But to run an opera house —still more, to create an opera company—requires something more than enthusiasm and business experience. One needs to have been, as our parents used to say, 'born and bred in the cabbage patch'; and unfortunately there was no such cabbage patch in England except for the excluded Glyndebourne. David Webster didn't really know the field and would not turn to anyone who could advise him in case he would be overshadowed. He chose as his musical director a minor figure named Karl Rankl, and for some years we put on performances which varied between mediocre and bad. Finally, the Trustees felt that they must talk to Rankl. He said "A conductor—the little man in the box—is of no importance". As we all knew that a conductor (to put it on a merely statistical basis) can make a difference of half an hour to the length of a performance, we were not much impressed. When Kleiber took the place of Rankl, and put on excellent performances of *Wozzeck* and the *Rosenkavalier*, things began to look up.

The Directors had decided that our operas should be sung in English. After all, Italian operas are sung in German in Germany, and vice versa. But these are the two opera languages, and star performers know their parts in those forms. They were reluctant to learn them in English. As a result we were largely restricted to English-speaking (chiefly Australian and Welsh) singers, which deprived us of some snob appeal. On the other hand, it forced David Webster to build up an English company with excellent results. Later the rule about singing in English was relaxed, and it was nice to hear the sound that only an Italian tenor can emit.

But the substratum of an English company was there, and this was Webster's great achievement.

Keynes, being married to a famous ballerina, was naturally more interested in ballet than in opera, and his greatest coup as chairman was to persuade Ninette de Valois to take the Sadler's Wells ballet to Covent Garden. Sadler's Wells was already a great name in ballet, and she did not like the idea of sinking it in the title The Royal Ballet. But when she saw the size of the stage, and the possibilities it offered of splendid productions, she agreed.

Maynard Keynes did not have long to enjoy his chairmanship of Covent Garden. One night, when I had gone on ahead to Cintra, Jane was with him in his box when a curious episode took place. The door of the box opened, in the middle of a scene, and a man in a black cloak stood there and put his fingers to his lips. "Who is that?" said Maynard rather jumpily—neither Jane nor Lydia knew, and the man disappeared. Jane told me the story when she arrived in Cintra next day. "That was death", I said, thinking of course, of the mysterious stranger who had appeared to Mozart and commissioned the Requiem Mass. Next day we read in the paper that Maynard had died.

The problem then was who should succeed him. There were several well-informed musicians on the Board, but we needed something quite different, a man whom the Treasury would trust—and respect. Such a man existed in the person of Sir John Anderson, who was, in the opinion of Whitehall, the greatest administrator of his day. His official duties had allowed him no time for music, but his wife saw that the chairman's box at Covent Garden was a social asset and she persuaded him to accept. Whether or not one knows anything about a subject, to be a chairman is a métier in itself; and John Anderson was an admirable chairman. He appointed a perfect secretary to the Board, Garrett Moore, who was later to become chairman himself. He recognised David Webster's weaknesses, but condoned them. The only trouble came when he had to speak about an actual performance; for example, the famous Wotan, Hans Hotter, fell off a rostrum in the *Rhinegold*, and when he appeared again in *Siegfried* Sir John was worried that he still had something wrong with one eye. No one liked to explain to him that this was part of Wagner's *libretto*.

My hope that Sir John could cope with the Treasury was not misplaced; he wrung from them incredible sums of money, and since in opera money is power, he was responsible, more than anyone else, for the development of Covent Garden from a doubtful experiment into one of the great opera houses of the world. I too drew a dividend, because the Andersons (or Waverleys as they had become) were often away on cruises, and I, as vice-chairman, fell heir to the Royal Box. I deserved it, because had I not acted so decisively when Boosey & Hawkes first came to the Arts Council, we might have had to wait many years for a national opera.

When I was at Oxford, a young Don, who believed himself to be a judge of character, said to me "You have no loyalties, outside your family". This was, and has remained true: with one exception: the Royal Opera House, Covent Garden. For thirty years I have not only enjoyed performances there, but have developed an affection for the whole place—the auditorium, the foyer and the members of the staff, which is like a family feeling. Not being able to go there during the seven or eight years of Jane's illness was the only deprivation that I really minded; and the fact that my daughter has become the first woman to be a director of Covent Garden, and loves it as much as I do, is one of the things in my life that has given me most pleasure.

★　★　★　★　★

After a year or two I returned to the Arts Council, and later succeeded Pooley as chairman. People used to confuse it with the British Council (which deals with arts outside England and the teaching of the English language). The British Council was believed to be in poor condition, and I received many congratulations on having taken it over, particularly from members of the government. Its chairman, Sir Ronald Adam, was a liberal minded General, whose support of the Army Bureau of Current Affairs probably did have some effect on the election of 1945. Many of my congratulations took the form "I'm so glad you have taken over from that damned old Bolshie, Ronald Adam". This shows how little serious politicians think or know about cultural façades.

I cannot say that the Arts Council prospered under my chairmanship, or that I enjoyed my spell of office. I sat at an empty desk in a large, dignified room (formerly Lord Astor's library), and once or twice a week had a short interview with the Director-General. Almost every day the directors of the departments burst into my room with grievances, and I gave them glasses of sherry. I was not allowed a secretary; the Director-General said that his own secretary would bring me in such letters as it was appropriate for me to see, together with his answers. I had not realised that a chairman's duties were so restricted, and apparently said so, as Sir William Haley was asked to invite me to luncheon in order to explain my duties. He said that the best chairman the BBC ever had, J. H. Whitley, had looked in on only two afternoons a week. In other words, a chairman's duty was to whitewash the decisions of his administrative officials when they were discussed by the Board. This is the bureaucrat's dream, as we know from Crossman's diaries. It did not suit me at all.

I enjoyed the Board meetings. If one must sit on a committee it is preferable to sit in the Chair, because one can not only expedite business but can observe the characteristics of members of one's Board and try to draw them into the discussions, sometimes all too successfully. The Board of the Arts Council was well chosen, and some of its members, especially the Welsh members, left over from the old Tom Jones days, were very helpful to me. But our activities were hindered by a chronic shortage of money.

Our main claimants, Covent Garden, Sadler's Wells and the leading orchestras, used up practically all our grant. As a result our meetings often had that negative and despondent character which has now spread to every branch of a bankrupt country. By a curious paradox the Arts Council's income is now immense, over ten times the size it was in my time, and I often wonder what I would have done (if I had been allowed any say in the matter) with such an enormous sum. The truth is that I find State patronage of the arts a baffling problem. From the consumer's point of view it is moderately easy. Stage companies and orchestras can be subsidized, and a good many local efforts, especially in the theatre, deserve support. It is easy to run exhibitions, and arguable that the Arts Council should have its own Collection as a supplement to that of the Tate. It can also support young singers or musicians, arranging for them to travel and to train. This is probably the part of its work which is least in dispute. But when one passes from the executant to the creator I doubt very much if there is anything the State can do. We know that certain writers, composers and artists go through bad times, but an Arts Council must not become a charitable organisation. This area should be left to bodies like the Artists General Benevolent Fund. Discovering and encouraging talent is a notoriously chancy business. It is, or should be, the principal function of publishers and art dealers, and they are more likely to succeed than the committee of a government body. Many earnest and intelligent men, like Sir William Rothenstein, used to advocate state supported schemes of mural decoration. The ability to bring off a large mural decoration has been, since Tiepolo, extremely rare, and practically the only nineteenth-century painter who succeeded in it was Delacroix. Even Munch, one of the greatest figure painters of his time, was less successful on a monumental scale. What finally killed the idea was the Federal Arts Scheme in the U.S.A., initiated in the 1930 depression, and run by conscientious men. It filled public buildings with mural paintings, most of which have now been whitewashed over. I write all this from the old-fashioned point of view that the aim of State patronage is to produce good works of art; but I am told that at a recent meeting of critics in Oslo it was agreed that the sole aim of painting was to support the political system of the state. Only the British dissented. Under these circumstances an Arts Council becomes unnecessary, and its functions can be handed over to a ministry of propaganda.

This was certainly not our trouble at the Arts Council. As I have said, the government was hardly aware of our existence, and we never 'got into the press'. We worked in a low key, and the only activities that I remember enjoying (apart from the Board meetings) were one or two concerts, and some small exhibitions which I arranged myself on such modest themes as the drawings of J. F. Millet and of Charles Keene.

Eighteen months after I had become chairman of the Arts Council I took on a gigantic and far from delicate operation, the founding of the Independent Television Authority, and enjoyed it almost as much as I disenjoyed the Arts Council. Is it too fanciful to say that, of the two sides of my inheritance, my father's pleasure in building up a business took over from my mother's love of economy?

Like all pseudo-intellectuals I had at first been hostile to the idea of television. It seemed to threaten the humanising predominance of books, which was the background of our lives. I remember vividly the moment in the garden at Upper Terrace when a forceful and intelligent lady named Vera Poliakov made me realise the enormous importance of television and its powers for good or evil. I was converted in a flash. During the long argument that had preceded the passing of the Television Act I had been in two minds. It was obvious that Commercial Television would produce a *cloaca maxima* of rubbish, but the television produced by the BBC was often extremely dismal. Even the most virtuous institutions cannot help taking advantage of monopolies. I realised that television was above all a popular medium, and believed that commercial television might add some element of vital vulgarity which is not without its value. Who would want to close down the *Daily Mirror* and the *Daily Express* and leave the average man with nothing to read but *The Times* and *The Guardian*? Added to which, my experience in the Ministry of Information had taught me that the *Mirror* and the *Express* often came out with truths that the establishment wanted to suppress.

When, therefore, Lord de la Warr, who as Postmaster General was the Minister in charge of installing Independent Television, asked me by telephone if I would be a member of the new Board, I gave a guarded assent. Next day he rang me up again and said "You might as well hang for a sheep as a lamb. Will you be Chairman?" This required more thought, and I asked to see a copy of the Television Act. Reading it carefully I saw a number of ways in which the Authority could intervene and prevent the vulgarity of commercialism from having things all its own way.

Why did Buck de la Warr invite me? I can only suppose that my name had respectable associations, and he thought that it might allay criticism in what might be called Athenaeum circles. In this he was mistaken. Their odium was not allayed, but was focussed on me, and when, soon after my appointment was announced, I entered the dining-room of the Athenaeum (as a guest) I was booed. To this general execration there was one paradoxical exception, Lord Reith. He had been the fiercest opponent of commercial television, and had made a speech in the Lords comparing it with the bubonic plague which, to those who knew anything about bubonic plague, seemed to be going rather far. But the day after my appointment was announced Reith (whom I had not seen since he left the Ministry of Information) appeared in my room at the Arts Council and announced that he would be happy to work under me on the ITA 'in any capacity'. Should I have been flattered? I don't think so. This was only a delayed by-product of Reith's grudge against the BBC. I replied as best I could—that it would be unthinkable for the creator of a great institution to take a subordinate position in a small one; that, far from working under *me*, he should hold some great public office and be directly responsible to the Crown. He was only half deceived, and left asking me to think it over. As I knew that no one would believe this story, I immediately rang for my secretary and dictated a full account of the whole interview. If I had read Reith's diaries I would have known that episodes just as incredible took place every few weeks. No wonder that reviewers of his book, who had not experienced the charm and intelligence that made up half his character, stated bluntly that Reith was mad.

Lord de la Warr had already appointed several other members of the Council, including my Vice-Chairman, a forceful man of business named Sir Charles Colston. He had also extracted from the Post Office staff an exceedingly able civil servant named Wolstencroft to guide my steps. He was a very modest man, but the ITA owed more to him than to all the rest of us put together. It was no use my thinking up policies until I had a Director General who would implement them, and thus began one of those searches for 'the right man', which seem to have occupied so much time in my life. On these occasions one has to fight on two fronts. The Treasury always hopes to get rid of some troublesome claimants, in particular disgruntled members of the armed forces. They gave me the choice of nine admirals, seventeen generals and six air-marshals, and said that they would be much disappointed if I did not find the right man among them. I interviewed them all, and things used to go quite well till I asked them the question "Are you interested in communicating with people?" The admirals did not know what I meant and were genuinely puzzled. The generals usually admitted that they were not. Only one air-marshal said that he was, and nearly got the job in consequence. The other group of applicants—journalists, cranks, do-gooders, do-badders—was much more difficult to deal with, as most of them had influential sponsors; and, although they often had more qualifications than the admirals, they were less agreeable characters.

Meanwhile, I had made up my own mind as to who the right candidate would be, but did not mention his name until, at a meeting of the Board, we seemed to have come to the end of our tether. This was Robert Fraser, whom I had known in the Ministry of Information, where he had seemed to me one of the ablest and most sympathetic of my colleagues. No one could say that he was unused to 'communicating with people'. He had been a leader writer on the *Daily Herald*, Parliamentary candidate for the Labour Party, and in 1954 was Director General of the Central Office of Information. My only fear was that I could not make the job of Director General of the ITA sufficiently attractive to him. I used all my powers of persuasion. Finally he agreed, partly because he could see possibilities; partly, I believe, out of friendship. I had got his agreement before putting his name to my Board, because I was afraid that, if his record were investigated, his early connections with Labour might prejudice my strongly Tory Board. I rightly surmised that none of them would have heard of him, and, if I could push his name past my exhausted colleagues at one sitting, all would be well. This in fact is what happened. I informed Bob Fraser next day, and he was duly appointed.

Much of my pleasure in founding the Independent Television Authority was due to the fact that I was working with a man in whom I had complete confidence. We had some very difficult decisions to make, but I knew that on each of these Bob would tell me exactly what was in his mind, and I would do the same to him. We had rooms next to one another and a really wonderful Scottish secretary, whose name, Alison Watt, I would like to record. The only point at which we differed was that Bob was too trusting. He is an Australian, and had retained something of the innocence which makes Adelaide such an enchanting town. Sometimes in discussing a proposition put forward by one of our companies he would say to me "Oh, what a nasty mind you've got".

I ought, perhaps, to say something about the structure of the ITA, which must seem almost incomprehensible to an American reader. The Authority built and owned the stations, and was technically responsible for transmissions, but it was not responsible for the content of what was transmitted. This was the responsibility (if one may use such a word) of the companies which we had appointed to make the programmes. The Act allowed us to appoint as few or as many companies as we wished; it looked to us at first that a correct number would be five or six. We had to allocate our companies so that each of them got a more or less equal share of advertising revenue, which at first meant splitting London into weekdays and weekends. One of the points upon which the Act was most insistent was that we should avoid anything that looked like a monopoly; no company should have a share in any other company. This turned out to be quite difficult because one character, whose name is entirely unknown to the public, and I have forgotten it myself, was determined to achieve a monopoly by forming companies under different titles, for which he himself provided the capital. Fortunately for me he had to give the names of the proposed directors, and, by reference to the Financial Times Library, it was possible to find if they were members of one of his parent companies.

By now the reader will have realised that I enjoyed my chairmanship of the ITA. In contrast to the dismal obstructions of the Arts Council, there was always 'something doing'. The best fun of all was appointing the programme contractors; of course one should not describe it like that, for they had millions of pounds at stake, but fun it was, all the same. The differences of approach and the revelations of characters were a feast for the student of human nature, and I now greatly regret that I did not immediately sit down and write a description of each interview. I should add that most of the applicants were likeable people; they were not, as is commonly supposed, arrogant and overbearing, and I got on with them rather better than I have done with some of my colleagues. I believe that the establishment attitude to figures in 'big business' has in it a large admixture of snobbishness. I remember General Sir Ian Jacob, when Director General of the BBC, who, by the way, behaved to me very generously, saying to me "Have you ever met that feller Roy Thomson? My God, did you ever see such a feller!" How can anyone who knew the friendly and straightforward Roy Thomson have made such an absurd statement except out of snobbery. Another example: when we were about to appoint the commercial television company later known as ATV, I invited its principals to come to my room and meet some members of my Board. They were Prince Littler, Val Parnell and Lew Grade. Prince Littler was very quiet and practical, and my Board swallowed him without difficulty. Val Parnell was everything they expected show-biz to be like. But Lew aroused their latent snobbery, and they all protested to me about his inclusion. "He's the best of the bunch", I said, and the subject was dropped.

We wanted our first three companies to represent, as far as possible, different aspects of 'communicating with the public'. We therefore chose a theatrical group (Prince Littler & Co.), a newspaper group of which the principal shareholder was the *Daily Mail*, and a film company, Granada, which had special ties with the north of England. This last gave me some trouble, as its boss, Sidney Bernstein, had, like most intellectuals of the 'thirties, formed affiliations with the Communist party, and I was asked to exclude his company. I said I would do so only if it could be shown by MI5 that he was still a signed-on member of the party. I had already found out from him that he was not. There was a good deal of protest and pressure from government circles, but they realised that for me to resign at this early stage would have been a serious blow to the infant ITA, and they let the appointment pass.

Being totally a-political I had no idea how much the Tory party had hoped that the ITA would off-set the more liberal (or, as they would have said, 'Bolshie') views of the BBC. The truth dawned on me gradually as I found myself briefly involved in political society. The matter reached a crisis when I was invited to luncheon by my deputy Chairman, Sir Charles Colston. I could tell that he had something on his mind, and his method of 'softening me up' was peculiar. "Are you interested in baby pictures?", he said, and, without waiting for an answer, produced an album of photographs of babies, which he looked at with a wolfish grin. A couple of whiskies would have been more effective. He then came to the point. He was the chief fund raiser for the Tory party, and he wanted me to think of ways in which the ITA could help him in this activity. I replied that the ITA was strictly non-political, and if it were known that we were indulging in that kind of activity there would be one hell of a row. He said nothing, showed his white teeth, the whitest false teeth I have ever seen, in an expansive grin, and let the matter drop. But I saw the dangers ahead, and went to call on Buck de la Warr immediately. He saw the dangers also, and, in what he later described to me as the most disagreeable interview of this career, he persuaded Sir Charles Colston to resign. Colston told the Board that he had urgent business interests to attend to, and in fact produced an admirable washing-up machine. His place was taken by Sir Henry Hinchcliffe, a *parfaitement honnête homme*, if ever there was one, who referred to his predecessor as 'that little beast'.

Colston should have waited a little longer before making his declaration, because in 1955 Anthony Eden became Prime Minister, and the whole Tory gang moved in. He immediately sacked his friend Buck de la Warr from the Post Office, and put in an ambitious (but ultimately unsuccessful) politician, Charles Hill. My brief foray into political society was over. Fortunately by this time the ITA was well established, and I did not need, to the same extent, the support of my minister. I say 'well established', but in fact during their first two years the programme companies lost a lot of money. It costs a very large sum of money to set up a television company, and at first advertisers, influenced, or even intimidated, by the press, shied away from television advertisement. In their embarrassment the companies proposed dropping their only current affairs programme called *This Week*, and putting in its place another piece of entertainment. I explained to them that this would be used against them by their enemies, but they refused to listen. In the Television Act there was a clause that enabled the Authority to spend a considerable sum (I think £75,000) on producing and exhibiting a programme if the occasion seemed to warrant it. This seemed to be such an occasion. I informed the Postmaster General, Charles Hill, who said he would oppose it. I replied that if I were not free to operate the Television Act in a correct and constitutional manner I would resign. He gave in. I then put my proposal to the television companies. They greeted it with a mixture of fury and astonishment: in fact it was the only time I had hard words with them. But, rather than see their autonomies eroded, they kept *This Week* on the air.

For at least six months there was much scepticism over the future of commercial television. The most remarkable instance was in Scotland. Roy Thomson had said that he would put up the money for a Scottish station, but, as he was already proprietor of *The Scotsman*, I thought it contrary to the spirit (if not the letter) of the Television Act to let him have the Scottish TV station as well. I therefore tried to induce some Scottish businessmen, probably quite as rich as Roy Thomson, to form a Scottish television consortium. My countrymen are cautious. After many disgusting lunches, followed by eloquent speeches, I had raised about £40,000. To start a television company required at least two and a half million pounds. I therefore reverted to Roy, who bore me no ill-will, and behaved to his Scottish station with his usual detachment.

During these years I was, of course, still Chairman of the Arts Council. I visited it regularly, and had been blessed with a perfect liaison officer, a young lady called Catherine Porteous, whom I had engaged as my secretary, but whom I soon discovered had diplomatic talents of a high order. Her charm was such that, when I went back to the Arts Council, I was rather better received than before, but the depressing fact remains that I cannot remember a single thing that I did there, whereas I can remember every event at the ITA so clearly that they could provide material for a short book. In writing an autobiography without diaries one finds that the memory is to a great extent a function of the body. One remembers hundreds of impressions and incidents so trivial that they are not worth recording. Why have they communicated themselves so vividly? I am reminded of the famous passage (later suppressed) in the conclusion of Pater's *Renaissance*, in which he writes of such impressions, and claims that when we have apprehended them we have achieved success in life. 'Any exquisite passion, any contribution to knowledge that seems by a lifted horizon to set the spirit free for a moment, or any stirring of the senses, strange dyes, strange colours, curious odours, or the work of the artist's hand or the face of one's friend.' Our memories record less admirable impressions, and so no doubt did the memory of Mr Pater. But, read with proper indulgence, his catalogue of the unexpectedly memorable is not far wrong, except that for 'the face of one's friend' for which I would substitute the face of some unknown person passed in the street.

In addition to such pure responses there are times in life when one's energies are engaged to the full, when, as Lord Reith was fond of saying, one is 'stretched'; and this takes place when one is thrown into a new job, and has to learn it as one creates it. Perhaps the simple truth is that the memory records achievements and suppresses failures.

But, the reader may ask, did you make any achievements at the ITA? The answer is Yes, and I will give one example. We had foreseen from the first that one of our chief difficulties would be the news. This is a programme that attracts a very large audience, and was therefore much coveted by all of the programme contractors. But I did not at all like the idea of three rival news services, each trying to attract audiences by going a little lower, and thought we might talk them into having a joint Independent Television News. It took a lot of talking. I remember one meeting when I watched the cigarette stubs mounting in pyramids on one ash tray after another. Fortunately these discussions took place when the Companies were beginning to recognise the weight of their financial responsibilities; no advertising revenue was coming in, and this, as well as public spirit, may have persuaded them to accept a joint venture in which each contributed a third. Our first choice as the editor of our News was Aidan Crawley who, in addition to his experience in journalism, had become a striking television personality. After a few months he found our news service did not allow enough comment on current affairs, which he had intended to do himself, and announced that he would resign. I fancy he thought himself to be irreplaceable, but nobody is; and in Geoffrey Cox we found an editor who made ITA *News at Ten* one of the best services in television.

But, apart from particular achievements, I created between the Authority and the companies an atmosphere of confidence that was more valuable than any written agreement. It may be an empty boast, but I believe that, if I could have stayed on the standard of commercial television would have been higher. But perhaps I am kidding myself, because could one aim higher than commercial television did in putting on Mozart's *Idomeneo* on Bank Holiday evening, 1976?

Last September I attended a banquet in the Guildhall commemorating the coming of age of ITA. What a different atmosphere to the evening when I had sat in that same place twenty-one years before. We had been defiant and secretly doubtful. Now the Chairman could refer to television, without hesitation, as the supreme means of communication, in which information, intellectual nourishment and entertainment reached millions of people who would never have enjoyed such a privilege without it. She quoted Aristotle twice! What would have happened to me if I had done that? I can imagine Randolph Churchill's comments in *The Evening Standard*.

I hated leaving the ITA; but to have stayed on there, and resigned from the Arts Council, would have taken a lot of explaining. In any case I was not asked to stay on. I had been a grievous disappointment to the Tories, and when I left the ITA I received no official thanks or recognition for having helped to create a very successful and non-controversial organisation.

# VI

# *Travelling*

I AM NOT A TRAVELLER in the sense that Robert Byron was a traveller. I do not know how to pack a rucksack or hire a team of mules, and the discomfort and bad food of genuine travel would outweigh any pleasure or pride in discoveries. I have, however, been invited to visit, under the best possible circumstances, several places I much wanted to see. The first of these expeditions was to Australia. I was adviser to the Felton Bequest, which buys pictures for the Melbourne Gallery with an income which was then considered enormous, but would not buy the trashiest nineteenth-century watercolour to-day. I had bought them some excellent pictures, but they were 'not exactly what they wanted'—too small, too big, too old-fashioned ( I had bought, for a derisory sum, a masterpiece by Landseer), too modern—and they were prepared to pay my passage out to Melbourne to look at the Gallery and recognise their needs, which were in fact what they saw reproduced in the fashionable art magazines. It happened that our dear friend, Colin Anderson, had one of his new ships setting out on a maiden voyage to Australia and he and his wife, Morna, were going on it. It looked as if I should not lack companionship on the voyage, and I therefore decided to go. By the worst possible luck Colin fell seriously ill before we had passed the Mediterranean and he and Morna had to go back to England. I was therefore left to spend the next three weeks alone. This is not an experience I would recommend to anyone. Although I was no longer the sheltered, priggish young director of the National

K.C. in Saltwood library

Jane

Gallery, I had no idea how shameless women could be. In those
days cabins were not air-conditioned and, as it was excessively hot,
I had to sit on deck. Immediately an unknown lady would sit
down beside me and try to fall into conversation. I was writing
*Landscape into Art* (painfully turning the spoken into the printed
text), and the young lady would lean across me and point to a
word, saying "What's that mean?" As I have already indicated,
I am fond of young ladies; but I am even fonder of work and
independence. It was difficult to maintain what my dear head-
master at Winchester called 'our laws of chivalry'. Then the concentration of a long sea voyage produces not only love but hate.
A number of people conceived the most violent hatred for me,
and never passed me without a muttered word of abuse. Amongst
them was a rich middle-aged couple who had great faith in a
medium they had found on board. By some unfortunate accident
I was invited to one of his seances, and I had the opportunity of
seeing how these impostors work. They learn what they can by
asking questions, and, as people's hopes and fears are usually much
the same, they can build on this information quite convincingly
when they come to tell their victim's fortune. The medium had
not asked me any questions, and had no idea who I was. When,
therefore, at the seance he was asked to speak about me, he had to
improvise. "He very gooda boy" (for some mysterious reason
mediums have to talk with a bogus Chinese accent) "and he write
gooda novel; but will he find publishah? Shiki (that was the
name of the medium's 'control') doesn't think so." His two sponsors were disappointed at their favourite's lack of insight and this
naturally increased their hatred of me.

On the last night of a voyage all enmities are forgotten and the
reign of universal love, that collapsed about three weeks earlier,
is revived. As one leaves the ship one hears innumerable insincere
promises of reunion.

We went first to Sydney. The degraded word 'exciting' may
be used quite accurately of Sydney, with its twisting harbour, its

great bridge, and its charming old Regency street. I at once took a great liking to the Australian people, which I have never lost. They are the only truly democratic and non-hypocritical people of the world. The settlement of Anglo-Saxons in a semi-tropical climate has produced a magnificent physique. Had it not been for Gallipoli, they would have been a race of gods. Wealth plays much less part in Australia than in the U.S.A.; in fact there are relatively few rich people and, thank God, even fewer smart people. What is known as 'sophistication' does not suit the Australian character at all, and the only unpleasant experiences I had in Sydney were a couple of dinners with socialites. The fortunate visitor to Australian cities stays in clubs which, when I was there, had not changed their character since the mid-nineteenth century. Such clubs still exist in Boston, but nowhere else. Eating was a difficulty. One was given an enormous breakfast, including a dish with the ominous name of 'lambs' fry', and no food was served after 6 o'clock at night, which was hard on actors. Sydney was full of talented young painters, but the public galleries were Augean stables; I expect they will have been cleaned up by now, and it must have been a Herculean task. In Sydney the favourite exhibit was a picture of a naked young woman with red hair, and cats crawling over her, entitled *Les Félins*. As one walked round the gallery visitors from outback used to say "Excuse me, can you tell me where I can find les fellins?" I was taken to visit an exhibition of contemporary landscape painting, and it was sad to see how the excellent Australian landscape painters of the late nineteenth-century had exhausted the genre. As I was leaving the exhibition I noticed, hung high up above the entrance stairs, a work of remarkable originality and painter-like qualities. I asked who it was by. "Oh, nobody." "But you must have his name in your catalogue." "Let's see; here it is, Nolan, Sidney Nolan. Never heard of him." I said I would like to see some more of his work. "Well, he's not on the telephone." "But you must have his address." More angry scuffling finally produced an address in a suburb of Sydney. I took a taxi there that afternoon, and found the painter dressed in khaki shorts, at work on a series of large paintings of imaginary birds. He seemed to me an entirely original artist, and incidentally a fascinating human being. I bought the landscape in the exhibition, not that it was necessarily the best, but in order to annoy the exhibition secretary, and was confident that I had stumbled on a genius.

Compared to Sydney, Melbourne is rather staid and conventional; in a minor way, there is rather the same contrast as between New York and Washington. Life is perhaps more peaceful, but a trifle boring. It has one fine street, a magnificent botanical garden, and some attractive nineteenth-century ironwork. The Gallery, which was the object of my expedition was badly housed (I believe it is now admirably installed), but it included some famous paintings, among them an enormous canvas by Tiepolo representing Anthony and Cleopatra, that had been bought from the Hermitage by the National Art-Collections Fund, and rejected by the London National Gallery as an incident in the quarrel between staff and Trustees. Facing the Tiepolo was a stuffed horse named Pharlap, which was the supreme attraction of the Gallery. Pharlap had been, without doubt, the greatest racehorse of all time. It was the god of Australia. My friends the Andersons had been married (Morna is an Australian) standing in front of it; and the director of the Gallery owed some of his unique authority to the fact that he had actually ridden Pharlap. This sacred animal had been sent to race in America, and had died mysteriously. Everyone in Australia believed that it had been poisoned: indeed this incident prevented, in the 1940's, the Americanisation of Australia. The Americans may have prevented the Japanese from conquering Australia, but if one spoke a good word for them the answer was always "Americans, Oh no; ye see they poisoned Pharlap". After its death there arose a violent controversy between Sydney and Melbourne as to which should have its remains. Finally its heart (the biggest heart ever found in a horse) was consigned to Sydney, and its stuffed body was exhibited in Melbourne. Around it was a fair collection of impressionists (some excellent Manets), a Rembrandt and a few other 'old masters', including a van Eyck *Virgin and Child*, which was the great treasure of the Gallery. Alas, the moment I saw it I was convinced that it was a copy.

The chairman of the Gallery pictured himself as a great proconsul. I went to stay at his house in the foothills of the Blue Mountains, and was not surprised to find in his hall a cast of the so-called bust of Julius Caesar in the British Museum that, in those days, was so often found in the front halls of headmasters' houses. This is a most gratifying object for self-identification, and now turns out to be a forgery, created precisely for that purpose. Although this was Australian mid-summer, it was extremely cold, but I managed to drag myself out of bed at dawn, and went shivering down to a pool in the hopes of seeing a duck-billed platypus. And I did. It swam and landed and waddled with perfect insouciance. This was worth the trip.

If I may digress, nothing in Australia is more surprising than the variations of heat and cold, depending on whether the wind is blowing from the desert of Central Australia, or from Antarctica. While staying with the chairman the water froze in my glass at night. Two days later the wind was so hot that I could not walk in the street. The Australians are evidently so used to this that they do not mention it.

The head of the Gallery was Daryl Lindsay, who had been at the Slade under Tonks and had an admirable, consistent set of values. He would not 'take on' modern art, and I did not press him to do so, because I felt that the average visitor to the Gallery needed to be brought up gently. He treated me with the utmost kindness, had me to stay in his charming house near the sea, and drove me about the country.

The Australian countryside is unlike that of anywhere else in the world. The whole impression is very light. Most of the gum trees (what in England we call eucalyptus) have light trunks—some actually a golden white—and their leaves hang downwards, so that the sunshine filters through them, and there is no forest darkness. The earth, even in the habitable parts, is reddish, and, in the uninhabited parts, which occur quite suddenly and stretch for thousands of miles, it is a powerful red. Flowers, birds and animals are also different from anywhere else in the world. Green parrakeets whizz round one's head in a friendly manner, wallabies hopped around in the scrub behind Daryl Lindsay's house, and on one occasion I had the thrill of seeing a procession of large grey kangaroos (the great red kangaroo is almost extinct). The koala, which is so popular as a toy, is actually rather a bore, as it never moves from a fork on a gum tree, where it makes itself completely tight by eating baby shoots. The only tiresome animal is the possum, which spends its nights on the roofs of houses, stamping about with a thunderous noise. Nearly everything that has been imported into Australia has been to its detriment—notably the rabbit and the crow. But two imports have been to its advantage, sheep, on which its economy depends, and grapes, from which is made a certain amount of excellent wine, which is drunk *in situ*, and a quantity of inferior wine, which is exported to the big French wine growers.

In between these pleasures I did my duty as advisor and gave a lecture on 'The Idea of a Great Gallery'. Whether or not it had any effect I cannot say, as I have never seen the great Gallery that was built after my visit. I then went on to Canberra, which at that date was an odd experience. We drove from the air-strip through a beautiful undulating landscape, full of imported trees, dark green and entirely un-Australian. After about twenty minutes I asked the driver when we should reach the city. "You're in the middle of it now", he said. Soon after, we reached some terraces and crescents, built to house diplomats and civil servants. They were graded in conformity with the status of the inhabitants. The whole concept was as un-Australian as the landscape. But Canberra does offer one genuine expression of Australian feeling, the war memorial. Instead of some meaningless symbolical piece of 'art', this consists of a gigantic diorama of Anzac Beach. A quantity of research went into its preparation, so that as far as possible every man is in his right position, and people whose sons or brothers had been killed could often identify them. This seems to me the only real war memorial in the world.

From Canberra I went to Adelaide, which is (or was) one of the most charming small cities in the world. I use the word city because it was conceived as such. Its founder, a young soldier named Colonel Light, looking down from a hill on to a piece of empty scrub, drew a plan, which still exists, of a *citta ideale*. Here he would place the theatre, there the art gallery, there the main street, and there the indispensable club, in which, as usual, I stayed; and of course Government House and the House of Parliament were not forgotten. There they all are, exactly as he placed them. It must be the only city of the nineteenth century planned from scratch, except, perhaps, for Hampstead Garden City, and it makes me sad that the word 'planner' has fallen into disrepute. It is surrounded by vineyards, planted by Germans. These all had German names, as elaborate as the names of the vineyards of the Rhine. During the first war it was thought patriotic to give them English names; after the war they took back their German names. Then came the second war, but nobody bothered to change their names again. The best of their wines are delicious. For some reason that I cannot now remember I had been asked to buy pictures for the Adelaide Gallery, as well as for that of Melbourne, and as the grant was quite small I was much more successful.

It was also in Adelaide that I became fully conscious of the fascination of Australian aboriginal art. I must have seen some in Melbourne, but it was more plentiful in South Australia, and the Adelaide Museum was full of it. When I say full, I mean it. Paintings and sculpture were piled on top of one another in a disgraceful manner. Apparently no one had looked at them with an appreciative eye. The bad conscience that now afflicts most decent Australians over the first settlers' treatment of the Aboriginals was just beginning to take effect in 1947, but was directed understandably against cruelty and injustice. No one had observed that these poor, harmless, stone age people had been sensitive artists. A few paintings were exhibited, and I managed to extract some more from the debris in the surrounding cases. They were more interesting than the carvings, which were not so different in style from those of New Guinea. They were done in delicate colours, perhaps because they were the only colours available, or perhaps as an expression of genuine delicacy of feeling; at all events, they were totally unlike the crude colours of 'primitive' art. Like the fauna and flora of Australia, they seemed to be completely cut off from the rest of the world. Most of them represented animals, but without any of the vitality of Stone Age art in Europe, or the Bushman's painting of South Africa. The animals were spread out quietly, and may have been painted after they had been eaten, as a sort of memorial, for the pictures always included a record of their insides as well as of their outer appearance. They were like very primitive X-rays, and, although they varied in quality, the best of them were moving works of art. They are still hardly known outside Australia, as a lunatic Act of Parliament has prohibited their export, as if they were fragments of the Parthenon frieze. In consequence there are far more of them in Australian museums than can be properly shown.

From Adelaide I went on to Perth, flying over the interminable red desert, which increases one's already enormous admiration for the pioneer explorers like Burke and Wills. Everywhere else in the world discoverers have penetrated to places where there have been people, or the remains of human habitation. In Australia there was nobody and nothing. The sight of this terrible desert made it all the more of an enchantment to arrive in Perth. No doubt Perth will have changed in the last thirty years, but when I was there it was arcadian, and also completely Victorian. To stay there was like a journey in time. The town itself was very unpretentious—not unlike the setting of a Western—but facing the Swan River was a row of large nineteenth-century houses, including an hotel and the usual archaic club, and in front of them stretched about 150 yards of green sward, which ended with the river bank; and two black and white jetties in the Caledonian style (Perth was largely inhabited by Scots). The rush-hour took place between 10.30 and 11.00, when two black and white paddle steamers, worthy of MacBrayne, drew up at the jetties, and the passengers walked in a leisurely manner across the sward to their work. Most people lived in a suburb of the city, on the way to the University, and, although the architecture of their houses was not very distinguished, their gardens were fuller of flowers than any I have ever seen. Perth is said, statistically, to have the best climate in the world, and it also has an inexhaustible supply of water. The words I heard most often spoken there were "I'll just go and move the spryer". At that time the art gallery of Perth was totally neglected, and contained only two or three large pictures of birds in flight before a red sky. But to my amazement I found a good collection of drawings by Aubrey Beardsley, which had been bought by Joseph Pennell when, for a year, he was buyer for the gallery.

Like Adelaide, Perth is surrounded by vineyards, and by huge fields of gladioli. I can't imagine what happens to the gladioli, but I know what happens to the wine. I was given by the local growers a magnificent *vin d'honneur*, in which sherry, white wine, red wine and brandy all came from the locality. As I had never seen for sale a wine described as Western Australian, I asked my host what became of all this vast output. "We sell 90 per cent to Bordeaux", he said, "but mind you, not like the stuff you've been drinking to-day."

I felt I could have stayed in Perth for a long time, and I very nearly did because the ship on which I was going home had failed to take note of the fact that I would join it at Fremantle (the port of Perth), and when I drove up there, an hour before it was due to leave, I found that the gangways had been raised and the ship was under way. Fortunately it was in earshot. I must have been a grotesque sight, carrying my baggage, and cluttered with aboriginal carvings which I mistakenly thought would amuse my children, shouting from the dock; but it came back, and I returned home bursting with health.

★   ★   ★   ★   ★

My next long journey was to India, and it took place in 1956, the Year of the Buddha *jayanti*. This was supposed to celebrate the 2500 anniversary of the birth of the Buddha but, as nobody knows when the Buddha was born—probably not before 270 B.C.—it was a purely fanciful excuse for a celebration. There was to be an East–West Conference, and the Foreign Office was asked to send three special representatives, David Eccles (then Minister of Education), Isaiah Berlin and myself. The fact that none of us had ever been to India was not considered a drawback: that was the way in which ambassadors used to be chosen. On the other hand, I think it might have been an advantage if one or two members of the official delegation had had some knowledge of Indian affairs; but they hadn't. As ill luck would have it, a fortnight before we were due to join the conference the Suez Crisis took place. It had been rumbling in the background for some time, but no one could believe that the statements made during the summer were anything but bluff. Of course there was a sort of spurious legality about the English position, but the idea that we should actually start a war in order to maintain this vestige of our old imperialism seemed to me incredible. I was still chairman of the ITA at the time, and the Prime Minister sent for me to tell me how the matter should be treated on the News. I explained that under the Television Act we were not allowed to influence the opinions put forward by our companies. One more nail in my coffin from the Tory point of view. I then went to see my friend R. A. Butler, and said that, if I went to the Delhi

Conference, it would be impossible for me to disguise my opinions about the Suez adventure. He said that this did not matter at all. There were two political parties in England; one of them was in favour of war with Egypt, the other was against it. It was quite reasonable that the second opinion should be represented. Fortified, but not convinced, by this piece of casuistry, I went. In the end I was the only one of the 'special representatives' to do so. Isaiah, with his usual intelligence, backed out at the last moment. David Eccles said "When this little business is over I'll come out and join you". (Those were his actual words). Thank Heaven he never did. English politicians had no idea what indignation the Suez adventure had caused, particularly in the East.

After a troublesome flight, with many stops, starts and returns, and the company for 24 hours of the most inexorably boring man I have ever met, I arrived in Delhi, and went to a comfortable hotel. Our delegation was staying there, but I have no memory of a friendly welcome; it was more like a first day back at school. I can well understand that they resented the appearance of an intruder. Next day we went to the Conference Hall, which was admirably designed and equipped, and I had my first experience of what it must be like to be a member of UNO or UNESCO. It is horrible. One has to sit there patiently while one delegate after another discusses points of procedure. The French have brought this exercise to a fine art, invoking logic, precedent, and objections so trivial and pedantic that one cannot believe one's ears. I am a conscientious man, and at first felt it my duty to sit there while all this piffle was being debated. I later realised that my presence was quite unnecessary. Nothing was going to happen. All that can be said for those boring and expensive farces is that they are a pretext for bringing together people of different nations and races, who can meet each other in the corridors and establish some kind of useful contact. I did this myself with the Nigerian, and even with the Russian delegate. Our High Commissioner at the time was Malcolm MacDonald, intelligent, open-minded, and a lover of art. People often asked me why this remarkable man would never return to politics in England. One reason was that he had enough political experience to see that neither party would have taken him on; and without a party no one in English politics has a hope. It took a world war to bring back Mr Churchill after years of exile: and even then it was an act of popular will, the *volonté générale*, one of the few examples in history, and much resented by the politicians. But there was another reason: that Malcolm MacDonald only felt at home in the East. Actually India was not quite far enough East for him, and he brightened up considerably when he had visitors from Indonesia, Malaysia, China or Vietnam. When I first arrived in Delhi he was so upset by the Suez affair that he had taken to his bed. I found him, unshaven, in a small, bedroom without a window, almost unable to speak for mortification. He asked me to come and stay to help entertain his guests which, after a decent interval with my delegation, I did. He gradually recovered (I think the Suez adventure was almost over), and I spent a happy week with him.

During that time I had myself to make a speech at the Conference. I spoke with feeling of the long history of relations between East and West, and the infinite value it had been to the West; and an extraordinary thing happened: the bored and disillusioned members of the Conference rose to their feet and broke into loud applause. For two days afterwards the hall of the High Commissioner's house was filled with flowers. My delegation felt that I had broken the rules, and washed their hands of me. But, before actually leaving them, I made one useful intervention. Shortly before Suez the Hungarians had rebelled, and this rebellion had been put down by Russian tanks with the utmost savagery. The Foreign Office had the bright idea that someone in the British delegation should make a speech setting off Suez against the Russian repression of the Hungarian rebellion. To equate an unsuccessful act of antiquated imperialism with the brutal repression of a free people fighting for its independence was a piece of folly so grotesque that I could not stand for it. Every morning we had a briefing, and on this occasion the head of our delegation said "It is a Foreign Office instruction. We must comply with it." I said "Then you do it without me. I'll take the next 'plane home and explain why." The speech was never made. No wonder my delegates were not sorry when I told them that I had done all I could in the Conference Chamber, and would now go on to see something of India.

Delhi is a splendid city, planned imaginatively and with a sense of greatness; but it does not contain many delights for the eye. The most attractive is a pink minaret, about four miles away called the Qtab Minar, which at sunrise looks even pinker and I drove out to it when I could. The greatest building in Delhi is Lutyens's Government House, which is a work of genius, but it bears no more relation to India than Washington does to the deep south. I made several Indian acquaintances in Delhi, who asked me out to dinner, but they were half-Americanised, and I had to sit through an interminable cocktail hour before sitting down to a very hot curry. These curries are made extravagantly strong in order to try out strangers, rather in the spirit of our eighteenth-century ancestors when they gave their guests too much to drink. As I hate being defeated, I ate them, and my digestion was impaired for another fortnight. At one of these dinners I made friends with a ravishingly beautiful girl, who was the Indian lawn-tennis champion. She used to take me out shopping, and I used to go to watch her play tennis at the leafy courts just round the corner from our hotel. In retrospect I recognise that I was not an altogether satisfactory member of a delegation.

I saw practically none of my own countrymen—I had not come to India for that—but amongst them was one of those rare and priceless Englishmen who are able to identify themselves entirely with an alien culture. He took me out for drives in the plain round Delhi. It is studded with tombs, which are small, but beautiful, thirteenth- and fourteenth-century chapels, full of bats.

One of the finest was in a sort of oasis, and as our car drew up it attracted all the local children, who surrounded us. My host discovered that they spoke a dialect of Urdu, which of course he could speak himself. He spoke to them of love and forgiveness, and they listened like little angels. As we were going, one of them held out an upturned palm and I put my hand into my pocket to give him a tiny coin. "Don't, don't", said my friend. It was too late. In a second our audience of little angels was transformed into a mob of little fiends. They attacked the unfortunate recipient of the coin with appalling violence. We drove away, leaving behind a scene of carnage. This taught me the lesson that good behaviour is the outcome of latent wealth, however small, and that the Indians are unbelievably poor.

I went on to Agra in a small aeroplane that landed in a field. Not a car in sight. After a while a jeep appeared and took me to a bad hotel, kept by two German ladies. I found my way to a room, which was immediately entered by nine Indians. They brushed my coat, polished my shoes and tried to open my bag. There are too many people in India, and they are all as curious as animals. The dreadful thing is that sooner or later one is reduced (or exalted) to the level of a sahib, and has to bellow at them "teek hi", which means 'get out'. All go except two or three who believe themselves to have a moral right to remain. One of these said to me "You need a haircut", which I did, and in a flash a hairdresser appeared who gave me an excellent haircut, on the path outside my door, followed by one of the best shampoos I have ever had.

This, perhaps, is a suitable place for a few reflections on the Indian character. It has been described with much sympathy both by E. M. Forster in *A Passage to India* and by Joe Ackerley in *Hindoo Holiday*. It would be unbecoming of anyone who has spent so short a time in India to add to these descriptions. But I might add that the Indians themselves do not like them, and much prefer Kipling's *Kim*, and I see why. The Indians are in many respects a ridiculous people, but both Forster and Ackerley make them a little more ridiculous than they are. Indian men are, it is true, very unsure of themselves; but Indian women are not. Both Forster and Ackerley were homosexuals, and Indian women play very little part in their books. But in fact they run the show, and know it. I said this to an Indian lady and she said "We like to think that is so; the men talk too much". When I was in India the head of Broadcasting was a woman, the Governor of Bengal was a woman (and said to me "Do not talk like that, or I will have you thrown into the Ganges and eaten by crocodiles"), and, since my time there, the Prime Minister has been a woman. I think the lady who said "They talk too much" was right. They are like the Russian intellectuals of the 1870s. Even on the lowest level Indians are dangerously unrealistic. If one wants to take a taxi and the driver cannot be found, any man will push himself forward and get into the car, even if he has never driven one before.

But this lack of realism is complementary to a thirst for the spiritual life. Soon after I had arrived in Aurangabad and was eating my breakfast, two or three hungry sparrows on my tray waiting politely till I had finished, I was wanted on the telephone. The call was from the Rotarians of Aurangabad, who asked if I would speak to them on the spiritual content of European art in contrast with the spiritual content of Indian art. I tried to imagine the Rotarians of Folkestone making such a request. When the evening came, about thirty grave-looking men with beards and turbans came to hear whatever nonsense I had to say, and made some searching replies.

Agra contains two sublime works of art, the niche in the Red Fort known as the Pearl Mosque and the Taj Mahal. When I was in India it was fashionable to say that Hindu art was all that mattered, and that Moghul art was merely decorative. This was partly an expression of the belief in 'plastic values'; and partly a justifiable feeling that Hindu sculpture was truly Indian, whereas Moghul art was imposed by a conquering race. But aesthetically this is nonsense. The finest works of Moghul art, whether in architecture or in such exacting media as jade, achieve a perfection that has never been surpassed. How this style was evolved in less than fifty years is a mystery. Granted that it was basically Persian, where did the craftsmen come from? About forty miles from Agra is Fatapur Sikri, the Sakara of India. It was built on a splendid scale (seven miles round) by Akbar in 1569; then the water supply proved inadequate, and it was abandoned. It is almost completely preserved, and one can see the overlap of Hindu and the Moghul style; and the Moghul is already superior. I will modify this heresy later when I come to Elephanta, but in northern India it is undeniable. All this is an introduction to the statement that the Taj Mahal is exactly what it is said to be, one of the most beautiful buildings in the world. The first surprise is that it is not at all the little ivory toy that one is accustomed to see on postcards, but extremely large, like the Duomo in Florence; the second is that its beauty does not depend on frippery, but on a superb sense of proportion. It is true that the decorative inlays, constantly and faithfully restored, are attractive; but the building would be great without them.

From Agra I went on to Bhopal. I went there partly because R. A. Butler had given me a letter of introduction to the Nawab, who he said was the ablest man in India, and partly because it was the place from which I could visit the earliest Buddhist shrine, the Great Stupa of Sanchi. The Nawab was indeed an intelligent man, very un-Indian in his realism. He told me that conflict with Pakistan over the question of Bangladesh was inevitable. He said "I hope Mr Eden will stay in Jamaica. He does your country great harm." But as he was interested only in politics and shooting our conversation was quite short. He put me up in his guest house, saying apologetically that the hotels in Bhopal left much to be desired. So, alas, did the guest house; the sleaziest pension in Estoril would have been luxurious by comparison, and the food was the worst I have ever been offered. The reality of staying with a Nawab is very different from the concept. The drive to Sanchi, on the other hand, was like a heavenly sequence of all that one loves most in European landscape. During the seventy miles one seemed to pass through Warwickshire, Wiltshire and end up in Umbria. The Great Stupa is on a little hill, with Umbrian landscape stretching away on three sides, and reminding one of an affinity between the Buddha and St. Francis. It is much earlier than any other building in India, first century B.C., is almost perfectly preserved, and bears very little relation to later temple styles. Instead of being a solid mass of sculpture growing out of a heavy and often magnificent base, Sanchi is light and lyrical. The Stupa itself, 'a mere lump', is surrounded by arcades, so that one's eye is continually turned outwards, over the landscape. The gates are decorated in relief, with scenes from the life of the Buddha. These reliefs are not only very confusing as narrative, partly because the Buddha himself can never be represented, but aesthetically disappointing, and an inscription tells us why; they are the work of ivory carvers, and are without any feeling of weight or space. But at the corners of the gates are carvings of women, generally referred to as fairies, which are really beautiful, and foreshadow, with greater refinement, the holy sensuality of later Indian sculpture. A visit to Sanchi can be done quite easily, as the mainline trains from Delhi to Bombay stop there; and I recommend it as an experience only one degree less inspiring than a visit to Olympia.

From Bhopal I went on to Bombay. We flew over hundreds of miles of villages, with their surrounding cultivation just sufficient to keep the inhabitants of the villages alive. If a single stranger had visited one of these villages there would have been nothing for him to eat. Gandhi was right in thinking that these are the substance of India. Miss Popham of Cheltenham had arranged that I should stay with an Indian family, whose daughter had been in the Ladies' College, and they met me at the airport, bearing garlands of flowers. The girl's parents were in England, and I was looked after by that well known Italian figure, *il mio*

First meeting of the ITA: *from left:* Sidney Bernstein,
K.C., Spencer Wills and Stewart McClean

Jane and Colette in Venice

*povero fratello*. I had thought it would be interesting to see what life was like in an Indian family, but in retrospect it was a mistake. They were not Indian enough. In fact I might just as well have been staying with an American family in the mid-west. Things began badly, because when I passed into my bedroom, out of the steaming heat of Bombay (and, my God, it *is* hot in Bombay), I was met by a blast of air-conditioning so cold that I saw myself rapidly catching pneumonia. I asked if it could be modified, and was told that my host's nephew was manager of an air-conditioning plant and that this was his masterpiece. This was the first brick I dropped, and thenceforward I dropped two or three every day.

Bombay is a terrifying place. The sweep of the harbour is grander than that of Naples, but behind it is a more than Neapolitan squalor. I have never seen such obvious and afflicting poverty. At night everybody leaves his house and finds a place to sleep in the streets. The most favoured position is under the wall of the street that runs round the harbour for about five miles. By evening it is entirely full of sleepers. All this is taken for granted, and my hosts were surprised that I noticed it. For the lover of art the only thing worth seeing in (or near) Bombay is the cave of Elephanta. It is on an island, up a steep ascent, and must once have contained the grandest of all Hindu sculptures. The instinct to destroy images is very strong, and the more impressive they are the stronger it becomes. The Reformation teaches us that. The carvings in Elephanta were so magnificent that the Portuguese dragged a couple of cannons up the steep hill to destroy them. But they didn't altogether succeed as the carvings are very large and cut out of the rock of the cave. Before they were damaged they must have been truly magnificent.

From Bombay I went for several days to Aurangabad, accompanied, which was very boring, by *il povero fratello*. It is a charming place in itself, and within comfortable motoring distance of Ajanta and Ellora. It had the added merit that it was then in the independent state of Hyderabad, and so was not subject to the prohibition laws, very strictly enforced in the rest of India. The signs of a bar warmed my heart. "Please come in, Sir. You are in the Nizam's dominions. What will you have?"

The wall paintings of Ajanta, which fill about seventy caves, should be one of the great 'sights' of India. The ravine in which they are situated is of staggering beauty, and puts one into a good frame of mind. They were discovered in 1819 and the problem was how to get into the caves because of the bats, who had lived there undisturbed for 1,500 years. No wonder that the frescoes, when at last they were visible, seemed to be damaged beyond repair. In fact they were quite well preserved, but after they had been cleaned and varnished they were on the road to ruin. They were copied, but nearly all the copies were burnt on their way to the South Kensington Museum.

This was a disaster, as Ajanta had been to Indian painting rather what Assisi was to Italian. Indeed I was constantly reminded of Assisi when I was there. I found Ellora rather disappointing, except for one splendid group in the Kailasa and preferred the gentle Buddhist carvings in a cave on a hill beside Aurangabad itself. It is a stiff climb, and to my great relief *il povero fratello* did not feel up to it. On the way back I was reminded that I was in a profoundly different culture. A blond heifer was sitting on our path. We could have scrambled round her, but one of our number (presumably a Muslim), anxious to do me honour, gently lobbed a piece of turf at her. Immediately my other four guides set on him and would have beaten him severely if I had not intervened. Let me add that sacred cows were to me one of the chief pleasures of India. They are like famous beauties, gentle, friendly, and sure of themselves. If they take a fancy to one they will follow one in to a shop, always behaving impeccably. The only trouble is that if they decide to sit down in the middle of a main road, they hold up the traffic.

Altogether Aurangabad was my pleasantest memory of India.

Even in the town the people weaving and dyeing textiles seemed to be happy. I returned to Bombay without enthusiasm.

While I was in Bombay I gave a lecture under the auspices of the British Council. I had done the same thing in Delhi, and it had been attended by twenty-three persons. There was no sense in declaiming a lecture to such a small group, so I beckoned to them to sit round me and talked to them informally. I asked the British Council representative in Bombay where my lecture was taking place. He said that he didn't know. I asked him if he would be so kind as to find out, and let me know at least half an hour before the lecture was scheduled to begin. He seemed distressed by this call to action; however, twenty minutes before the lecture was due to take place he appeared, and said he had found out that it was to be in the University. I was talking to a group of intelligent Indian ladies, and one of them offered to take me there in her car. The British Council representative came with us.

Bombay was run by the Parsees. They were originally Zoroastrians from Persia, driven out by Islam; now they are chiefly men of business, and have a drive and realism that the Indians lack. They were known by the names of their callings, or characteristics. One whom I met was called Mr Soda Water. The character whose name in the London Telephone Directory so greatly delighted Constant Lambert, Mr Trampleasure, was no doubt a Parsee. I dined with one of them whose official name was Sir Jehangir but whose real name was Mr Ready Money, and whose palatial house (which reminded me of Philip Sassoon's house at 45 Park Lane) was still called Ready Money House. I must confess that after the shifty benevolence of the Indians I enjoyed the clearer heads of the Parsees. Whether I should have enjoyed doing business with them is a question that did not concern me.

I was not sorry to leave India. I had had many marvellous experiences—Sanchi, Ajanta, Elephanta, the Taj Mahal—and gained something from witnessing such a different way of life. But in the end the insoluble social problems of India and the universal evidence of poverty began to weigh on my mind. There are simply too many people about. One feels that one can never be alone for a second. And the Sahibs' view that they jabber and can only be controlled by harsh words is, alas, true, as Nehru himself would have been the first to admit. He always carried an elegant black cane, and often used it. One could say in extenuation that they have been subject to a succession of conquerors. But the Egyptian *fellahin* have been slaves for 5,000 years, and often have a dignity that the Indians lack.

★ ★ ★ ★ ★

My next long journey was to Japan. I have described in *Another Part of the Wood* how Japanese art was my first love, and an album of Japanese drawings my most precious possession. I had collected Japanese prints when I was at school, and had also bought odd numbers of an art magazine called the *Kokka* which showed me that the prints of Utamaro and the drawings of Hokusai, beautiful as they are, came at the end of Japanese art, and the great works of the middle ages and the sixteenth century could be seen only in their country of origin. I was therefore delighted when the Japanese government invited me out to visit their country for a month. I went on September 18th, 1963. By this time Jane had begun to develop a series of illnesses, which continued in almost unbroken sequence for over ten years. She was recovering from one of these and could not have undertaken the journey. In any case she would have found the routine of my life in Japan intolerable; but I missed her sadly, as I had no one to talk to. In India everyone speaks English, but in Japan the language barrier is insurmountable. Except for our old friend Yukio Yashiro I did not meet a single Japanese who could speak more than a few necessary words. The Foreign Office supplied me with a guide-companion called Mr Maeda, who had spent seven years in Bombay and nine in Washington, but he spoke and understood less English than an air hostess or a taxi driver.

# Travelling

Many people find the flight of 24 hours very exhausting, but I did not mind it, because it involved no disturbing change of hour on arrival: just a day gone out of one's life. Quite early on in the flight we were exactly over the north pole, and I thought of all the heroes who had suffered unbelievable hardships to reach a point which I had reached while eating an ice-cream. We stopped for refuelling at a place in Alaska called Anchorage, and spent an hour in a room containing six stuffed huskies and one enormous stuffed bear. The view from the window made me realise how lucky I was to live in Europe—a dozen houses in an icy wilderness. What can the human relations of the inhabitants be like!

My first disillusion with Japan was the drive from Tokyo airport to the centre of the city. It takes over two hours, most of which are spent in traffic blocks. The architecture is simply non-architecture. There is not a single building with any character, let alone style. I was taken to a large, impersonal, American-type hotel called the New Imperial. I remembered that the Old Imperial was by Frank Lloyd Wright. It was still standing*, and was one of the very few buildings to have survived the 1921 earthquake. I determined to be transferred there as soon as possible. My hosts thought they had done me honour in putting me in the New Imperial, and my desire to move to the old one was the first sign they had that I was incomprehensible. However, they allowed me to do so (it was much cheaper), and I spent my evenings marvelling at the ingenious use of space and the inexhaustible contrivance that, in his early years, this spoiled genius could command. I should add that Aldous Huxley said that the Imperial Hotel was 'sadistic', perhaps because the ceilings were rather low and Aldous Huxley was tall: or perhaps because he could not detach himself from the fashionable Corbusier style of architecture, which Frank Lloyd Wright's building so courageously opposed.

* Yukio Yashiro, when he was head of the Ministry of Fine Arts, had it registered as a National Possession, but said that he knew the site was so valuable that the decision would be overruled. It has now been pulled down.

# Travelling

Inevitably my first day in Tokyo was spent in official visits. There seemed to be an endless number of bodies, as well as the Foreign Office, which had to be thanked and recognised, but I never discovered what they were. I made my speeches in English, which was not understood, and listened to replies in Japanese, which I did not understand. Whether there was no interpreter available, or whether it would have involved a loss of face to employ one, I do not know. Thank Heaven at lunch time dear Yukio appeared and, after an affectionate greeting, I was able to ask what had been arranged for me.

We were going first to Nara, which, although it is only a short way from the terrible Osaka (the 'Chicago of Japan', as was often said), still remained a charming old university town, authentic and slightly rustic, built round a large deer park, full of inquisitive and rather too self-confident deer. My guide and companion, a wizened little old man, was to accompany me. As I have said, his command of English was very limited and he had not the faintest interest in art. Fortunately Yukio also came with us. He had spent the war years in Nara, living in convents, and so was on good terms with all the Abbesses, and most of the Abbots, and could persuade them to show me treasures of painting and sculpture which could in no other circumstances have been seen. A lover of art who visits Japan without some such guidance will see only gardens, the exteriors of temples with their monotonously threatening 'guardians', and a few 'art galleries', for the most part very badly arranged, great pieces of sculpture all higgledy-piggledy one behind the other. Without Yukio to cajole the Abbesses and exert his authority on the Abbots I should have had a very incomplete picture of Japanese art. The one well-arranged gallery, Yamato Bunkakan, had been built by Yukio himself, a few miles out of Nara. It shows how marvellous the treasures of the temples could look, if anyone took trouble over them; but even in Yamato Bunkakan only a few things can be seen at a time. In Japan there is always a pretext for not showing a picture.

The commonest is high humidity; no pictures can be seen on a rainy day and, as it rains a great deal in Japan, one may often make a long journey in vain.

The first day in Nara we naturally went to the Horyu-ji, the oldest temple in Japan. I had known its contents in reproduction since I was a child (my old companion had never heard of it), and was trembling with excitement. The majority of Japanese temples are very sympathetic because they are not at all imposing (exceptions are the Todai-ji in Nara, and the Nishi Hongwan-ji in Kyoto). One walks up a wide, untended road between two walls of irregular plaster work, with thatched roofs, and comes out into a sort of park, with relatively small buildings in a consistent style grouped together, as if they were a beautifully calculated village. Many of these buildings are extremely ancient—eighth or ninth century—but, as the Japanese very sensibly remake their old buildings every fifty years or so, imitating exactly the originals, they look quite new. The absence of patina, moss, and other signs of age, is at first disappointing to the western eye, but, having made up my mind to it, I was rather glad not to be misled by the deceptions of the picturesque. The greatest treasure of Horyu-ji, the painted hall, was burnt down in the last century, but many of the temples contain sculpture of great beauty, and, to move across a lawn from one building to another, expecting in each to find some ancient and beautiful work of art, is one of the pleasantest forms of sightseeing I have experienced.

Let me make a general confession which, now that dear Yukio is no longer alive, I can do with an easier mind. I find a great deal of Buddhist sculpture monotonous. It is derived from Chinese art of the seventh century, filtered through Korea, and is often the work of Korean craftsmen. The earliest Japanese bronze group, the Shaka triad in the Golden Hall at Horyu-ji, signed and dated 623, is a boring work, without any sculptural vitality or invention. I suppose that a western analogy would be the imitations of Byzantine painting found in provincial icons.

## Travelling

Temple after temple; they seem to be havens of peace, but when they were built they were centres of disruptive power, and their armies of monks were the most brutal and savage in Japan. How I would love to describe the beautiful contents of the Kofuku-ji, the Todai-ji, the Yakushi-ji, and how bored the reader would become! But I must mention one other building in Nara, because it is the oldest surviving museum. It is called the Shoso-in, and contains the collection of a connoisseur of the seventh century, who bought objects from all over the world, from Persia eastwards. They are all perfectly preserved, for the simple reason that the museum is open only for a fortnight in November, and even Yukio could not get me in. A museum curator's dream.

I may also allow myself one observation on Japanese art, which may come as a surprise to those who have not visited Japan. They are supreme portraitists. Portraiture did not exist in Europe until the very end of the fourteenth century, but from the eighth-century portraits of the priests Gangin and Gyoshin to the thirteenth-century portraits of the Kamakura period there are portraits that in their sense of human character seem to me to surpass almost anything in European art. The paintings are comparable with Holbein, but the sculpture is even more impressive. In the Kofuku-ji are two full-length figures executed in the first decade of the thirteenth century by a sculptor named Unkei, which combine truth and idealism in a manner worthy of Donatello. They reminded me of the prophets on the Campanile in Florence and would, I genuinely believe, withstand the comparison. As for the portrait of the priest Chogin (Shunjo) in the Todai-ji, I cannot think of anything in European art that so movingly unites realism with a profound feeling of veneration.

After a few days Yukio had to return to his duties, and I was left alone with my little old wisp of a guide (who turned out to be three years younger than I). Meals were extremely boring. I could not make him understand anything. Finally I got through with the question "What are you most interested in?" He replied "Baseball. I follow a team", which did not get us much further. He once managed to speak to me in English. It took place in Osaka airport, where he had insisted on going an hour and a half early to wait for our plane to take us to Kyoto, and I saw that something was working in his mind. At last he came out with it. "A small, shoddy place", he said. I was so delighted by his use of the word "shoddy" (which was perfectly accurate) that for an hour or two I felt more kindly towards him.

After the provincial rusticity of Nara, Kyoto seemed metropolitan (and has in fact a population of 1,500,000 people). The Japanese Foreign Office had thought it would be a good experience for me to stay at a typical Japanese inn, instead of the excellent international hotel (the Myako), and on the whole I was glad of their decision. Yukio told me that it was not a good example of its kind, and it was indeed rather grubby and slovenly, with a landlady exactly like those who figure in nineteenth-century English comic songs. One's shoes were taken away at 6 p.m.; I don't know how people manage who have a taste for night life. I was quite happy to write letters home and practise calligraphy. I had a book on the subject, and the hotel provided brushes, an ink-stone and paper. I kept it up for the rest of my stay, and believe it increased my understanding of Japanese art. Of course there were no chairs, but one soon gets used to sitting and, ultimately, lying on the floor. The great joy was the enormous wooden bathtub, the size of a small swimming-bath, which was filled for me at 6.30, and in which I was supposed to disport myself for about half an hour. Water, even hot water, is not my element. I have very seldom bathed in my life, and my morning bath takes three minutes. But I stayed in my wooden tub for ten. As no one could speak or understand a word of English the choice and time of supper and breakfast were taken out of my hands, and they were brought to my room by an extremely plain young woman, who also made up my bed on the floor at precisely

8 o'clock. Most Japanese girls are very attractive, but I see that it was prudent of the landlady to entrust this duty to a plain one.

After two or three days we were transferred to the Myako, which must be one of the best hotels in the world. Kyoto itself is a flat, uninteresting city, but it is surrounded by gentle slopes, which reminded me of the Euganean hills, and on one of these stands the Myako. Nearly all the others are occupied by temples in huge gardens. We visited two or three temples a day, and could have gone on doing so for months without repetition. They differ from one another, so that one feels that each one is prettier than the last. But these experiences were not as idyllic as they should have been because every quarter of an hour there drew up outside the temple seven (always seven) bus-loads of schoolboys, dressed, strangely enough, in the uniform of West Point Academy, who were marched round the temple to the accompaniment of a commentary bellowed through a megaphone. They looked at nothing, took each other's photos, and were gone in a quarter of an hour, when the next seven bus-loads arrived. Anyone visiting Kyoto should try to find out if there is a close season for these schoolboy tours, as they interfere with one's responses to what should be visions of delicate beauty. I realised how much I had missed when I visited the few temples that were not on the young men's itinerary. One of these is the Chishaku-in, and it perfectly illustrates the Japanese temple scheme, which is an architectural invention equal, in a lighter vein, to the frescoed rooms of the Renaissance. It consists of a sequence of large bays, joined by a gallery, of which three sides are painted with flowers or landscapes, and the fourth is open to the garden. The garden is related to the paintings, and great qualities of imagination go to its design—in fact, one of them, in the Sambo-in, was designed by the great warrior-statesman, Hideyoshi. I sat on the floor and prepared my mind for long contemplation. If the words 'aesthetic experience' have any meaning, this was an aesthetic experience.

I must add that to a Japanese amateur the aesthetic philosophy of the west is almost entirely meaningless. Far from thinking that the sensations aroused by art and nature are basically different, he considers nature herself as a sort of artist. Certain old trees and rocks are venerated as supreme works of art, and such rocks are brought for hundreds of miles to suitable situations. Their arrangement in a garden is, so to say, an extension of their personalities. Venerable trees, often at the point of collapse, are propped up, so that, to the profane eye, only the props are visible.

The other temple to which the West Point boys were not admitted is the Nishi Hongan-ji, the headquarters of a powerful sect called Shinran, which has six and a half million followers in Japan. The Abbot is married to a niece of the Emperor, called the Lady Ohtai, and she did me the great honour of receiving me and showing one of the temple's greatest treasures, an anthology of poems in six volumes, said to have been written by some aristocratic calligrapher in about 1118. It is the most ravishing example of the fusion of drawing and writing I have ever seen, and I would gladly have spent the whole day looking at it. Of course I could not read the poems, but nor, I was delighted to find, could the Japanese. The calligraphy is so exquisite as to be incomprehensible. The Lady Ohtai spoke a little English in the quiet, modest voice of a genuine aristocrat. We seemed to be in sympathy with each other, when she said "There is one more question I must ask you. What is the state of calligraphy in your country?", and in a flash I realised what deserts of incomprehension exist between our two cultures. I sometimes believe that I can distinguish between good and bad calligraphy; but I expect I would be easily taken in by a showy or an archaising piece. I remember seeing over the door of a temple in a very remote part of the country what looked to me like a magnificent piece of calligraphy, and asked my companion what it said. He replied "Coca-Cola".

The Nishi Hongan-ji is so rich and powerful, that its general effect is rather vulgar. The Zen temples are a reaction against this kind of display. No doubt Zen sects are also very rich, but they make the entrances to their temples as inconspicuous as possible—often no more than a small winding footpath. In contrast to the courtly splendour of the Lady Ohtai, visitors to Zen temples make themselves at home, brew tea, change their shirts and sleep on the floor. There is something sympathetic about all this—also an element of spoof. I found that the twittering sparrows were on tape.

My second morning in the Myako hotel I came down to the hall to find poor Mr Maeda looking extremely ill. He had been worried that I was not always doing exactly what was written in his book of instructions and this had given him a stomach ulcer; also the fact that all his meals came out of an expense account had tempted him to eat hugely. Although less than half my size he ate twice as much. He would even eat the little cakes of coconut that are given out at tea ceremonies as a formality, and are never eaten. As I approached him he put his head in his hands and said "Oh my stomach, my duty, my stomach!" "Come along", I said, "you must put your health before your sense of duty. Up to bed." He protested shakily, but he was in genuinely poor shape, so I half-carried him to the lift, and got him up to his room. I never saw him again. I suppose he felt disgraced and slunk back to Tokyo. Of course I was glad to be freed of him, but I feared that the Foreign Office would send a replacement, which in course of time they did. He spoke even less English, and lacked the touching naiveté of my first companion. On my last day in Japan I asked if I could go to see him to thank him for all that he had done for me. "Noh, noh, no obrigation." I persisted. "Noh, noh." The Japanese at their worst. I did not need a guide, partly because all hotel porters speak English, and partly because by this time I had embarked on making three films for television, and my director, Ian Mutsu, had a Scottish mother, and spoke perfect English. His grandfather had been Foreign Minister, but when his father married a Scottish lady he could no longer be employed in the public service, and Ian had become a film director. Great luck for me, as he turned out to be an intelligent companion, and also a good director.

My new freedom allowed me to visit a department store. My poor little guide would never allow this, as it was not in his book. He would look frenziedly through its pages, and say "Noh, noh shopping", and would not even allow me to pause in a street and look at a shop window. I wanted to go to a store, partly in hopes of finding a present for Jane, and partly out of curiosity. We had all been brought up on the legend of Japanese 'good taste', which had been illustrated by some pretty matchboxes. But what I had seen so far did not sustain it. The trinkets and *bondieuseries* which were sold in booths in front of temples like the Todai-ji were as vulgar as those in Toledo or Assisi, and appeared to be almost identical. I did find one very humble booth that sold sweets and pickles in charming pots—blue and grey, with touches of yellow, so that the whole effect was like a Braque. I paused to admire them. "You want to buy?" said my guide. "No, thank you, but I think them beautiful." "Beautiful", for, alas, he understood the word. "You think beautiful", and he went off into screams of laughter. He continued to whinny all the way round the temple, repeating the word "beautiful", and starting to laugh again. I was therefore not surprised when I found the most famous department store in Kyoto, showed considerably less evidence of good taste than Harrods or Selfridges. There was not a single presentable object.

It has become fashionable to say that the words 'good taste' are meaningless. The people who say this, often quite clever people, should be compelled to buy all their carpets and curtains in a co-operative store. Good taste is not the prime mover in art; we should not think of using the words in front of a Michelangelo or a Rembrandt. But we should in front of Piero della Francesca's *Baptism*, or Watteau's *Ensigne de Gersaint*, so the concept is not without value, and it would be foolish to impoverish our limited vocabulary of criticism by discarding it for what are very largely reasons of inverted snobbery.

## Travelling

A history of bad taste would be a fascinating subject. Of course it has always existed, but for some mysterious reason its expansion over half the world took place at about the same time in the first years of the nineteenth century. This cannot be blamed on the usual whipping-boy of the period, the industrial revolution, because triumphs of bad taste appeared in India and Japan before either country had been touched by industrialism. What had happened to change the exquisite harmony of Moghul architecture into the hideous cacophony of the nineteenth-century Indian interiors, or the line and colour of Ukio-ye prints into the unrelieved vulgarity of a modern Japanese store? Although the Ukio-ye is always described as a 'popular school' the answer must lie in the word vulgarity. Popular taste is bad taste, as any honest man with experience will agree. But the two cases I have cited are different. Bad taste in India is all-pervading because the traditional style of decoration, superbly encrusting Hindu temples, cannot be assimilated to more modest aims; whereas in Japan the bad taste that permeates the big stores is the *revers du médaille* of the almost embarrassingly good taste of certain earlier buildings and their surrounding gardens. The best Japanese architecture, like the Katsura Summer Pavilion in Kyoto, or the Hoke-do in the Todai-ji, use space and interval with a perfection and an economy that existed nowhere else in architecture until the time of Mies van der Rohe. And since these buildings are rebuilt in exact facsimile every thirty years they are still part of a living tradition. As for the 'good taste' of their surroundings, where except in Japan would people gaze with reverent admiration at areas of raked sand? I must admit that I looked at the most famous of these, the Ryuan-ji, with a pleasure bordering on excitement. To the lover of abstract art it must seem like a masterpiece. But I am a gross feeder. I need something more to nourish me than this subtle and self-denying purity. I found myself thinking nostalgically of Europe, and wondering how people who are dedicated to these sand gardens could swallow Bernini. Surely he would make them feel sick.

# Travelling

Japan arouses very different emotions in different people. Several men whose memory I revere, Edmund Blunden, Laurence Binyon, William Plomer, have loved it more than any other country. Others whom I admire, like Peter Quennell, have hated it. I must try to draw up a balance sheet of my own responses.

On the credit side, I have already written enough of the temples and their gardens; for the visitor these will always be an endless joy. I saw a fraction of them, and my only sorrow was that I could not converse with the humane, often jovial, abbots, or the exquisite abbesses. I had a strong impression that what is best in Japan goes into the religious life. It is a life dedicated to beauty and contemplation and, for better or worse, seems to be very little concerned with those acts of social benevolence which take up almost all the time of an English parson. That women play an equal part with men adds a quality of gentleness and self-sacrifice.

I would also put on the credit side an adjunct to contemplation which has spread from the temples to ordinary life, the tea ceremony. The Japanese are a nervous people, and the strain of their intensive business dealings often drives them to a condition bordering on hysteria. If they are rich enough they play golf (entrance fee to a club costs at least £1,000 and many people play at night by arc-lights), but the humblest can partake of the tea ceremony I did so almost every day. The ritual of the tea ceremony, if correctly performed, involves long delays; I am by nature impatient, but for some reason I found that the endless wiping and arrangement of the bowls was soothing, and when a Zen priest, either to spare my time or out of pure Zen irresponsibility, cut down the time of the ritual, I felt cheated.

Complementary to the tea ceremony is that unique entertainment, the Kabuki theatre. Kabuki grew up as a sort of popular protest against the aristocratic No theatre. I have met Europeans who say that they prefer No to Kabuki. I can only marvel at their patience, which is not shared by a majority of Japanese. In a No play the actor may stand totally still for ten minutes, then slowly raise one hand and emit a long "Oooh". It sounds quite easy, and I used to do what seemed to me like a passable imitation of it. But an acquaintance told me that he once lived in a house next to one in which No actors were being trained to emit this sound, and that it was a course of instruction as long and as exacting as the training of a soprano. Owing to its great antiquity and unbroken tradition one watches No drama with a kind of solemn reverence, and it produces a feeling of long-drawn-out expectancy, so that when at last something happens (and terrible things happen) it strikes one with irresistible force. Also it is full of ghosts, which gain from this severely formalised treatment. But four hours!

Kabuki on the other hand is a grandiose riot. It takes place in enormous theatres (No theatres are as small as dissenting tabernacles), which are always packed by a participating audience, including a quantity of children whose squawks are almost indistinguishable from those of the actors. Although one sometimes has the impression that 'anything goes', Kabuki has inherited from No a strict sense of tradition and even of dedication. Some of the plays date back to the seventeenth century, but most of them are early nineteenth century, and their style of production has not changed since the prints of Kyonaga and other masters of Ukio-ye. The Japanese cannot really understand the plots. They come to see the actors. The actors all belong to families who have been in Kabuki for generations, and no outsider would be admitted. The part of the stage on which they act is sacred, and one of the reasons why Kabuki will not go on tour* is that they cannot bring their sacred boards with them; also they could not support the respectful silence of a western audience. 'Grandiose riot'; the riot takes place on the stage, with singers and drummers and a profusion of gorgeous costumes; then suddenly there is a hush, and a terrible cry is heard from the back of the auditorium.

---

* Kabuki was put on at Covent Garden in September 1955, but although it gave pleasure, it was a very tame affair compared to the real thing.

# Travelling

A high platform leads through the stalls to the stage, and along it moves the principal character, raising his feet with appalling deliberation. He is weighed down by enormous cloaks and a bizarre head-dress, but this does not prevent him from making a variety of threatening gestures which chill the blood. The singers and drummers are subdued, and there totters out to meet him a beautiful woman, who is of course a man, whose sidelong glances and entreating voice appease his wrath.

The actors are superb. Some idea of their range of expression can be gained from the prints of Sharaku. The 'ladies' are of an ideal femininity, which is said to have had great influence on the behaviour of real women in Japan. Kabuki only attained its quality when, in the seventeenth century, women were forbidden to act, and their parts were played by men. Whether or not this is true, I must put on the credit side that Japanese women are charming, and look enchanting in their kimonos. The Geisha is an excellent institution. She is not, as ignorant westerners have sometimes supposed, a tart, but a respectable lady who joins a dinner party predominantly male, and is placed next to the humbler and more obscure guests at the bottom of the table in order to cheer them up by her conversation. How much more agreeable civic life would be were there Geishas in Bradford and Huddersfield; but I fear that no young English women would be modest enough to undertake this essentially feminine task.

While on the subject of dinners, I must record that Japanese food is nearly always excellent and exceptionally healthy. During all the time I was in Japan I never suffered from those tummy-aches that so often diminish one's pleasure in India and Egypt. And then, the convention followed in most restaurants outside Tokyo that luncheon is served even to a small party in a private room, with its own very small garden, is extremely agreeable, and would have been even more so if we could have spoken each other's language.

Finally, the landscape. There is a great variety. A place called

Hakone lies among hills which might be Scotland, and for that reason was so much admired in the nineteenth century that a huge Scottish baronial hotel was built there, and Rudyard Kipling stayed in it. (I went there because it has the finest of all small collections of Japanese and Chinese ceramics). I have already compared the landscape of Kyoto to the Euganean hills, and this relationship of hill and plain covers a good deal of southern Japan. The inland sea is a dream. What would I not have given to board one of the boats that go up and down it! But it was not on my itinerary. Towering over all the surroundings of Tokyo, and one of the wonders of the world, is Mount Fuji. Hokusai's famous book of 'The Hundred Views' is correct: it gets in everywhere. Sachie Sitwell says that during a fairly long visit he saw Fuji only once for half an hour. I was lucky. I saw it almost every day, watched it turn every colour, and can guarantee that Hokusai's prints are correct. Actually it is black. I discovered this on a flight to Osaka, when we flew alarmingly close to it. But it is so huge and so far away that its colour is entirely dependent on light and atmosphere, and in consequence Hokusai can truthfully represent it as either red or blue.

A heavy balance on the credit side. What of the debit side? I am afraid the words are inescapable—the Japanese character. They seem to be almost entirely dependent on instructions, preferably written instructions, and a formalised code of behaviour. They cannot perform a spontaneous act of kindness or compassion; it would not be 'in the book'. There is a well-known story of an English lady who was seated in a tram when it had a slight accident. As she was not feeling well she fainted. When she came to she found herself alone in the tram, which had been put back into its shed. Nobody had had instructions to help her. "No obrigation, no obrigation": how often I heard those words. It is sometimes said that the Japanese have no imagination. In face of masterpieces of painting like the Blue Fudo in the Shoren-in, the Scroll of Hells in the National Museum, to say nothing of the

Japanese fairy tales that have delighted children all over the world, this sounds like a stupid generalisation. But it remains true of 99 per cent of the population.

But balancing this pedantic obedience there is a terrible streak of violence, the old Samurai violence, which has been diffused into the masses. I was naturally never allowed to meet a bellicose Japanese, but by all accounts they are no more amiable than the bureaucrats. So I am left in a state of confusion. Everything related to old Japan, including even the men and women crossing a bridge in Kyoto, and looking as if they had stepped straight out of a Hiroshige, is beautiful and moving. Almost everything developed in modern Japan, except in architecture, is heartless, inhuman and unsympathetic. It is a triumph of efficiency and obedience. I had come to fear that this impression might be due to racial prejudice until I went on to Hong Kong and met Chinese. What an incredible difference! The Chinese are subtle, observant, responsive, above all intelligent—a word one has simply to put out of one's mind in Japan.

It is arguable that someone who has spent only a month or two in a country has no right to expatiate on it. But I have often found that first impressions have a value that only a very long residence can supersede. After a year the obvious and unexpected differences from one's own country are taken for granted, and are not thought worth recording, even when they are of real importance. Although I have spent so much time in Italy my first impressions remain as true as anything I could write to-day. When one first visits a country all one's faculties are alive; afterwards they are dulled into acceptance. The reader will have discovered how vividly I have remembered every incident in India and Japan, even down to the complicated names of Japanese temples; and how little I remember about the Arts Council or my life at Upper Terrace House. This must be my excuse for writing at length about countries to which I paid short visits.

# VII

## *Saltwood*

UPPER TERRACE HOUSE had, from my point of view, one serious disadvantage. The library, which I used as my study, led out of the hall and was too small to contain more than a quarter of my books. I was within earshot of the telephone, and of everyone who rang the front door bell. My work had to be done either in bed, before breakfast (which it still is), or in the front seat of my car, which I used to park in a cul-de-sac near Kenwood. Both Jane and I had always wanted to live in the country, and one day, driving back from Barbie Agar's house near Petworth, we decided that we should do so. Next morning we saw, among the irresistible advertisements of houses for sale in the first pages of *Country Life*, the name of Saltwood Castle. To our astonishment it was only four miles from Lympne, where we had lived before the war; but we had never even heard of it. It lies in a triangle between the main London–Folkestone road and the coast road to Sandgate, and was so little known that, although it is a large mediaeval building with two magnificent towers, probably designed by the great fourteenth-century architect, Henry Yevele, it was not (and still is not) mentioned under Saltwood in the Shell Guide to England. It had belonged to the Deedes family who had owned huge tracts of East Kent, but given them away as an act of Christian socialism. When we were at Lympne it belonged to a lady called Mrs Levi Lawson, later Lady Conway, who was a recluse. She was clearly not a friend for Philip Sassoon, and I never heard him mention Saltwood.

# Saltwood

I had always wanted to live in a gothic house—perhaps some instinct left over from Winchester; and here was one for sale in a part of England where we had come to feel at home. One day when we were staying in Folkestone, Jane recuperating from 'flu, I drove over to Hythe, and looked at Saltwood Castle across the valley. The two towers were lit by a gentle afternoon sun and I have never seen them look more beautiful. I did not dare to tell Jane, as she would have wanted me to make an offer immediately; fortunately it was withdrawn from sale. But I recognised the hand of fate.

A few years later we were going as a family to Venice. When we reached Boulogne we were told that there was a railway strike in France, and there was nothing for it but to go back in the same boat. By a miracle we got into rooms in the Grand Hotel, Folkestone, and next morning, walking along the Leas, we met our old friend, Francis Queensberry. He said "Lady Conway is dead. You must go over and buy Saltwood". We went immediately, in our Venice clothes, not looking at all like serious purchasers. We drove under an outer gateway, its unstable arches overgrown with small trees, past an orchard which had long ceased to produce any apples, and an empty moat from which rose the sixteen-foot walls of the inner courtyard; finally we came to the two round towers that had so much enchanted me. We pulled a rusty bell, not expecting it to have any effect, but after an interval a lady appeared, dressed in that material which has such sinister associations in Victorian fiction—black bombazine. This was Lady Conway's companion, Miss Baird, and she was in fact a very tricky character. She had been in the secret service in the Middle East; "Delightful work", she said, and I could well understand why it had a special appeal to her. She greeted us with the words "Have you not heard that Lady Conway is dead?" We replied that this was precisely why we had come. "Is the Castle for sale?" "Yes, but it is already sold." This conflicting statement did not deter us. "We should like to buy it", we said. "But you haven't looked over it", she quite reasonably replied, "besides" (looking at our sketchy Venice clothes) "it is very expensive." "Oh, that's all right", I said. During the conversation I had been looking away from the towers to the valley which they dominate, and had become more than ever excited. "Well", said Miss Baird, "I suppose you had better look into the courtyard." That finished me off. It was, and is, one of the most enchanting spots imaginable: a high wall running round an oval lawn of about an acre, broken by various staircases and turrets, by the ruins of a banqueting hall and a chapel. It was a *hortus conclusus* if ever there was one.

I must write a few words about the strange character whose timely death was so greatly to change our way of life. She was an American lady of unknown origin, and had married in California a Mr Levi Lawson whose family were then proprietors of the *Daily Telegraph*. By a curious chance Beddy-ole-Man had been best man. She must have been nice looking, but she was camera shy, and the only representation I have seen of her is on one of the stone corbels supporting the beams of the Great Hall, done by a local mason. "I did it from life", he told me; but it is not very life-like. She was a romantic, and her whole aim in life was to own castles. Soon after buying Saltwood she persuaded the wretched Mr Levi Lawson to buy Hurstmonceaux as well; but it proved a bit too much for her, and she does not seem to have lived there. I called Mr Levi Lawson 'wretched': after a few years he went down into the woods and shot himself, and his widow was left to concentrate all her energies on Saltwood. She was not interested in gardening, but had a passion for building, and employed a resident mason full time: his restorations were harmless, partly because he was not very skilful. The restorations which gave the Castle its slightly Victorian air had been done in the 1870's by the Deedes family. The towers must have looked more authentic (and they are 90 per cent authentic) before they were given machicolations and what was then called 'honest' restoration.

Mrs Lawson personally supervised all the work, and would be down on the site at 8 o'clock in the morning. If a piece of masonry looked insecure she would push it over with her foot. Next to building her chief pleasure was interior decoration. The Castle was stuffed with furniture, objects, and above all tapestries, collected rather indiscriminately but with a genuine feeling for decorative effect. When I revisited Fenway Court in Boston I was reminded of the interior of Saltwood, only instead of the great masterpieces of painting that Mr Berenson forced on to a reluctant Mrs Gardner, there were dozens of tapestries.

Mrs Lawson saw practically no one, but her passion for castles led her to visit Allington, a castle near Maidstone, where she met Lord Conway, and decided to add both him and his castle to her bag. She married him in 1934. His weird old wife, always known as 'the mobled Queen', had died the year before, and I suppose he was lonely: otherwise I cannot imagine how a man with so keen a sense of self-preservation could have taken such a suicidal step. In his youth Lord Conway had been a genuine explorer of mountains, and had written some readable books on German and Flemish art. As Allington is large and uncomfortable, he came to live at Saltwood. He was seventy-eight years old, short, and paunchy, and almost blind. Lady Conway made him do exercises on the lawn. He survived for less than three years: then Lady Conway was once more left a widow, and she reverted to almost total solitude. Her only friend was Lady Melchett, and it was when travelling with her in the Eastern Mediterranean that she had met Miss Baird, and persuaded her to be her companion. Saltwood Castle had belonged to the see of Canterbury, and one of the buildings on the periphery of the courtyard had been the Archbishop's Hall of Audience. It was tolerably well preserved, and Lady Conway decided to restore it as a memorial to Lord Conway. She put on a roof with a carved ceiling, the work of the Hythe Cabinet Works and worthy of any craftsman in England, and made it into an enormous antiquaire's parlour, filled with tapestries, church furniture, choir stalls and altar rails. I saw that if bookshelves were put in the place of these decorations it would take my whole library, and became more than ever besotted with the idea of buying Saltwood. There were many complications before the deal was completed. Miss Baird claimed to have a more suitable purchaser, and enjoyed seeing our faces fall when she announced that a sale to this candidate had already been effected. Fortunately she was only one of four trustees, and the most reasonable of them was on our side. So finally we bought it, with all its contents and the beautiful valley that leads down to Hythe—the last of such valleys on the south coast not to be built over—for a sum which could have been covered by the sale of two or three of the better tapestries and carpets. But we did not sell them. We were reluctant to break this dream that had taken so strong a hold on us.

Rummaging in the rooms of the Castle after we had bought it was like something in a fairy tale. Every room from cellar to attic, was crammed with what were formerly called 'objects of art and virtue', and is nowadays usually described as junk. The cellar contained a large and impressive collection of old ironwork and pewter; the attic a number of gothic figures, casts mixed up with originals. In many of the rooms were chests containing fragments of velvet or brocade. After a month we came to the end of these treats and surprises, and had to decide what to sell. I am afraid we made a foolish choice and sold too much. In such matters my judgement is usually bad, and this is aggravated by a desire to save myself trouble, which has been the bane of my life. Enough remained to make the place look quite presentable, but to tell the truth I do not think we ever made the interior of the Castle look as attractive as Lady Conway had done. It is not a good house for pictures, and her profusion of fabrics and tapestries suited it better.

Our friends did not all share our enthusiasm for our new toy. 'Absurd', 'pretentious', 'gothic revival', 'all stairs', were some of

the milder comments that reached us. They had grown used to
our presence in London, and had decided, quite wrongly, that we
were urban characters. Moreover, their idea of a house in the
country was a snug little Queen Anne box, and the sight of two
tall stone towers made them feel uneasy. It was thought that one
of the rooms in Saltwood, suitably enough Miss Baird's old room,
was haunted, and I must confess that when I slept there I, who
normally sleep like a mole, felt uneasy and a little frightened; and
this was not auto-suggestion because, although several of our
friends had felt the same and told each other, none of them had
liked to tell me. But friends came down for the week-end, and a
series of photographs show happy parties in the courtyard. No one
liked it more than our old friend, the King of Sweden, who came
down several times, and I may digress to say that we in turn went
to visit him in Sweden. We stayed in a charming country house
called Ulriksdal; he seldom used the palace, except to house his
collection of Chinese art, and stayed at the beautiful, intact
palace of Drottingholm only in the winter, because at that time
he was not bothered by tourists. We have seldom enjoyed anything more than our visit to Sweden. Our host had a sweetness
and simplicity of character which I have rarely seen equalled. Mr
Berenson once described him as a 'human masterpiece', and I
agree. He was a considerable scholar, not only of Chinese ceramics,
but of his own country's antiquities, and on most days we went
on archaeological picnics. In Jane's interest he deferred the hour of
departure till 9.30, and brought two bottles of beer for lunch. He
had a weakness, but it was a very sympathetic one—an innate
modesty prevented him from making the gestures which people
feel they have a right to expect from a king. Driving away from
the Palace after a meeting of the Privy Council we passed a group
of citizens who saluted him. He made no response. Jane, charac-
teristically, said "Sir, you must wave to them". He did. Art-
loving kings have usually been assassinated or reviled—Richard
II, Charles I, George IV; but Gustav Adolph V was too evidently

a good and serious man to be the target of criticism, and even his socialist prime ministers loved him. Much later I was invited to make a speech about him at the dinner given on his eightieth birthday. I ended by saying "wherever scholars and lovers of art are gathered together, you, Sir, are our King".

Some years after we moved to Saltwood, Alan who had been travelling across the United States as a waiter in order to see what it felt like to have no money in a foreign country, had gone to live at Rye, and one day he asked if he could bring over a friend of his to meet us. She was a Colonel's daughter, the sweetest and prettiest little girl we had ever met. The moment we saw her we recognised that he had had the greatest piece of luck that can befall any man. He had found his natural protector. She was not only beautiful but, what was more important, she was absolutely straightforward and natural. Next day, when we saw Alan, we said "You obviously love her. Why don't you marry her?" He replied "Well, you see, she won't be sixteen till May, so I can't marry her till then". We said "Well, go ahead, and do it as soon as possible", which four months later he did. The wedding reception was held at the Arts Council's house in St. James's Square. This was an improper use of a public building, but there was no Colonel Scorgie to object, and the members of the Council who were invited seemed pleased. I certainly enjoyed the occasion more than anything else that happened in the Arts Council. Alan, with characteristic determination, went for his honeymoon to the battlefields of France and Flanders. He was already preparing his cry of indignation at the leadership of the British Army in the 1914–1918 war, which, when it was published as *The Donkeys*, aroused so much controversy. When he returned home he found awaiting him in the St. James's Club an insignificant looking envelope with blue typewriter-ribbon—obviously a bill for back-gammon debts. He shuffled it out of sight and left it for several weeks; finally he felt strong enough to open it, and found that it contained a letter from Lord Beaverbrook making him an extremely generous offer to write for him. Beaverbrook did not know anything about him, but had read an article he had written on the first war. What an extraordinary example of his editorial flair!

Colin's wedding was a very different affair, and was the only occasion on which the resources of Saltwood Castle were extended. He had fallen in love with a ballerina named Violette Verdi, whom he had met when she was dancing with the Ballet Rambert at Sadler's Wells. Later she joined Balanchine's company in New York. Colin, who had been ill, felt the need of a change, so he left Granada Television, where he had a good future, and flew out to New York in search of Violette. She was a well-brought-up French girl, not a star, but exceptionally musical and completely dedicated to her work. I liked her from the first, but, alas, like many ballerinas, she had a possessive and domineering mother. I doubt if she was in love with Colin—she thought only of her career*—but Maman had heard a rumour that I was incredibly rich, and pushed forward the match, supposing that Colin would wait every night at the stage door with a full wallet. The poor boy did at first wait most nights, but his wallet was not full, as he depended on his job as producer-director for the high-brow New York Television network, Channel 13.

However, his suit was accepted, and in due time Violette came to Saltwood for the wedding. Maman also arrived, with a number of her relations, who had walked straight out of de Maupassant. Violette's father remained a mystery. One side of Colin's character likes things to be done in style, and in order to please him we arranged for a party of about two hundred and fifty of our friends. The men were told to wear grey top-hats and tail-coats. The service, in Saltwood Parish Church, was conducted by the Dean of Canterbury, who made an inspiring address about the Union of the Arts. At the end there was a scuffle between the local organist

* She has now become Director of Ballet at the Paris Opera.

and one imported from Canterbury as to who should play the Wedding March. It ended in fisticuffs, so the bridal couple had to walk down the aisle in silence. We then adjourned to a magnificent banquet in the Great Hall and Undercroft of the Castle. Photographers prowled around, snapping Vivien Leigh talking to the Red Dean. Violette danced on the lawn. Everyone seemed happy. But I was not. This was not my idea of Saltwood, and from several signs I had a hunch that things would go badly. In fact they went even worse than I had anticipated.

While we were in Saltwood we had a visitor's book, given us by Irene Worth, whose name appears in it more often than anyone else's, and, although we sometimes forgot to ask people to sign it, especially the ones who came oftenest, it helps me to recall some of the happiness my friends have given me. If asked which has given me most pleasure in my life, art, writing or friendship, I think I would answer friendship. Many of my friendships have been with women, and I say this quite sincerely, although I realise that many people will think that such a relationship is impossible for a normal man, and that I am merely covering up love-affairs. Of course there are certain perils, and occasionally things have taken a dangerous turn; but only once has a friendship been lost. I think that the reason I have had so many friends of the opposite sex is that I do not think of them primarily as women, but as companions who, on the whole, are more sympathetic than men. In recent years I have come to see that this was an illusion. Women are more feminine than I had realised. I can't change now, and on the whole my illusion worked well.

Several of the friends whose names appear in the visitor's book I have attempted to describe in a previous chapter—Vivien Leigh, Ninette de Valois, Frederick Ashton and Edith Sitwell. I have also said something about William Walton, who had been such a stand-by to Jane when I was occupied with bogus war work. He had married an Argentinian lady, who looked after him to perfection. A house and a magnificent garden on the Island of Ischia seemed to be an ideal retreat; but gradually tension and emotion went out of his life, and then out of his music. On an early page I find the names of Julian and Juliette Huxley, and the date August 1954. I had known him since Oxford days, and delighted in his zest and energy and enormous fund of information. His name is also one of the last in the book, and what a sad transformation had taken place in less than ten years. He had become a stage Victorian, fussing about trifles in the querulous accents of the 1860's. His only remaining human trait was a touching admiration for his brother Aldous who, incidentally, stayed at Saltwood only a few months before his death. Aldous had remained far from Victorianism, and described in the high, astonished voice of the 'twenties incredible vagaries of human behaviour. Most of his sentences began with the words 'It's too extraordinary . . .'

I find that the names which appear most often in our book are those of Colin and Morna Anderson. Colin and I had had adjoining rooms at Oxford, and had seen each other without a break ever since. When we went to Upper Terrace House, Colin moved next door into the enchanting Admiral's House that Constable painted at least three times. With the exception of David Crawford, Colin did more for the arts than anyone in England. In his Orient Line ships he employed the best modern designers and, when the building of large passenger liners was no longer a profitable venture, he changed from patronage to administration. He became Chairman of the Royal Fine Arts Commission, Chairman of the English Opera Group, Chairman of the Tate Gallery, Chairman of the Royal College of Art, Chairman of the Contemporary Art Society and the National Council of Design, Trustee of the Gulbenkian Foundation. What a catalogue! Infinitely more extended than my own, which, God knows, seemed bad enough to me at the time. And in addition to the arts, one finds, if one looks in *Who's Who*, Chairman of about forty-five other Committees dealing with shipping, transport, pollution, and similar difficult topics. Let no one suppose that such chairmanships are a sinecure, like certain City directorships. I have held them, and know how much hard work they involve. I am sure that he did not draw a penny of income from any of these offices, and they gave him absolutely no added status nor power. They were done out of devotion to the public interest. We shall see if a socialist community produces anyone similar. If they do, which is unlikely, he will certainly not be as genial, fanciful and majestically eccentric as Colin.

Next to the Andersons the most frequent guests were Joan and Garrett Moore. We had known them before the war, when they were without question the most beautiful couple I have ever seen; and after forty years they are beautiful still. Garrett is a man with a passion for detail, applied quite ruthlessly but without malice. When we were all staying together in Portmeirion during the war, I heard him examining the local chemist about the contents of one of his bottles. After about ten minutes the wretched man ran out of the shop and disappeared down the village street. Garrett had not meant to be unkind: his mind works like that. So that when he became Chairman of Covent Garden, notes used to whizz round from the Royal Box to the producer, telling him of inconsistencies of dress or lighting which Garrett, with unerring eye, had observed. It might have caused a rebellion, but Garrett is naturally such a sweet character that no one minds his interference, and the frequent presence of a sharp observer contributed to the improvement of Covent Garden productions. As for Joan, she is not only a great beauty, an admirable pianist, an enchanting companion, but the most loyal friend in the world. Although she has had to enter the kind of High Society that stifles most people (Garrett is a Knight of the Garter) she has remained as frank and giggly as she has always been. For thirty years we have talked together about books, music, and occasionally people, and I cannot remember a moment that I have not enjoyed.

The next names that I find, in a mysterious variety of handwritings, are those of Yehudi and Diana Menuhin. To have been able to call such a man one's friend is something to have lived for. As he spins round the world, marvellously chosen postcards come in from Diana, covered with her large communicative writing; then Yehudi comes home again for a month, and often visits Saltwood. He stayed with us for two nights before a concert in Canterbury Cathedral, and for once had a day without travelling in which to practise. The next evening he played more beautifully than I have ever heard him do before. At the climax of the Bach Chaconne a little mouse ran across the floor in front of him. This conjunction of very exalted and very humble forms of life seemed to me extremely moving.

What other names do I find in the visitor's book? Frequently those of Cynthia and Sidney Nolan. The young artist whom I had found (not 'discovered') twenty years before had grown to be a great name in modern art. When time has weeded out his colossal output and the didactic snobbery of abstract art has declined, he will be of even greater renown. Sidney set out in his youth to be a second Rimbaud, and, although his natural gentleness has denied him this furious vocation, his mind is full of subversive ideas worthy of his model. Cynthia is, in her own way, his equal, a brilliantly observant writer and, as I know to my cost, remarkably perceptive of human shortcomings. There are also the names of many other artists who are well known, and one whose name may not be familiar, but I believe her to be a painter of exquisite quality, Mary Potter. Her husband, the noted humorist, left her. Of all the women in the world whom I would not have left, Mary Potter is the first. She accepted the law of nature, and went on painting better than ever. She lived in Aldeburgh, and was the devoted friend of Benjamin Britten. Whenever I have been ill (which, thank God, is very seldom) I have stayed with her to convalesce, and in her peaceful companionship have regained my health.

Who else? Obviously Henry Moore and the Graham Sutherlands. Very often Stephen and Natasha Spender, who on one occasion brought down Stravinsky, whom I had met in Los Angeles. The moment he set eyes on Jane he said "You must be one of us", and in fact Jane was often mistaken for a Russian. I think he enjoyed himself, and wrote a perfectly incomprehensible bar of music in our book. He was one of the most entertaining men I have ever met. If an aesthete were asked where and when he would like to have lived, he might answer in Rome in 1916, when Diaghilev had gathered round him Massine, Picasso and Stravinsky. The year of Verdun and the Battle of the Somme. No wonder that the average man regards aesthetes with contempt. Thank Heaven Stephen and Natasha are still alive (so many of our friends have died or gone to live abroad), and have shown us the most delicate sympathy in our last three unhappy years.

As I come to the end of the visitor's book, one name appears more frequently than almost any other, that of David Knowles. Many historians would agree that his history of the Religious Orders in England is one of the historical masterpieces of this century. I had met him when still at Oxford, but had lost sight of him, and as usual I cannot remember when we became such close friends. There are lots of good people in the world who are simple, or even stupid. David was that rare phenomenon, a very good man who was complex and highly intelligent. He had a sweet smile, but also a penetrating glance which saw through any form of pretence. I knew it was an undeserved privilege for me to be in his company, but he was so easy to talk to that I forgot my sinful state. We talked about history, poetry and nature. David Knowles loved nature as much as Mr Berenson had done and, on our walks in the valleys behind the Castle, he would pause before a tree or a turn in the valley and say "This is good!" He meant more than 'I am enjoying it'. 'Good' meant to him that it was the work of God. We sometimes talked about God, and he showed that width of reasonable understanding which had led him to the brink of excommunication. He once confided in Jane that the two happiest people he knew were a monk and a nun who were married. But he was so great a scholar that the Church could not afford to lose him, any more than it could Lord Acton. Although he knew that the thought of the Catholic Church played a great part in my mind, he never once attempted to influence me, still less to 'convert' me. He only went as far as to say that he knew I was looking for something. So I was, and still am.

Our friends came for week-ends, all but two, who stayed for a week or ten days. One of these was E. M. Forster. He had lived with his old mother near Dorking in a house designed by his father, which was the epitome of Victorian domestic architecture. I wonder if even John Betjeman would have swallowed it. When his mother died he was given rooms in Kings College, Cambridge, and made an honorary fellow. They were big rooms, furnished with the usual English lack of any visual sense, and he seemed rather lost in them. But he made friends with several Indian undergraduates and was, I suppose, happy enough. For a dreadful fortnight in August the kitchen at Kings was shut. Then he came to Saltwood. He was usually accompanied by Joe Ackerley, who was supposed to be looking after him—not that he needed any looking after except on the train down when he sometimes landed up in Maidstone or Canterbury instead of Folkestone.

Morgan Forster was a man with a genuinely free mind. At Cambridge Lytton Strachey had called him the 'mole' because you never knew where he would come to the surface or by what invisible means he had got there. But he was really quite consistent. Even his most surprising remarks revealed the same state of mind. He believed in human beings and human relationships and thought that nothing else mattered. He loved people, places and music. He disliked institutions, categories and hierarchies. When Kings College gave him a luncheon on his seventieth birthday he insisted on the condition that there should be no 'high table' and anyone could sit anywhere. It was snowing heavily when we arrived in Cambridge and, as his old friends were too high-minded to take a taxi, we walked from the station; twenty elderly snowmen entered, dripping, the hall of Kings. He called his collection of essays *Two Cheers for Democracy*. "One too many" I said to him, and he gave me a sweet smile of agreement. He had only recently realised to what foul indignities the once honourable word had been subjected, so that it may now mean anything from tyranny to vulgarity.

To have this lovable man, with whose opinions I was so much in sympathy, staying with us for a fortnight every year was something to look forward to. He used to sit curled up, with his eyes closed on the hardest seat he could find in the courtyard. I very seldom saw him open a book. But he was ready to talk and, like all good talkers, enjoyed an audience, particularly an audience of young people. They were enthralled by someone of his age who expressed their own feelings, many of which they had been taught to think were disreputable.

In 1956 he was seriously ill, and was sent to a Cambridge hospital. His friends were asked to go down to say goodbye. Although incapable of humbug I think he rather enjoyed these death-bed scenes. But he recovered, and came down to Saltwood for at least three more Augusts. After he had died his dear friend Joe Ackerley came by himself. He was moderately sad about Morgan, but very happy to be the principal guest. He was indeed a remarkable person in his own right, for he contrived to be at the same time fanatically truthful and courteous. Although his later books reveal him as a very active homosexual, he was, I believe, genuinely fond of Jane. He had a passion for animals, with which I sympathised, and when he was put back in charge of *The Listener* (he had been its editor for many years) while his successor was on holiday, almost every article and review was about animals, so that his staff protested. We looked forward to many such summer visits, but he died. Robert Lowell, asked by an interviewer, who wished to explain the complex melancholy of his poems, what worried him about life, said "That people die"—a statement that becomes more painfully true every year.

Our other long visit was that of Maurice Bowra, which took
place at Christmas. The kitchen at Wadham was closed. Maurice
had spent Christmas with us ever since the war, and at Hampstead
these had been very jolly occasions, as Maurice was then more
mobile, and was even willing to take part in charades, acting the
part of King Edward VII in the Tranby Croft affair. One of our
neighbours in Hampstead had actually been present, so we gave
a well-documented performance. For a charade of the Expulsion,
in which Jane and I played Eve and Adam, Maurice took the part
of the Almighty and appeared with a top-hat (heaven knows
where he found it) and an umbrella, which he shook at us in an
awe-inspiring manner. The only trouble was that he insisted on
going to church on Christmas Day, and disturbed Jane by his
loud, and not very tuneful, singing of the hymns. He did the
same when he came to spend Christmas at Saltwood, but this
was even more embarrassing to Jane, because we used to go to
service in Canterbury Cathedral and were given seats in the choir.
Maurice took the correct C. of E. view that the congregation
should join in the singing of hymns and bellowed away, to the
amazement of the very refined choir. He seldom came in summer; he said it wasn't natural, but in fact he was afraid that he
might be asked to walk. I once persuaded him to walk across the
courtyard to my library in the Great Hall, and he was quite
pleased, as he found a number of very obscure books of learning
that had been bequeathed to me by Edith Wharton. On another
occasion we went to visit our neighbour Elizabeth Bowen, who
was also an old friend of Maurice's. "You can't drive up to the
door", I said, "you have to walk about 60 yards." "Then I'm not
going", said Maurice. However, he went and Elizabeth's small
sitting-room was soon 'overflowing with the sound'. As time
passed he became more and more static, or rather sedentary,
establishing himself on a small red sofa in our panelled sitting-
room, talking. The problem was to provide him with an audience.
We asked down friends who were prepared to submit, of whom

the most devoted was Irene Worth; and we usually had John Sparrow to take a turn; but twelve hours is a long time. Most of the responsibility for keeping Maurice stoked fell on me, and I profited by it, because he took advantage of my smattering of information to give up being the famous wit, and became, what he really was, the man of prodigious learning. I knew just enough to egg him on, although when it came to Russian commentaries on Xenophon, I could do no more than make approving noises. Incidentally, Maurice was very fond of reciting Russian poetry, which he did with so much conviction that it was enjoyable, although no one could understand a word. In between these learned sessions he became his better-known self, and infected us all with his good humour and appetite for life. A few heads rolled in the dust, but fundamentally he was one of the most warm-hearted men I have known. When we decided to give Saltwood to Alan, and build ourselves a bungalow in the kitchen garden, we added a comfortable spare room, known as Maurice's room. We drove him round to look at it when the hóuse was almost finished. He gave it his strongest commendation "By no means bad". The very first day we spent in the new house the telephone rang with the news that Maurice had died. For both of us he was irreplaceable.

The names of two loved friends do not appear in the visitor's book because they could not write: they were dogs. Many people, and in particular orthodox Roman Catholics, will consider it shocking to mention animals in the same category as human beings; but, since I am writing from my heart and not in accordance with any principles, I must confess that I was fonder of our two dogs than of most of my fellow men. Strictly speaking, they were not our dogs. Plato, a magnificent Great Dane, had been bought by Colin while he was still at Oxford. Emma, a miniature Dachshund, had been given to Colette while she too was at Oxford. For various reasons they found their ways to Saltwood, and became our dogs. They adored each other, and used to play together in a way that reminded me of Michelangelo's drawing of Samson and Delilah, in which a gigantic Samson lies on the ground and a diminutive Delilah prances round him and teases him. Plato was a noble character, but not very clever. Emma was the most intelligent animal I have ever known; but if I were to give examples of her intelligence I would not only bore the reader, but I would appear in the all too familiar light of an animal-loving crackpot. Plato became ill with cancer and felt the hand of death upon him. One winter night he went into the courtyard to die in the snow. I should have left him, but the instinct to try to save life is over-riding; I put on a fur coat over my pyjamas and after about an hour (he was of course far too heavy to lift) I persuaded him to come back to the warmth of his barrel. I was rewarded, for the next day was fine, and we sat together on a bank. Plato put his head on my shoulder. The day after, he died. Emma survived him by ten years, in fact she lived to be twenty-one. What she liked best was a party in which she knew all the guests and greeted them individually with yelps of delight. I have never known a more convivial being. At last she grew old, and when she felt death approaching she did just the same as Plato—she ran out in the middle of the night to escape, and, as before, it took well over an hour for me to catch her and bring her in. She died next day. Being so close to a very intelligent animal leads one to speculate on how the human race has achieved its state of superiority. A dog has memory, intuition and curiosity, not to mention the moral virtues of courage and affection. The answer seems to be simply the power of articulate speech. 'In the beginning was the word' is true in the plain English sense, as well as in the original meaning of that profound Greek concept, the logos. The study of man should begin with the study of the origins of language. This seems, unfortunately, from numerous and contradictory books, to be an absolutely incomprehensible subject.

★　　★　　★　　★　　★

During our first ten years at Saltwood I was chairman of the Arts Council, and I was already living there when I was asked to become chairman of the ITA. I was also a member of many time-consuming committees, and only began to shed them in the late 1960's. I suppose that is how the world saw me as I recently received a note on my life from the Royal Institution which, after giving a list of public offices and meaningless honours, adds 'He has also written several books on art', but does not name them. Both India and Japan were visited from Saltwood. Looking back, I am ashamed to think that I left Jane alone so often. Her health had begun to decline during the last years at Hampstead, but at first Saltwood did her good. She turned her attention to the garden, which Lady Conway had neglected, and in an amazingly short time the tall stone walls of the courtyard, inside and out, were covered with climbing roses. One can walk round the top of these walls and enjoy the view over the unspoilt country to the north-east; and for several months the roses grew up level with one's knees. I loved this walk, and I showed it with pride to visitors. I remember taking round three civil servants, representatives of the Department of Ancient Buildings. The roses were at their best, and the scent of Wedding Day and The Garland was in-toxicating. The civil servants walked round in total silence. After a time I could bear it no longer, and said tentatively "Don't you think it's rather nice?" To which the senior member of the trio replied "Oh no, not with all this vegetable growth". They did not actually instruct us to cut down the roses (I suppose this might have involved administrative difficulties), but they used to send over a representative, who padded silently round the Castle, to report if we were planting any more. Fortunately there was no more room for any.

I love writing as much as Jane loved gardening, and I had a perfect room to write in, just off the Archbishop's Hall. It was hung with the best of Lady Conway's tapestries, and was as far removed from modern taste as it is possible to be. I used to sit at the window (I always write on my knee), looking down the terrace, with roses climbing up the wall on one side, and falling down towards the valley on the other. My large library was in the next room, and when I came to write the script of 'Civilisation' I found myself reading books which I had bought forty years ago and had never opened. Ideal conditions: but, happy as we were at Saltwood, I think we were even happier when we were travelling together. I am a confirmed sightseer, and if I go somewhere it is to look at the works of man. In visiting a church or gallery I do not like to be alone. I want to express my joy or disappointment to a companion, to point out unexpected details, sometimes, I fear, to give a mini-lecture. Jane was the perfect sightseer's companion. To visit Santa Croce or San Miniato in her company was to have every pleasure enhanced by her quick perception, and by a diligence which exceeded my own. She went at exactly the right speed, a very important attribute in a sight-seeing companion. I tend to go too fast, and Jane made me look longer. We were so happy on our travels that I sometimes wonder if the desire for Saltwood that came over us in 1952 was not like one of those passionate love-affairs that end in tears. On the whole I think not, because the valleys and the library were two joys that never palled. But of course there were problems of upkeep, and an oppressive feeling of nimiety, or too-muchness. I have suffered from it all my life—too many possessions, too many books, too much to eat and drink. On the opposite side of the empty moat that once surrounded the Castle was an old kitchen garden, which had been totally neglected in Lady Conway's time, but Jane had put back into good working order. I formed in my mind a dark design to build a small house there, and hand over Saltwood to our son, Alan. This would be a rare case of being able to eat one's cake and have it; the library and courtyard would still be there for me to enjoy, but I would not have to feel responsible for them. I nursed this idea for several years before trying it out on Jane. To my astonishment she agreed immediately. This turned out to be almost the only good idea I have ever had in my life. We were exceptionally fortunate in our architect. He was recommended to us by a friend who was Librarian in the Bournemouth School of Art, and said "There is only one man in this country who I would trust to build a house for me, and that is John King". As he was lecturer in the same school of art I might have been suspicious; but for some reason, perhaps my friend's exceptional honesty, I was convinced. People who visit the house say "I suppose you built it yourself". Let no amateur ever make such a claim. Three quarters of the work involved in building a house, from foundations to 'detailing', can be done only by a highly trained professional. But I did have the idea of making it a bungalow consisting of three pavilions, one for living, one for sleeping and one for eating; and I was determined that the exterior should be white board on brick. I saw that this could be used with rather the same fenestration as in Japanese architecture, and showed John King reproductions of the Katsura Summer Palace in Kyoto. I believe that a serious architect is glad to have certain conditions laid down by his patron. Gabriel was a very great architect, but he accepted advice from a man as stupid as Louis XVI. John King did everything I asked of him, and added a good deal of his own. The result is the most harmonious and comfortable house I have ever lived in.

Alan and his wife (who is also called Jane) have made the courtyard of the Castle even more beautiful than it was in our time, and have turned the entrance into a sort of *manoire* in the Normandy style, with cocks and hens, ducks and pigeons, and eleven peacocks. This has had a humanising effect on the mediaeval exterior, and is the aspect of the Castle that visitors like best. How my daughter-in-law copes with all these birds as well as the garden and the cooking I can't imagine. But, as many of us discovered during the war, we can do, and are glad to do, things that would have seemed impossible to our parents. So my crazy love-affair with Saltwood seems to have ended well.

# VIII

## *Television Performer*

I PROLONGED my chairmanship of the Independent Television Authority in order to be present at the opening of the Scottish station. This took place on August 31st, 1957, which was to be my last day as chairman. In the evening there was a dinner, followed by a very long entertainment of the usual kind, made more distressing by the routine inclusion of local colour: Scottish comedians, girl pipers, and the communal singing of Scottish songs. At last this unpleasant experience came to an end, and I was invited on to the platform so that Roy Thomson could present me with a small, modern silver quaich. I made another laudatory speech, my third; and stepped down a free man. As I walked towards my table I noticed Lew Grade and Val Parnell looking at their watches and beckoning to me. I went over to them, and Lew said "It's after midnight. You're no longer chairman of the ITA. You can come and work for us—we've got a contract for you." I was not only flattered, but delighted by a display of quick action, which reminded me of Dr Horowitz and Mr Berenson. This was a perfect justification of free enterprise. I agreed, and thus entered a field of activity which was to occupy much of my time for the next twenty years.

I had in fact done one television programme already. This was in 1937, and was the first 'art' programme to appear on the new medium. I was chairman of a panel in which four artists tried to guess who wrote certain lines of poetry, and four poets guessed, from details, who painted certain pictures. The poets won. I suppose about 500 people saw it. It was done in the Alexandra Palace, and I must say that the lights were extremely hot. These hot lights passed into the mythology of television, so that when I was doing 'Civilisation' elderly people used to ask me if I didn't mind the heat of the lights, and when I replied that they were never hot enough, thought I was joking.

My first programme was a total disaster. This was not altogether my fault. The member of ATV's staff who was supposed to look after me was a clever man called Bob Heller, who had been at Harvard and listened to my lectures there. He was almost the only university man on the staff, and was kept on, even after his health was failing, because he could compose the kind of conventional letter that was outside the range of Lew Grade. He should have told me some of the ways in which a television performance differed from a lecture; instead he handed me over to a miserable director who, in retrospect, seems to have been going slightly out of his mind; or perhaps he was simply drunk. At all events, the poor man died after my second programme. He never explained to me that a live programme must run to a split second, and in consequence that it must be scripted and rehearsed down to the last detail. All he did by way of rehearsal was to put me into a chair raised up on a pile of bricks, so that he could shoot me from below, and tell me to say something. "What?" "Oh, anything." In the event I never sat in a chair. But I was also to blame, because with consummate vanity, I thought I could go on ad libbing, and amusing the viewer with my speculations. Moreover, I had chosen a subject that involved the kind of abstract speculation which only Dr Bronowski has been able to put across on television. I had been struck by the fact that, as Plato, the Great Dane, sat outside Alan's house in Rye, the passers-by used to say "Isn't he beautiful?" I thought it would be interesting to find out what they meant. So my programme turned into an examination of the word 'beautiful', and I remember asking could a pig be beautiful, or a crocodile. My unhappy director, hoping to swamp me, introduced a number of more experienced performers into the programme, who, of course, had no idea what was going on. The result was a shambles. It must have been one of the worst programmes ever put on, and was generally recognised as such; in fact ATV decided to cancel my contract, but someone, perhaps Bob Heller, asked that I should be allowed one more try.

My next programme was directed by the same pathetic character, but I had chosen a fool-proof subject, a visit of Henry Moore and myself to the British Museum at night. It was also unscripted, and Henry and I found ourselves standing in front of a detail of the Parthenon pediment with nothing much to say; but we just got away with it by patting appreciatively the magnificent forms. I will not weary the reader by describing the stages by which I gradually came to terms with the medium. The first stage was to learn that every word must be scripted; the second that what viewers want from a programme on art is not ideas, but information; and the third that things must be said clearly, energetically and economically. In so far as I became a competent television performer I owe everything to a director called Michael Redington. He had been an actor, and often after my first rehearsal would say "I went to sleep"; after the second he would say "You overplayed it!" The third usually went quite well. The old days of live transmission had a certain excitement. If one made a 'bish' one had to live with it. This gave to one's performances a tension which diminished with the introduction of tape. Now that they are on film it is 'money for jam' because every fluff can be cut; but I might not have been able to do the filmed sequences of 'Civilisation' with as much vivacity if I had not 'come up the hard way' of live transmission.

I stubbornly continued to do programmes on general topics, and some of these were quite amusing. I remember one called 'What is Good Taste?', in which I had constructed a bad-taste room and a good-taste room. The bad-taste room contained almost everything that was then to be found in the average home, a flight of china birds and a carpet from the Co-op. The good-taste room was all white. I occasionally have naughty impulses, and one of these attacked me during this film. I said "This isn't the sort of room in which you would dare to open a bottle of stout, or, as they say on the BBC, a bottle of Guinness". Of course it wasn't in the script. At the time the BBC, which is supposed not to advertise, was widely accused of crypto-advertising, and my light-hearted insertion was discussed by the Governors. They seriously considered a legal action, but had the sense to drop it.

Gradually it became clear to me that what people wanted was to know about individual artists, and my first real success was a series called *Five Revolutionary Painters*. At that time the ITA was still thought of as 'the people's programme', and a surprising number of people were interested. A friend of mine told me that in a pub in Covent Garden he found two of the market porters discussing Caravaggio; he thought he was suffering from an hallucination. The railway porters at Charing Cross used to sit up with their children long after bedtime to listen to talks on Michelangelo. After my visit to Japan I did a series of three programmes on Japanese art, directed by my friend Ian Mutsu, and filmed by one of the best Japanese cameramen. I usually sit on the occasional seat of a taxi in order to enjoy the driver's conversation, and on one occasion I remember a taximan pulling up a book on Zen Buddhism, and saying "That's what you've let me in for". I said "Don't you find it rather difficult? I can't understand half of it." He said "Oh, I understand it all right, and I like it, but my wife doesn't like it because I won't kill spiders. She says 'You old b.b. buddhist.'"

The forty-eight programmes I did for ATV were probably more widely seen by the British people than 'Civilisation' and had more influence in England. Latterly I became more ambitious, and planned a series of programmes called *Temples*. Three were completed and shown; on Chartres, St. Mark's in Venice and Luxor. I had hoped to do one on the temples in Guatemala and on Angkor-Vat. Unfortunately Michael Redington was no longer available, and I had different directors for each film. This is a serious matter, because the relationship between the author-performer and the director is of vital importance, and in Luxor and St. Mark's I more or less directed myself, which gratifies the ego but is very seldom satisfactory, on stage or screen. The Luxor film was my first introduction to Egypt, which I loved so much that I have been back many times, and have done another film on the earlier period. Working with a half-Egyptian crew, I have come to love not only Egypt but the Egyptians, and my dream of bliss, which I shall never now achieve, would be to go from Cairo to Assuan on a Nile steamer.

Why I never got any further with the Temples series was that I was persuaded to do a programme on Royal Palaces. This was a joint venture by the BBC and the ITA, and naturally the ITA was anxious that the author-narrator should be one of their men. In many respects I was the obvious man, as I had been Surveyor of the King's Pictures and knew the palaces well, and the Temples series had given me experience of this kind of conducted tour. But my instincts were very strongly against attempting the programme. Anything said about Royalty must be free from criticism of any kind, and give a feeling of boundless enthusiasm. I have a bump of criticism that I find it hard to conceal. The script should have been written by Arthur Bryant and narrated by Richard Burton. In the end I accepted, chiefly because I felt I owed it to Lew, who had so generously backed all my earlier attempts. The subject abounded in difficulties; how much history to put in, how much architectural criticism, how to give the programme any shape. Looking back, I do not think I took enough trouble about it. I should have visited each palace many times alone with my director, Tony Lotbinière (who had made an excellent film on Eton College), and worked out with him a precise shooting script. But in the end these technicalities were unimportant compared with my failure to catch the right tone. This was not an occasion for irony or throw-away lines, and I indulged in both. In order to have access to Buckingham Palace and Windsor, we had made the film when the Queen and the Duke of Edinburgh were out of the country for a longish time, and I had had no opportunity of consulting them. When they finally saw a rough cut it was without sound, and I had to speak the text from my script while the royal corgies bit my ankles. It was a total failure. The Queen and the Duke of Edinburgh disliked it so much that they would, I believe, have liked to veto the whole film. She was persuaded not to do so by Kim Cobbold, the Lord Chamberlain, and I suppose that the programme went on the air, although I do not remember seeing it. I have described this failure at length, because by a curious irony it led to a success. The controllers of the BBC must have seen it in the way of duty, and someone there, perhaps Huw Wheldon, had the idea that I might be employed on a more extended scale. David Attenborough invited me to lunch, saying that he would like to discuss a project with me. He wanted to do a series of fifteen films: "What shall I call it? Say Civilisation". I don't think he really intended to use that word, but it slipped out. I was munching my smoked salmon rather apathetically when I heard it, and suddenly there flashed across my mind a way in which the history of European civilisation from the dark ages to 1914 could be made dramatic and visually interesting. I said "Let me think about it for half an hour". I seemed to remember someone saying that I need only be chairman of a committee, and someone else that I need not write the programmes, only narrate them; but my mind was occupied and I did not answer. When we came to the coffee I said "I will do the programmes. I will write and narrate them. I do not need any outside help." At this moment Huw Wheldon had joined us and gave me full support. His colleagues felt a little uneasy, but there was nothing they could do about it. A few days later I went down to stay with Alan in Wiltshire, and in the course of a very wet walk told him precisely how the programmes (now cut down to thirteen) would work out. In the event they hardly varied at all. When I told David Knowles what I had undertaken he said, with his usual historical insight "What are you going to do about Spain?". This was exactly the problem that had been worrying me. If I had been writing a series on the history of art, Spain would have had an important and honourable place. But how to fit the Spain of the Conquistadores, Philip II and the persecution of the Spanish Erasmians, the Escorial and the Inquisition into the rational humanistic plan which had occupied my thoughts? In the end I simply left it out, saying (which was true) that I did not know enough about Spanish history.

I then had to meet my directors. The senior one was Michael Gill, and our meeting was naturally a moment of strain to us both. I have a fancy that Michael thought I would be 'grand'—a common delusion of those who do not know me—and was prepared to resist; but I was charmed by his enthusiasm and intelligence, and the interview ended happily. My second director, Peter Montagnon, is someone who inspires immediate affection. He is silent and sympathetic. Only after an acquaintance as close as he will permit does one realise what a deeply mysterious character he really is; but that does not make one love him any the less. The third person with whom I had to deal was Ann Turner, who made the impression of senior tutor in a ladies college. She directed only one programme, and it seemed to cause her too much anxiety; but she was the most marvellous researcher I have ever known. My three directors said that I must produce a sample treatment. I should have liked to begin at the beginning, but they insisted that it should be on the Italian Renaissance, as they thought I knew more about that period. I wrote a harmless, but slightly commonplace piece, which they turned down, saying that it was like something out of a colour-supplement. I tried again, and the result was more or less similar to the programme that was actually filmed.

More or less; one merit of the 'Civilisation' scripts was that they were in a continual state of evolution. First I would write my draft, which would be discussed, usually over lunch, in the Television Centre. Heaven knows how many lunches I took off the BBC, and what fun they were! After two hours of unsparing criticism, I went home and wrote a second script. I always took my points of departure and based my arguments on things seen— towns, bridges, cloisters, cathedrals, palaces. But when I actually arrived at my visible subject, it often looked slightly different from what I had expected; sometimes it was unfilmable, more often it revealed new possibilities; and then a third version of the script had to be prepared. Considering this entirely visual approach it is surprising that the scripts, with very little alteration, could finally be printed, and furnish a tolerable book. But how much was lost, not only the rhythmic flow and contrast of the images, but also the music. When I set about the programmes I had in mind Wagner's ambition to make opera into a *gesamt kunstwerk*—text, spectacle and sound all united. We chose the music ourselves. Peter had a good knowledge of plain chant; I am particularly fond of polyphonic music, from Josquin to Monteverde; we all united for the eighteenth and nineteenth centuries. It was my idea to end the series with the closing bars of Stravinsky's *Apollon Musagète*. We ran into one unexpected difficulty. It was absolutely necessary to include the Marseillaise in programme 12; and no record of the Marseillaise had been made by any French or English company. I wanted to go down to the Renault works and have it sung for us by men on strike, but time was running short. In the end we found a Russian record, in which the French was sung with a strong Russian accent. Everyone took this to be a Marseilles accent, so all was well.

\*    \*    \*    \*    \*

We went first to Florence, where I met my crew. I liked them all, but two were outstanding, the senior cameraman responsible for lighting, called Tubby Englander, and his assistant, Ken

Celebrating the conclusion of the television programmes
of 'Civilisation': Michael Gill, K.C., and Ken Macmillan, 1968

K.C. as Chancellor of York University conferring
an honorary degree on Lord Crawford

Macmillan. I can't think how Mr Englander came to be called
Tubby, for no nickname could have been less appropriate. He is
a small, compact man, with a neat moustache and horn-rimmed
spectacles, always impeccably dressed in a dark suit, which con-
trasted oddly with the conventionally unconventional garments of
the crew. He looks like a figure from a Moghul miniature, one
of those elegant, silent men whose presence in India must have
been almost as foreign to the original inhabitants as that of the
English. He has a passion for tidiness and order, and before each
shot he used to flick almost invisible pieces of fluff off my coat.
But the chief thing, from my point of view, was that I recognised
a maestro and had perfect confidence in his lighting. It is very difficult for the amateur to tell the difference between what looks like
acceptable lighting and television lighting. I am all too prone to
interfere, and with anyone but Tubby I would have been tempted
to do so. But I soon learnt to keep my mouth shut. Ken Macmillan had an eye for a 'frame' slightly better than either of my
directors. He was an artist, silent, withdrawn and independent,
and latterly, when I saw him taking a position different from that
suggested by the director, I would give him a wink and a nod of
agreement.

As far as I can remember the first shot we took was of Michael-
angelo's *David* in the Accademia, in which I emerge, looking as
small as possible, from behind the gigantic figure. It was still
fashionable among film directors to place the narrator on an improvised erection, which wobbled and made him feel nervous;
and this evidently affected my speech because Michael shook his
head gloomily and said that I would have to take a course in
voice production. I readily agreed, but, as I had made forty-eight
films without any complaints about my diction, I thought that
this particular difficulty would be forgotten. Michael continued
to have doubts about the programmes throughout the whole of
this first Italian expedition, and, after a piece that I spoke in Rome,
on the Campidoglio, which when I heard it again did strike me

as rather too analytic for the popular ear, he seemed inclined to call the whole thing off and suggested cutting down the programmes from 50 to 35 minutes. As usual I agreed. Inwardly I felt quite confident. I believe that the first time that Michael and the crew felt that they had got on to a good thing was in a sequence in front of the Pont-du-Gard in Provence, that was to be part of the first programme. Whether it was the beauty of the setting, or something I said that suddenly convinced them, that was the moment in which, for them, the series ceased to be just another job, and became a campaign.

Many people have asked me what is required to be a good television performer. The first thing is not to be frightened of the camera. I was taught this by Arthur Askey, almost the first man to appear on television, on the opening night of Granada TV. He said "I'll show you", and went right up to the lens and shook his fist at it. I don't know what the viewers made of this performance. The lesson is easily learnt, and since my first programmes I have never thought of the camera for a second. I have felt that I was talking to a friend or, more often, soliloquising. As a young man I used to take long walks across the moors and had formed the habit—said to be a bad habit—of talking to myself. I believe that these soliloquies were the foundation of my success as a television performer.

The second, and far more important, requirement is patience. I am said to be an impatient man. I look repeatedly at my watch, and hate being kept waiting. But when I am doing a job my patience is limitless. This is absolutely essential for 'location shots', in or out of doors. A camera crew, by union rules, consists of twelve men; they are not all strictly necessary (I have done good sequences with only five men), but they have to be kept busy, and for an hour they lay rails, carry up extra batteries, move the position of the sound equipment (for some reason sound is always the poor relation of a TV crew), change the positions of the lights at least six times, and finally install the camera—well, not quite 'finally', because there is still the narrator to be fitted in somehow, and if he walks into the shot, as I so often (perhaps too often) did in 'Civilisation', there are more difficulties of lighting. If one is out of doors clouds suddenly darken the sky. Everyone surveys them gloomily through dark glasses, and prays, like Cézanne for 'un temps gris clair'. If one is indoors there are unexpected reflections. And always there is the problem of noise. I have often thought that making a television film would be pure pleasure were it not for sound problems. Aircraft noises one can anticipate, but the sensitive ear of the microphone picks up traffic noises which one has taken for granted. The majestic silence of the Sistine Chapel is broken every ten minutes up to midnight by the sound of cars roaring up the hill outside. It is practically impossible to shoot a film live anywhere in Paris. In the middle of the Tuileries Gardens there is a thunderous roar of traffic. And, apart from such obvious hazards, there are sounds of which one had been totally unaware— a honking barge, a distant saw-mill or a barking dog. When sound problems prove to be insupportable the location has to be abandoned and the long process of setting up has to begin somewhere else. *Pazienza.*

A major difficulty for the performer is that sometimes he will have been waiting for two hours on a location, but he has to walk into it with an air of surprise, and speak as if the whole experience was fresh and exciting. He must to some extent be an actor. People often ask me if I used any sort of a prompter. The answer is that one can—indeed must—describe buildings without a prompter, and one can also tell a story. But when it comes to thoughts and reflections one soon gets into trouble; a 'telecue' saves one from the 'ums' and 'ers', and repetitions. Some performers, especially politicians, can never use a telecue without revealing the fact that they are reading. Television is not for them.*

---

* I may record one use of a telecue which fascinated me. Lyndon Johnson, when he addressed an open air meeting, had a telecue hoisted up in the air, out of shot, so that he could keep his head erect and give the impression of speaking to the back of the audience.

For me one of the unexpected pleasures of making 'Civilisation' was seeing great works of art that I had known all my life under conditions that had long become impossible for the ordinary visitor. The Sistine Chapel is now so full of tourists that one cannot move, and is deafened by guides barking out banalities in four languages. We had it to ourselves for five hours, during which Tubby contrived to light parts of the ceiling that I had never seen. The prolonged company of Michelangelo is marvellous, but very exhausting. In fact the only time during the whole series when I could scarcely go on was standing before the *Last Judgment* in the Sistine ceiling. By contrast Raphael's *Stanze*, also revealing, under Tubby's illumination, unforeseen beauties, was cheering, and revived one's faith in humanity. It had happened once, it might happen again. Filming in the Vatican costs £1,000 a day, so one has to move quickly, make no fluffs, and fill every second. When we had done everything on our schedule there remained forty minutes. I suddenly thought of the last words of programme 7— "I wonder if any thought that has helped forward the human spirit has been conceived or written down in an enormous room" —and, although the long corridor of the Vatican isn't precisely a room, I thought it would make the point. "Quick, follow me!" and we all streamed upstairs from the Belvedere, and set the camera up at one end of the corridor. We had no need of lighting, as evening sunshine was pouring in through the windows. I walked away from the camera the whole length of the corridor and, still visible, disappeared through a door. As I vanished the Vatican officials appeared to turn us out. In some ways it is the most effective shot of the whole series.

Television lights produced two other revelations, one bad, one good. The bad one was to reveal the incredibly bold restorations that Corrado Ricci had inflicted on the mosaics of San Vitale in Ravenna. Some of these were already known from early photographs, but, under the relentless glare of our lights, it was apparent that these famous images, which appear as frontispieces to so many books on Byzantine art, were executed, and to some extent conceived, in the late nineteenth century. More impudently still a number of them are not even composed of tesserae, but painted to simulate mosaic. It is often said that history is an agreed fiction, and nothing (except perhaps Arthur Evans's 'frescoes' in Crete) illustrates this old truism more graphically than the mosaics of Justinian and Theodora in San Vitale. The good revelation was the altar of the Santo in Padua. The monks of the Santo, known as Antonini, are not a very co-operative brotherhood, and are notoriously offensive to lovers of art who want to inspect more closely their high altar. But £100 from the BBC made them look as genial as the monks on an old-fashioned calendar, and we were allowed to shine our lights on Donatello's reliefs of the *Miracles of S. Antonio*. I thus saw something that I fear very few people have seen since they were transferred to their present position. Everyone knows that they are masterpieces of dramatic invention and of design; but it is impossible to tell from photographs how these qualities are enhanced by the incredible beauty of their execution. The bronze is cut and polished with a goldsmith's precision, and there is a frequent use of gold inlay. This brilliant craftsmanship does not destroy, but rather enhances, their impact as an inspired interpretation of human behaviour.

Filming 'Civilisation' gave me the opportunity to revisit places, like Moissac and Vézelay, that I loved and might never have seen again. The chief of these was Urbino, where the beauty of the Palace and the surrounding landscape redeemed what might other-wise have been one of the dullest programmes of the series. Evidently my enthusiasm for that enchanting place made itself felt, for in the last few years hundreds of people have made the long journey to Urbino, and only its inaccessibility has prevented it from becoming a tourist centre. 'Each man kills the thing he loves.' In addition to these happy returns we went to places which were new to me; Aachen, where the Cathedral, although copiously restored, still represents that point where the Barbarian north turned to the civilisation of Byzantium. It may seem like a vulgar impulse, but to have sat on Charlemagne's throne (or, as I did later, at the desk where Napoleon wrote the Code Napoléon) is a moving experience. I am used to handling precious objects, but when in Aachen I carried the Cross of Lothar from the Treasury and placed it on the high altar of the Cathedral, I will confess that my hands trembled and tears poured down my cheeks.

Another place that we had never visited was Conques. My pretext for going there was that it had been a major stopping place on the pilgrimage route to Compostella, and pilgrimages played a considerable part in programme 2. My real reason was that I wanted to see the Treasury. Conques is as inaccessible as Urbino, and is consequently quite unspoilt; when we were there there was only one modern house, at the top of the village street, large, white and ridiculous. The Treasury is indeed a marvellous spectacle, and contains one of the most weird objects that have come down from the middle ages—the reliquary of Sante Foy, whose well attested miracles had made the village famous in the twelfth century. This little Christian Antigone, who was put to death for refusing to change her faith, is commemorated by a jewel-studded idol, the face of which is an antique gold mask, probably made in Egypt. Nothing could show more clearly how symbol and probability were separated from one another in the mediaeval mind. But in the end what one remembers about Conques is not its Treasury, but the way the village is tucked into its valley, and how the only street twists round the Romanesque church. Peter Montagnon, Tubby and I got up at 6 o'clock one morning to film it from a neighbouring hill. The crew were asleep, we took their camera and they never discovered that it had gone, so there were no union troubles. It is the best shot in programme 2.

Perhaps the happiest time that Jane and I had together in the whole making of 'Civilisation' was our visit to Germany to film the Rococo churches. I had been to some of them before without

Jane, and it was a joy to see how rapturously she responded to them. But I had never been to the finest of them all, the Vierzehnheiligen. What a masterpiece! This church and the palace of Würzburg tempted me to call Balthasar Neumann the greatest architect of the eighteenth century and, much as I love Gabriel, I will stand by that rash judgement. I believe that the Rococo churches of Bavaria are still underrated, not only as architecture, but as the discovery of a new truth, that the faithful may be persuaded by joy rather than fear.

In addition to visiting towns we went to the places where the great episodes of civilisation had taken place. I had decided that when I said "I am on an island on the Lac de Bienne" I should be on that island. I only cheated once, in programme 12, with disastrous results. The Lac de Bienne was the only place where Rousseau was allowed a few months' peace, and it was there, listening, as he tells us, to the flux and reflux of the waters that he had the sensation of being completely at one with nature. I thought I might recapture some of the emotions which attended this famous moment in the history of human awareness by filming on Rousseau's island. But in the end the only shots to be printed showed me paddling about in a boat which might just as well have been on Virginia Water. One cannot exaggerate the extravagance of television; it makes opera seem frugal by comparison. Tubby spent seven hours lighting the Invalides for my fifty seconds' talk at Napoleon's tomb; and then it showed only as a distant background. We stayed for three days in Angers, filming the only surviving series of fourteenth-century tapestries which seemed to me absolutely essential to any survey of late gothic art. In the end we never used an inch of it—"Too much wool", said Michael. It was the sign of a great director. I was the only beneficiary of these extravagances. The peace that had inspired Rousseau to write his *Cinquième Promenade* still pervaded his island, and I could sit in the actual room in which he catalogued the flowers that grew so abundantly around him.

The other landscape location that I loved was Iona. I had visited it every year when I was a young man, as it was not far from my father's home in Argyllshire, but had always gone in a boat, and so had no idea of what a nightmare journey it is to get there by car; and, as with Urbino and Conques, this has kept it unspoilt. Every few days a boatload of tourists arrive from Oban at about 11.30, and leave at 4.00, disgusted as there is not even a postcard shop in the village. I can only repeat what I said in 'Civilisation'. Iona gives me, more than anywhere else I know, a feeling of peace and freedom; and the strange thing is that my crew, who were by no means a pious or superstitious body, had the same feeling. Once they got over the shock that there was no booze to be had on the island, easily remedied by fetching a case of whisky from the mainland, they entered into the spirit of the place. Only one member of our crew was disappointed, a tall, handsome man known as 'Grips' whose job it was to carry heavy equipment. He was a passionate golfer and had carried his clubs all over Italy. He had liked Assisi the best of our locations because in front of the Basilica there is a grass slope of about 150 yards which was ideal for practising mashie shots. For some unknown reason he had not brought his clubs to Iona, and there, just behind the hotel, were several miles of light, springy turf which would (impious thought) make one of the most perfect golf courses in the world. I used to come on him in the evening gloomily contemplating this tempting surface.

Almost our last expedition was to America. There were two motives for going there; one to show how the eighteenth-century doctrine of reason had spread to a new continent, and turned into action; the other to show what in my last programme I called heroic materialism at its most spectacular. The first objective took me to Charlottesville. I had long admired Jefferson, but had never been to Monticello; and until one has visited that extraordinary creation, a naïvely beautiful Palladian house, built on the side of a hill, overlooking what was then Indian territory, one can form no conception of his character. One thinks of him simply as a very intelligent man, who wrote the Declaration of Independence. At Monticello one realises that he was an eccentric of genius, who had to do everything his own way and no one else's. He even compiled his own New Testament and had it printed in four different languages in parallel columns. He was a renaissance man, and I was frequently reminded of Leon Battista Alberti. No one could have fitted more perfectly into the end of 'Civilisation', as I had conceived it.

In New York there occurred the only misadventure of our whole expedition. I had thought of speaking my piece about the wonders of heroic materialism from the Staten Island ferry as it approaches the skyscrapers of Wall Street. The ferry goes every half hour. Michael told me the wrong time—half an hour too early. I meekly got on to an empty ferry, expecting to find the crew on Staten Island. No crew. I therefore got on to the same boat and returned. Meanwhile the crew had come on the other boat and found no one. As the ferries stop for only five minutes one could not wait for the next one to arrive. We passed each other, waving wildly at a distance of about 300 yards, and finally Michael persuaded the captain of his ferry to send a telephone message to mine, so that at last we were united. But by then the light had gone.

The last programme was obviously going to be the most difficult. I had to indicate how the brutalities of the industrial revolution were mitigated by the rise of humanitarianism, and the trouble was that neither of these subjects provided much televisual material. We had to show the gloomy squalor of an early industrial town, and went to Huddersfield; but it was a fine day, and the whole place looked cheerful and sunny. We should have gone to Manchester, for the most heartless exploitation of labour began there, in the textile industry. Also it was the town of Engels; but I thought of this too late.

While we were doing a shot of the Clifton suspension bridge

in the last programme Michael said to me "You know, you must end the series with a summary of your beliefs". This was a blow. I had hoped that my beliefs were sufficiently revealed in my comments throughout the series, and I dreaded the idea of summarising them in a few banal sentences. However, I sat down dutifully in the bedroom of my Clifton hotel and wrote the summary which appears on the last page of my book. It contains nothing striking, nothing original, nothing that could not have been written by an ordinary harmless bourgeois of the later nineteenth century. But I believe that some people were glad to have these truisms restated at the end of such a long journey in history.

The last words of the programme were shot in Saltwood, in my study. As if in sympathy the camera broke down, and a new one had to be sent from London. But at last the final words were spoken, including the prophetic lines by Yeats, which I had heard him read soon after he had written them; I walked in to my library, patted a wooden figure by Henry Moore, as if to imply that there still was hope, and out of shot. It was all over. The crew came over to the Castle for a drink. We had become a band of brothers and were not far from tears at the thought that we should not meet again. I may be fanciful, but I think something of this feeling of comradeship is perceptible in the film. It seems ridiculous to say that the happiest years of my life took place when I was sixty-eight, but so it was.

\* \* \* \* \*

I had naturally seen some of the 'rushes' when they had been assembled by our brilliant cutter, Allan Tyrer; and they didn't look too bad. By the time we had got half way through I suddenly thought "This is jolly good", and I expected the series to be successful, but I wasn't in any way prepared for the impact it made on people of every shade of thought or education. The newspaper criticisms were not particularly favourable, but the letters I received were overwhelming; I used to get 40 or 50 a day.

What pleased me about them was that they didn't address me as a star, but as a friend. The writers ranged from very simple, almost illiterate people, who could not have understood a quarter of my allusions, to letters from cabinet ministers (including Jim Callaghan) and three Cardinals. The most afflicting were letters from people who said that they had been on the point of committing suicide, and that my programmes had saved them. I think I had nine in all and, although people who threaten to commit suicide do not always carry out their intention, some of the nine may have been genuine. What a terrible responsibility! I tried to write more or less personal answers to these letters; it was six months' work. I did so partly because I was grateful, and partly because people often seemed to have misunderstood what I had said, and I wanted to explain myself more clearly.

A success like this is always hard to explain. I believe that the average man (and I know that there is no such man, but the expression is irreplaceable) was pleased when someone spoke to him in a friendly, natural manner about things that he had always assumed were out of his reach.

This communication with simple people was one of the things about the programmes that particularly annoyed intellectuals of the left, who believed that they had a prescriptive right to speak to the working classes. Academics were furious at the simplification of their labours, and would have liked to catch me out in mistakes, of which there are a certain number. But they never wrote to me about them; perhaps they thought I was beneath contempt. In fact my approach to history was unconsciously different from that now in favour in universities, which sees all historical change as the result of economic and communal pressures. I believe in the importance of individuals, and am a natural hero-worshipper. Each programme had its hero—Charlemagne, the Abbot Suger, Alberti, Erasmus, Luther and Montaigne, Mozart, Voltaire, Jefferson, Rousseau, Wordsworth, and finally Brunel. One whole programme is called *The Hero as Artist*. The majority of people share my taste for heroes, whether football stars or pop singers, and so were glad of an historical survey that emphasised outstanding individuals rather than economic trends.

When the series was shown in the U.S.A. things got out of hand. The number of letters quadrupled, and some of them were rather dotty. We opened a crackpot file which soon overflowed. A number of young ladies, some of them very pretty, sent me their photographs, but Catherine Porteous sternly forbade me to reply. Unsuspectingly I went to Boston to give a lecture at Harvard, and was initiated into the embarrassment of stardom when the coloured porters at the airport jostled each other for the privilege of carrying the luggage and would not take a tip. To be followed in the street, and stopped by every passer-by in the Park, places a strain on one's geniality. I was sincerely grateful, but ultimately rather exhausted. I remember going into a chemist's shop in Boston and a lady who was there said to the chemist "Do you realise you have the greatest man in the world in your shop?" The chemist answered impassively "Sure I do". It is comical that such treatment should have been handed out to a Wykehamist; an Etonian would have been better able to cope with it. Readers of *Another Part of the Wood* will recognise that these demonstrations had not the slightest effect on my self-esteem. I think I know more or less what I am worth; it isn't much, but it is something. How my small talents came to arouse this kind of mass hysteria I shall never understand. After ten years the effect has not entirely worn off, and in summer I cannot walk many yards down Piccadilly without being stopped and thanked by elderly Americans. I confess that I find this very touching. My fans are surprised, and perhaps a little shocked, when I stretch out my hand to them in gratitude. I suppose they feel that a genuine 'star' would have treated them more haughtily.

The series was shown several times in the National Gallery at Washington (a special copy was bought by the Senate and shown in the Capitol), and our Ambassador had suggested earlier on that I should come out to make a personal appearance. "Things like that begin to go flat about half-way through", he said. When I arrived in Georgetown to stay with my old friends David and Margie Finley, Carter Brown, the Director of the Gallery, rang me to say "For God's sake don't go in through the front door. You'll be mobbed. I went in by the back door and down a long underground corridor to a press conference. After it was over I was led back along the same corridor so that I might walk the whole length of the Gallery upstairs. It was the most terrible experience of my life. All the galleries were crammed full of people who stood up and roared at me, waving their hands and stretching them out towards me. It is quite a long walk, and about half way through I burst into tears at the sheer pressure of emotion. I thought "What do I feel like? I feel like some visitor to a plague-stricken country, who has been mistaken for a doctor: but is not a doctor." I had somehow to control myself, stand on a platform, listen to *The Star Spangled Banner* and make a speech (which was inaudible as the amplifying system broke down; something I have in common with the Mona Lisa). I did it, and was proud to have done it and the speech, which was later beautifully printed, is to be found at the end of this book. Incidentally, my camera crew, which was doing another job, were present, so I was able to give them full credit. They took a film of this extraordinary scene, but needless to say it was never shown. I then went downstairs and retired to the 'gents', where I burst into tears. I sobbed and howled for a quarter of an hour. I suppose politicians quite enjoy this kind of experience, and don't get it often enough. The Saints certainly enjoyed it, but saints are very tough eggs. To me it was utterly humiliating. It simply made me feel a hoax. I came up to lunch with red eyes, and tried to put the experience out of my mind. But, as the reader will have realised, it would not go, and has not gone. and I record it because I must be one of the few ordinary, normal men on whom this kind of experience has been inflicted. The

Finleys drove me home in silence. They felt as embarrassed as I did.

I was brought up to believe that any work of art, music or literature that is enormously popular must have something seriously wrong with it. I see no reason why 'Civilisation' should be an exception to this rule. But I have never discovered precisely what is wrong with it, if not taken too seriously. I used to think that its success in the U.S.A. and Canada was due to the re-assurance it gave to bourgeois values. But this does not account for its equally great success in Poland and Roumania. I think I know the answer, but will not pursue the question further.

★   ★   ★   ★   ★

I did a number of television programmes after 'Civilisation'. The first of these, called 'The Origins of Modern Painting' was not a success. It was directed by my son, Colin, and perhaps un-wisely we followed the same form as 'Civilisation'. I walked into the shot, said my words, and walked out. It seemed like a repetition done with rather less expertise, and I tried to stuff too much into each script, so that there was no time for music or for the wandering eye. But it had a good idea behind it: to show how the painters, from whom modern art derives its freedom, were not 'born free', but drew their inspiration from visual experience and even actual places. This involved another series of happy journeys. We went to Aix-en-Provence to film Cézanne's quarry of Bibémus, and the little house above the Château Noir, where Cézanne painted, a holy spot to me. We went to Monet's house and waterlily garden at Giverney, and to Munch's tiny house at Askgardstrand.

This was, in a way, the most fascinating of all, because, although Munch does not look like a realistic painter, in fact every tree, every fence, every rock by the shore, is copied immediately from a thing seen. A comic element was provided by our search for Rousseau Douanier houses in the suburbs of Paris. His own Octroi has long ago disappeared, but, with the help of an intelligent chauffeur, we found some unspoilt nineteenth-century common-places. The jungle scenes we shot, as Rousseau saw them, in the Grande Serre of the Jardins des Plantes from which he could hear the lions roaring in their nearby cages. I learnt a lot from all these experiences, but apparently no one else did.

Two later television series, also produced by Colin, were more successful. One of them was based on my old lectures on classic and romantic art, with additions on Blake, Turner and Rodin, and was called by the deceptive title of 'The Romantic Rebellion'. I was glad of the opportunity to talk about Turner, since the admiration of his genius has grown so amazingly in the last twenty years that my early pages on him in *Landscape into Art*, once con-sidered too laudatory, now seemed lukewarm. I cannot remember anything that was said about it in England, and I doubt if I received a single letter about it, which shows how much the reception of 'Civilisation' had depended on a kind of self-identifi-cation by the viewer. But it seems to have had a measure of success in the U.S.A. The other series was a final summing up of my thoughts on Rembrandt, commissioned by a Trust set up by our dear friends, John and Anya Sainsbury. I think this was a good series, and the last episode, 'Rembrandt and the Bible', perhaps the best script I have ever written. It was shown on the BBC and, although it was not widely seen, I received a number of warm and intelligent letters, which showed that a few people understood what I was trying to do. However, as I have said before, these two series were not really television performances, but filmed lectures. My last performance was a film on early Egypt called 'In the Beginning', and I made it after the disaster which will be described in the epilogue. The concept of this programme meant a lot to me. On successive visits to Egypt, and especially to Sakara, I had grown more and more impressed by the suddenness with which civilised man had made his appearance. By evolutionary standards it should have taken millions of years for the primitive hunter, with low forehead and crunching jaws, to turn into the graceful, intelligent-looking man whom we find in the earliest Egyptian sculpture. In fact it took only about 500. Most people close their minds to this irrefutable fact, either because they cannot explain it, or because it smacks too much of special creation. It was on account of this second suspicion that I called my programme 'In the Beginning'. I wanted it to make people reflect on what I believe to be the greatest miracle in history. By the year 2750 Egypt had developed nearly all the qualities that we value or used to value, in our own civilization: a belief in the individual as moral being; pride in the merciful execution of justice, a well organised system of government, a sense of the beauty and dignity of man, who had a soul that would survive him after death; an awareness of animals as something very close to ourselves, which could be lovable as well as useful; geometry and its application to stone architecture; and above all an art that combined grandeur with humanity. All this emerged in what we call the Old Kingdom, which lasted over 700 years, and to which Egypt looked back for the next 200 years, rather as China looked back to the T'ang Dynasty. As we know most of this from visual records, architecture, sculpture in the round, and reliefs, it should have been a perfect subject for television. But it didn't turn out as I had intended. Colin, who produced it, had persuaded Michael Gill to direct it. It was his first experience of Egypt, and he was so much impressed by the visual possibilities of the landscape, and of Ramassid temples like Karnak, that the programme turned into a kind of glorified travelogue. A more effective film? Yes, of course. But my 'message', which had obsessed me for five years, hardly emerged. I should have called the film 'Sakara', but then Colin could never have persuaded *The Reader's Digest* to finance it.

This was, and will remain, my last television performance. I was seventy-two when it was made, and I know that after seventy a man loses that power of projecting his subject and

K.C. in the Katsura Summer Pavilion

K.C. in Garden House, Saltwood

himself on which a successful performance in any medium depends. I remember that when I was a boy my father took me to see the most celebrated comedian of his day, named Arthur Roberts. He had long ago retired, but had been persuaded to come back and do some of those old turns which had kept his audience in fits of laughter. He repeated them word for word, used all the old winks and gestures, and never got a single laugh. I suppose he was in his late sixties. The fact is that communicating with an audience depends on physical attributes, and when they decline no amount of expertise has any effect. I was lucky to be still capable of this power of communication when I was sixty-eight, and must not tempt the fates, who had so successfully tempted me, any longer.

*Epilogue*

*Appendix*

*Index*

# Epilogue

ON MY SEVENTIETH BIRTHDAY my friend Jock Murray, who has published my books and looked after my affairs for many years, gave me a luncheon. I asked if it might be at the Café Royal. I had gone there before the 1914 war. My youthful steps were illegally directed to the Long Bar (now the Grill Room) when my father dropped in for an unauthorised drink before luncheon; and as a school-boy I had sat in the Café (now the restaurant) in hopes of seeing the artists and writers who were my idols, although when it was hideously redecorated in a modern style, they had ceased to go there. Jock allowed me to interfere in the choice of guests and accepted most (but not all) of my suggestions. Those that he did not accept have borne me a grudge ever since. The sight of so many old friends gave me enormous pleasure; like Emma I yelped with delight as each one entered the room. Only about three or four close friends could not come. William Walton was in Ischia, and Ben Britten's health was already precarious. Jane had bought a beautiful new hat for the occasion and sat between her two dearest friends, David Crawford and Henry Moore, with Yehudi beside her at the next table. We had no photographers and no *placement*. At the end I said a few words of thanks to Jock, who replied with touching warmth, and told us that as a memento of the occasion he had printed a copy of my Romanes Lecture, *Moments of Vision*, in a beautiful new type called Janet, designed by Reynolds Stone, who had also done two wood engravings of Sudbourne and Iken. We were gloriously happy.

Crossing Regent Street on the way home Jane said "Wouldn't it be a good thing if we could be run over by a 'bus". As things turned out she was almost right, although in that case I should not have written *Another Part of the Wood*.

## Epilogue

During the summer I was invited by the Smithsonian Institution, the intellectual dynamo of Washington, to go on a cruise to the Eastern Mediterranean. Both our fares would be paid, and I would be given a generous tip. In return the author of *Civilisation* was expected to talk luminously to his fellow passengers, and give a few informal lectures. The plan was that the cruise should go to Egypt, calling at Crete and Cyprus on the way out and at Sicily on the way home. I had never been to Crete or Cyprus, and had given up all hope of ever doing so. It was an irresistible opportunity and I accepted. The only trouble was that Jane's health had seriously declined and, although she loved Egypt as much as I do, I was afraid that the noisy delays in that disorderly country might be too much for her; but she had always enjoyed cruises, and I hoped that the sight of so many new places would do her good. We were to embark on our Greek cruise-ship at Athens, and flew out there a few days earlier. Jane seemed quite happy and was even strong enough to climb up the Acropolis. To walk once more past those great golden columns that conceal so calmly the secret of their unequalled beauty, was the fulfilment of a vow we had taken forty years earlier—to visit either Chartres Cathedral or the Parthenon every year of our lives. We spent over an hour in the Acropolis Museum, rearranged to perfection, and totally recaptured the joys of our youth. A friendly Acropolis guide helped, or rather carried, Jane down to our car. She was also able to visit the National Museum, and once more we stood dumb before the 'Zeus of Histea'. Alas, she could not climb a stair that led to the fantastic wall-paintings from Santorin, and I began to doubt the wisdom of taking her on this expedition. When, in two days, our fellow passengers began to assemble, I became even more apprehensive. They were nearly all elderly people who were devoting their retirement to the pursuit of culture; but age had not subdued their voices or moderated their terrific heartiness. I love Americans, but I hate noise, and no one can deny that Americans en masse make a great deal of noise. As we drove

234

down to the harbour in a bus full of yelling old ladies, I saw in Jane's face ominous signs of distress, and when we were shown our very small cabin, she burst into tears. "You must get me off, you must get me off". Too late. The gangways were already being raised. I could not change the cabin, as the boat was full. In any case all the cabins were equally small, as it was assumed that passengers would not use them except to sleep in, but would spend their time convivially in the public rooms. Jane wept literally all night, and most of the next day. I took down her meals to the minute cabin. It did not look as if the cruise would be a success. The kind, hearty, leader of our flock, Dick Howland, had explained that when we entered the dining-room we should sit down at the first vacant seat, so that we could all make friends. I cheated in so far as I sat down next to men rather than women, but otherwise obeyed instructions.

Things continued to go badly till we reached Cyprus. Then, going ashore at Kyrenia, on a warm sunny morning, our spirits began to revive, and we enjoyed the gothic ruins of Bellapais, like an English abbey in Mediterranean light, and the marvellously preserved cathedral of Famagusta. Jane said "Now I feel it's something like a cruise". To our great relief war broke out between Israel and Egypt, so we were deflected to Anatolia. What a piece of luck for me, as I saw Priene, Didyma and Ephesus, which in my wildest dreams I had never expected to do. It was interesting to discover that over half the ladies on the cruise had been there already. By this time Jane had recovered her equilibrium, and we walked down the long, winding street of Ephesus in much the same state of astonishment as we had felt when, forty years earlier, we had first visited Pompeii; astonishment because, in these large, well-preserved towns the essential vulgarity of the Hellenistic world is made so disturbingly clear. At breakfast a fellow passenger took porridge with milk, cream, butter, sugar and salt. I asked to taste this unholy mixture. She said, "What do you think of it?" I replied, "It's exactly like the architecture of Ephesus". She was delighted.

## Epilogue

How wonderful to see Knossos in its beautiful setting, which compensates for the unarchitectural complex of poky little rooms, and what a pleasure to contemplate the great Minoan oil jars in the museum at Heraklion. As for the famous frescoes, it is a miracle that Arthur Evans ever 'got away' with them. There is one authentic head (shown separately) and a few fragments of authentic drapery. All the rest is blatantly the work of a restorer. Arthur Evans, whom I knew and greatly admired, was an extremely intelligent man: what was his state of mind when he superintended these fabrications? Perhaps great archaeologists are really creative artists manqué, and are bored with 'finds' like the Mildenhall silver, which are perfectly preserved.

We then went to Malta, and I made the interesting discovery that the present Italian cult of Caravaggio had not penetrated to Washington, as no one on board had heard of him, and I had to give an off-the-cuff lecture to try to persuade my companions that the *Beheading of St. John the Baptist* in the cathedral was one of the great pictures of the world.

From Malta we floated, in perfect sunshine, to Sicily. Few places have fallen more catastrophically victim to the vulgarities of the present time; which in Sicily had evidently been equalled in the fourth century as we can see in the mosaics at Piazza Armerina. However it is still a joy to pass from the quarry in Syracuse into the theatre built from its stone, and the more remote temples like Selinunte are as enchanting as ever.

Our cruise was to end at Palermo. We moored to a jetty late one evening and next morning when we woke, the weather had broken. It poured with rain all day. We hired a car and went to our favourite places. I could not face Monreale in a downpour, as I had always remembered its cloister (an encyclopaedia of Romanesque carving) in brilliant sunlight; but we sat in the Capella Reale till the spirit of Byzantium began to sink in. When we went back to the harbour the rain had turned into a deluge, and the boat had begun to bump ominously against the jetty. Our cabin was on that side, and the noise became a nuisance, so we went up to sit in the lounge. After about half-an-hour, Dick Howland's voice came over the loud-speaker. "There is no cause for panic, but the Captain wishes all passengers to leave the ship immediately. Please do not try to go down to your cabins. I repeat, there is no cause for panic". Clearly there was. We went down to the disembarkation deck, Jane in a thin evening trouser-suit, I in summer clothes, but fortunately wearing a cardigan. The way down to our cabin was barred. No money, no passports. Our fellow passengers were staggering along the bumpy gangway, but Jane was too frightened to make the attempt; a very small, but evidently very strong, Greek sailor picked her up and carried her ashore. The jetty was awash with about six inches of water, the rain coming down in buckets, but we sploshed along towards some sort of shelter. Having found in the customs office a bench on which Jane could sit, my irresponsible curiosity led me, against all orders, to go out and see what was happening. It was a memorable sight. A tidal wave, no doubt caused by an earthquake out at sea, had broken down the harbour's outer mole. Of the thirty-nine ships anchored in the harbour, nearly all had come adrift, and were rocking about in the waves, banging into each other, and occasionally blowing up. The captain had ordered our immediate disembarkation because he saw that one of these ships, an enormous tanker, was bearing down on us. It would have crushed us like a fair-ground toy. Fortunately, a very large repair ship, with two tall metal towers carrying cranes drifted between us and the tanker, and as I ran up the quay I could see the tanker collide with it. The towers crashed down, with minor explosions and superb flashes of light that momentarily illuminated the whole scene in the harbour. It was appalling—small boats overturned, large boats passing over them—absolute chaos. But although I was appalled, I was also exhilarated. I have led a sheltered life (except during the bombing of London) and this great affirmation of nature's contempt for human contrivance was something I was glad to have witnessed. I returned reluctantly to a small disconsolate group of fellow passengers waiting in the dreary office of the customs house. The problem was what to do with them. As I was the only member of the party who spoke Italian, I had to take charge. I remembered a second-rate restaurant in the Corso Vittorio Emanuele about a mile away. Nothing for it but to walk there. We waded along the jetty, Jane perfectly calm and resolute; we pushed through the crowds of sightseers who were enjoying the spectacle of chaos and destruction as much as I had done, and climbed the hill to the restaurant. Naturally it was shut. Persistent banging brought an angry proprietor, who at first refused to let us in, but seeing our deplorable condition—we were all wet to the skin—finally consented, and we sat down in fairly good spirits. We were saved from pneumonia by a curious piece of good fortune. Instead of towels, the lavatory had a device that blew hot air on one's hands. By inserting a quantity of coins, we succeeded in drying ourselves, and were ready for the meal when at last it arrived. But where to go for the night? I sent out sentinels to stand at the door of the restaurant in case any other members of the cruise should pass, and sure enough one did. By a miracle Dick Howland and the travel agency responsible had found us all accommodation; they had opened up a summer hotel on the outskirts of the town that had just closed. Jane and I were given a room in a large, seedy hotel in the centre. There we had to stay all the next day, Jane wearing my cardigan, waiting for news about our ship. By evening we learnt that it was still afloat, although at an angle, and I could go and retrieve our belongings. This proved to be the most disagreeable part of the whole episode, as the cabin was still half-full of water. However, I managed to squeeze most of our clothes into cases, and struggled upstairs and into an impatient taxi. The invincible travel agent had succeeded in hiring a 'plane to take us to Rome, and we set out from Palermo airport next evening. It is never a cheerful spot, and on that occasion the scene was exactly like one of those reconstructions of refugee camps made familiar to us on the television screen. I drifted away from our bewildered group to see if I could discover a quieter corner, and suddenly found myself face to face with Mother Teresa and some of her nuns, who were on their way to visit the Vatican. My first instinct was to fall on my knees, but I was afraid that one of our cruise companions might see me, and feel embarrassed, so I knelt on one knee, kissed her hand, and received a smile of such radiant beauty and goodness, that all the misfortunates of the last twenty-four hours fell into place.

Our hotel in Rome seemed to be expecting us, and the comfort and security of our usual room, with its window looking on to S. Agnese, was almost uncanny. No one had heard of the disaster in Palermo, which, in the interests of tourism, had been kept out of the newspapers.

Next morning Jane seemed miraculously recovered, and we set out on our favourite walk. We crossed the street into the Piazza Navona and went on to the Sapienza. I remember Jane commenting on the tact with which Borromini has fitted his façade on to the colonnade of della Porta. Then to S. Andrea to gaze at the splendid Domenichinos in the semi-dome; then back to the Chiesa Nuova, where the sacristy is one of the most beautiful rooms in the world, and the small chapel of S. Filippo Neri had always filled us with feelings of devotion, finally to S.ta Maria della Pace, that inexhaustible façade, in which we had continued to find new felicities of design for over forty years. I remember our saying, as we had said to each other since 1928, that Pietro da Cortona was the most underrated of European artists. In the evening we went into S. Agnese where a children's service was taking place, and the whole interior was full of balloons, flying up to the ceiling. How they would have delighted Borromini! Next day we flew back to London.

Naturally there was a reaction, and Jane spent one or two miserable weeks. But by mid-December she was well enough to go down to stay with John Sparrow in All Souls. This has always been, to me, one of the pleasantest experiences in life—a warm and beautiful house, a superb collection of books, flowing over into every room and passage, good college food, and a friend whom I have known for almost sixty years, and to whom I can say anything. There was some College festivity that evening, so that John and I had to dine in Hall, leaving Jane to have dinner alone in the Warden's Lodgings. Halfway through our dinner the head of the staff, known as the Manciple, whispered something in John's ear. Jane had fallen off her chair, and had been carried up to bed. I went back, to the Lodgings, saw her safely tucked up, and returned to my festive dinner. Next morning she had forgotten about the whole incident, and we went to the Ashmolean. We had gone there together before we were married and the years when I was Keeper of the Department of Fine Art had been the happiest in our lives. For an hour some memories of those days floated round our heads. Jane felt strong enough to walk back to All Souls, and we set off, down the Broad, through the Bodleian quadrangle, and as usual we stood in admiration of the Radcliffe Camera. In the afternoon we returned to Albany. I was cooking some pasta, and Jane telephoning when I heard a crash. I found her lying on the floor, with one arm stretched out limply behind her like the arm of a rag doll. She had clearly suffered a stroke. The doctor came, and next morning found her a room in University College Hospital. For about three weeks she hung between life and death, able to recognise me, but practically no one else. It was Christmas, and the nurses were exceedingly festive. I have never been more miserable. Even if she lived, it was clear that she would never recover the use of her left side. These thoughts occupied my mind, as I walked twice a day (for there was no means of transport over Christmas) from Piccadilly to Gower Street. I had the uncanny experience of walking down Tottenham Court Road without seeing a soul or a vehicle. After a few weeks the doctor thought she could be taken by ambulance to a nursing home in Hythe, where she had a large sunny room.

# Epilogue

But the brisk vulgarity of the nurses upset her. She grew steadily weaker, and the Hythe doctor told me that she could not live for long. She had always said that she wanted to die in her own bed, so I decided, under pressure from the children, to bring her home. Our kind doctor said he would not be responsible, and would give up the case; she would die in the ambulance on the way up from the nursing home. In fact her heart did stop beating for a few seconds. She was put into her bed and lay in a sort of coma for three hours. Then she suddenly opened her eyes and said, "I'm at home". It had the quality of a miracle. The engagement and installation of four nurses, and all their necessary apparatus, was done by Colin's wife, Faith, to whom I feel eternally grateful. Then there began a vigil which lasted for almost three years, with many alarms and complications. I gave up all my London commitments and settled in the Garden House, partly to be with Jane when she wanted me, partly to act as a sort of Matron to the nurses. I learnt a lot about 'human nature'.

My only consolation was in writing. I was offered the absorbing task of producing a new edition of Botticelli's illustrations to Dante, which not only made me look more carefully than I had done before at these beautiful visions, fluttering yet precise, but gave me a pretext for delving once more into the *Divine Comedy*. Dante had always been Jane's favourite author (followed by Racine), but her mind never became strong enough to read him again; in fact for three years she did not read at all. Fortunately my edition appeared, with a dedication to her, shortly before she died, and gave her more pleasure than anything else in the last month of her life. As she spent much of the day in sleep I had plenty of time to write. I made my Rembrandt lectures into a short book; I wrote an introduction to Vasari, which meant rereading the *Lives*, and the little read *Proemio*, and I did a number of long reviews, including one on the life of Edith Wharton. Finally, after two years, I was persuaded to write this book, which, whatever its defects, has turned out to be an excellent piece of therapy.

# Epilogue

Well-wishers urged me to take occasional holidays, but these were not a success. I went back to Rome, partly because I have several friends there whom I had not seen during our last brief transit, and partly because Jane had left her jewellery in the hotel safe. But visits to our favourite places increased my melancholy. I thought that the sparkle of New York would revitalise me, but it had the reverse effect. I could not stop worrying about Jane, and I am afraid that this came out in my conversation and in a certain lack of responsiveness. My only successful holidays were short visits to Dorset and Aldeburgh, where I could bury myself in the company of undemanding old friends. In the end I was least miserable at home, where I was looked after by a kind, practical helper named Lindley, who had been engaged as a chauffeur, but became a cook. He did everything. I should have been lost without him. There were good days on which Jane was clear in the head. She was even able to come up to London for a party given by Jock Murray for the publication of *Another Part of the Wood*; she could sit in the garden in her wheeled chair, and often said "I am happy". This made all our efforts seem worthwhile. But far more frequent were the bad weeks when she and everyone around her was miserable. Finally there were critical days when she developed new and apparently lethal symptoms, and had to be taken to London by ambulance for treatment. The last of these was a skin disease which could be warded off only by enormous doses of cortisone that clouded her mind. By one of those ironies of which life is so prodigal, she would not believe she was in her own bed.

My isolation should have given me the opportunity to learn something about myself, but as the reader of these pages will have seen, I cannot go very far in that direction. I have no aptitude for self-analysis, and when I try to examine my character, I soon give up in despair.

As time went on, Jane grew weaker but she never spoke about death. Then one day when I was away from home, she asked for writing-paper and wrote, in a perfectly clear hand (her writing had previously been indecipherable) letters of farewell to me and the children. I foolishly did not recognise this as a premonition of death. A few days later her mind, which had been very confused, suddenly cleared. We looked through a new volume of photographs of quattrocento art, and she identified every one. Then I read her Keats' *Eve of St. Agnes* and she seemed to enjoy it. When I came to the end I said, "What shall we read tomorrow?" She answered, "I shan't be alive tomorrow", calmly and gratefully, and immediately fell asleep. She never woke up. This time I had recognised the symptoms, because my mother had had a similar moment of clarity immediately before her death, and I was not surprised when the nurse came to tell me that she had died.

It now remains for me to see what I do with my life.

# *Appendix*

*Response to Mr Carter Brown on receiving
the National Gallery of Art medal for
Distinguished Service to Education in Art
(Washington, November 18th, 1970)*

CARTER BROWN, your excellencies, ladies and gentlemen:
Ever since the programmes first 'took on' I've felt a
terrible fraud. It's really quite an uncomfortable feeling.
The 'Civilisation' programmes were not made by a single person,
they were made by a unit, some of whom I'm glad to say are here.
And all the praise that has come my way should have gone to the
unit and to the BBC. Unfortunately, people have a habit of person-
alising, and just as in the 1914 war they spoke about fighting the
Kaiser and not the military machine which faithfully expressed
the ambitions of the German people, so they have personalised
these programmes and directed their kind and grateful and very
touching words to me.

Education! . . . well, my producer Michael Gill will support me
when I say that when we started off on this series we never for a
moment thought about educating people. We simply hoped to
entertain them. And we thought that if we worked away together,
we might make an evening's entertainment, which, as the poet
Yeats says, would 'keep a drowsy senator awake'. Michael Gill
ought to have half this medal, but it's so pretty it would be a
shame to cut it in two.

On thinking it over I do see that it's a mistake to draw too
sharp a line between entertainment and education. I fancy that

education has two complementary aspects. At one end of the stick is learning to do what you don't want to do. That is the most important part of education. It's absolutely vital to the conduct of life, and it's absolutely vital to the action of the mind throughout the whole of the rest of one's life. We used to achieve it by having people learn Latin, the most disagreeable thing I've ever done in my life. I did it for ten years and hated it all the time. But I did get some sort of—well, I suppose one can only call it intellectual discipline out of it. You know, old-fashioned writers on education in the sixteenth and seventeenth centuries used to speak of the necessity of young people being 'birched into their Latin'. I don't know how that would go down in modern schools.

And later, I had the same experience when I tried to read the great German philosophers. I turned over the pages of Kant and Hegel, and I couldn't make head or tail of them. I felt absolutely frustrated and humiliated, but I had to go on until I thought I understood something, and at least I had acquired a new mental process.

Now although I believe that this part of education is the most important part, it has one great defect. One may achieve intellectual discipline, but one doesn't remember a single thing that one learnt in that way, because one doesn't absorb it. I can't translate the simplest Latin inscription, and if you ask me what Kant's *Critique of Reason* is about I couldn't tell you.

Education has another aspect—what you learn through delight. It is a pity that the Nazis spoilt, by adopting it, a very good slogan: 'Strength through joy'. And in fact it is by falling in love with a subject, a period, a style, an individual hero, that one absorbs something so that it becomes a part of one's living tissue, and one never forgets it. 'Give all to love,' your great underrated poet said. It's true of education as well of life. And the first advice I would give to any young person is, when you fall in love with Roman baroque or with the essays of Montaigne or with whatever it may be, give up everything to study that one, all-absorbing theme of the moment, because your mind is in a plastic condition. A plastic period usually takes place between the ages of about fifteen to the age of twenty-two; and anyone who is learning at that moment will never forget what he has learnt. Read and read, look and look; you will never be able to do it so intensely again. I often wonder if in the last fifty years of grubbing away and reading in galleries and libraries I've learned anything compared to what came to me in those plastic moments.

Well, what I put into the programmes may not be written with much knowledge—they contain a good many mistakes and slips of the tongue—but they are written with love. And that, I hope, will have some effect on people who see them and read them. They will find something to kindle their enthusiasm. Thus far I believe they *are* educational.

A second way in which they perhaps could be educative is they give a feeling that history is a continuous process. Well, that's obvious to anybody with any brains; but I'm told, although I never met them, that there are people who think that the new world is something completely different from what has ever happened before and that it's cut off from the history of the past. That's a very bad idea. It's not only silly, but constricting and life-diminishing. And of course it's entirely unphilosophical, because past is present and present is past—in the twinkling of an eye, what I've just said has become the past.

And so, I hope that the programmes will help to get out of people's head the idea of 'born yesterday'. Of course there has been a great change in the world; we're probably going through the greatest change that's taken place since the Neolithic revolution, and how are we going to find our way through? Our only guide is history. In spite of the emphasis on mechanisation that dominates our daily life, I still believe that man hasn't changed very much. I'm a great believer in faces. And when I look at the faces of those Egyptian civil servants in the Boston Museum, those state employees of the year 2500 B.C., they might be people working in the Fogg or in the Massachusetts Institute of Technology. Man is trying to change himself, he's come more into the open, he's let out things that he's kept to himself. That may be a good thing or it may be a dispersal of energy. We shan't live to see.

What else can I say in excuse for this idea of giving me—or rather of giving me and the BBC unit—a medal for education? Well, that although these programmes, you tell me, give people something to believe in, I hope that they will also give people a healthy scepticism. If you listen to them carefully you will find there is a good deal more scepticism in those programmes than most people allow for. And the central quotation of the whole book is Montaigne's words "Que sais-je?—What do I know?"

I believe that one of the purposes of education is to balance scepticism and belief. Of course that can be done by what we call common sense. Quite simple people, usually women, have lots of common sense and aren't taken in, and maintain a balance of scepticism and belief. But to suppose that the majority of people balance scepticism and belief is not borne out by advertising, or the modern world in general. My goodness, if people really began to be sceptical and use their minds, in order to see through cant and humbug and self-seeking lies, advertisers and public relations men and a number of the politicians, and even a few fashionable philosophers, would be out of business.

One of the great points of education, I think, is to acquire intellectual honesty and to see through cant and humbug. And the way that education does this is not only by training people to use their minds, but by teaching them history. When you read history you learn that people in the past were just as clever as we are, in fact at some periods they were a good deal cleverer. The audiences that sat for seven hours in the sun listening to the dramas of Aeschylus must have been a good deal more intelligent than I am. And the people who went to the Socrates show were certainly also very, very bright in the head. And yet all these people who were much cleverer than we are believed in things like animal sacrifice which we think absolutely absurd.

I would like to think that these programmes have done two things: they have made people feel that they are part of a great human achievement, and be proud of it, and they have made them feel humble in thinking of the great men and women of the past. Also, I'd like to think that they are entertaining.

# Index

# Index

# Index

# Index

American forces in England, 56–7, 70; and E. Sitwell, 62–3; and Ezra Pound, 88; President of London Fashion Designers, 127–8; illness, 168, 202; Russian appearance, 196; gardening skill, 202, 203; and 'Civilisation', 218–19; declining health and last years, 234–5, 239, 240

Clark, Kenneth Mackenzie, Lord (KC), Surveyor of the King's Pictures, 2, 209; visits Manod caves, 8; aestheticism, 8, 84, 91–2, 94, 113, 114; and MOI, 10–15, 18–19, 20–2, 34, 42; Controller of Home Publicity, 14, 15, 19–20; in Paris, 16–17, 70–3; in air-raids, 20–1, 33–4, 36; and war artists scheme, 22–4; London homes, 30, 33–4, 36, 69–70, 126–8, 184; liking for feminine society, 34, 58, 192; tendency to weep, 55, 218, 225; committee membership, 55; self-assessment as Director of NG, 77–8; and 'restoration' of paintings, 77–8; Slade Professor at Oxford, 79, 80–4, 92; *Sunday Times* articles, 93; on himself as lecturer and writer, 94–5; in Portugal, 96–102; religious experience, 108; on treatment of 'local' pictures, 113–14; melancholy, 115, 196; honoured by France, 119, 123; on the Council of the Louvre, 119; opens Chicago exhibition, 125; and his children, 127, 190–2; dinner at No. 10 Downing Street, 128–9; booed at the Athenaeum, 138; a-political, 143; adviser to Felton Bequest, 148; on Hindu and Moghul art, 162–3, 165, 178; love of Japanese art, 168, 170, 172, 174–5; and Buddhist sculpture, 171; concept of good and bad taste, 177–8; reactions to Japan, 179–83; and his dogs, 200–1, 206; on rapid appearance of civilised man, 227–8; 70th birthday luncheon, 233; Eastern Mediterranean cruise, 234–6; disaster at Palermo, 236–9; and Jane's last years, 241–3; on education, 244–6; learning through delight, 245; history as a continuous process, 246, 247; *Another Part of the Wood*, xi, 22, 79, 98, 242; 'Art and Society', 93–4; 'Civilisation', 6, 212; *The Gothic Revival*, 79; *Horizon* (essay on Edith Sitwell), 62; 'If the Invader Comes', 19 and n; *Landscape into Art*, 81–2, 86, 95, 149, 227; *Moments of Vision* (Romanes Lecture), 93; *The Nude*, 81, 86–7, 91, 105–6; *Piero della Francesca*, 84–6, 95; *Ruskin in Oxford*, 80; *Ruskin Today*, 68, 79–80; 'Value of Art in an Expanding World', 93–4 *see also* Arts Council; ITA; Television

Cocteau, Jean, 115

Colston, Sir Charles, and ITA, 139, 143

Conques, Treasury, 218; Sante Foy reliquary, 218; Christian Antigone, 218; Romanesque church, 218

Constable, John, 193; Swedish attributions, 51–2

Contempoary Art Society, 193

Conway, Lady (formerly Mrs Levi Lawson), and Saltwood, 184, 186, 202; life and character, 186

Conway, Lord, owner of Allington Castle, 187

Corbusier, Charles-Edouard Le, 169

Council for the Encouragement of Music and the Arts (CEMA), founder members, 25–6, 55; absorbs Art for the People, 26

Council of Industrial Design, 55

Courtauld Institute, 4

Covent Garden, Royal Opera House, 194; as a National Opera, 101, 131–4, 136; singing in English,

# Index

Covent Garden, Royal Opera House, (contd.) 132-3; and the ballet, 133; Kabuki, 180 and n; Trust, 132

Cox, Geoffrey, and ITA News, 146

Crawford, (David) Earl of, 55, 73, 193, 233

Crawley, Aidan, and ITN News, 146

Cripps, Sir Stafford, 29, 32

Cuttoli, Mme, and Picasso, 71, 72

Cyprus, Bellapais ruins, 235; Famagusta Cathedral, 235

Daily Mail, and ATV, 142

Dante, xi; KC and Botticelli's illustrations, 241; Divine Comedy, 241

David-Weil, David, President of the Grand Conseil, 120, 121

Davies, Martin, work at Manod caves, 7, 8

Davies, Sir Walford, and CEMA, 26

d'Arcy, Fr, SJ, 64

de Gaulle, General, 70; in wartime England, 54

de la Warr, (Buck) Earl, 25; PMG, 138; and ITV, 138-9, 143

de Segonzac, Dunoyer, 72-3; etchings of Vergil, 73

de Valera, President, 34, 35

Degas, Edgar, 117

Delacroix, Ferdinand, 136; KC's lectures on, 83, 84

Dent, Alan, Vivien Leigh, A Bouquet, 61 and n

Department of Ancient Buildings, 202

Desboutins, Père and Mme, 117, 118

di Gaspari, Mme, 128

Diaghilev's Ballet company, 196; surviving stars, 46; KC's exhibition, 54-5

Digby, Pamela (later Churchill; Harriman), 56

Domenichino, S. Andrea, Rome, 239

Domenico, Veneziano, Madonna, 105

Donatello, 84, 172; Miracles of S Antonio, 217

Dublin, KC's mission, 34-5; Coole, 35; Abbey Theatre, 35

Duff Cooper, Alfred (later Viscount Norwich) and MOT, 18

Duveen, (Joseph), Lord, and Berenson, 103

Eccles, David (later Viscount), 156, 157

Eden, Sir Anthony (later Lord Avon), 143; and Suez crisis 157

Egypt, 218; Luxor film, 209; KC's film, 227-8; early development of man, 228, 246-7; Karnak, Ramassid temples, 228; Sakara, 227, 228

Ekwall, Eilert, 51

Eliot, T. S., 52, 58; Pound revises The Waste Land, 88

Englander, Tubby, senior cameraman, 212-13, 216, 218

English Opera Group, 193

Evans, Sir Arthur, Crete frescoes, 217, 236

Eugene, Prince, 51

Eyck, Jan van, Virgin and Child, 152

Fatapur Sikri, 163

Ferguson, Howard, 28

Finley, David, 87, 225

Flint, Russell, 23

Florence, 85, 86; Academy of Fine Art, 94-5; Baptistry, 111; Campanile, 172; Or San Michele, 111-12; Santa Croce, 111; 'Civilisation', 212, 213

Fonteyn, Dame Margot, 46

Forster, E. M., 57, 115; at Saltwood, 197, 198; in retirement at Cambridge 197; A Passage to India, 161-2; Two Cheers for Democracy, 198

France, attitude to World War II, 16-18; German Occupation, 70,

# Index

India, (contd.)
167; bad taste, 178; Bhopal, 163; Great Stupa of Sanchi, 163–4, 167; Delhi, 160–2; tomb/chapels, 160–1; Ellora, 165, 166, Kailasa, 166
Ingres, Jean Auguste, KC's lectures on, 83, 84
Italian Renaissance, 84, 211
Italy, enters the War, 103; transfer of 'local' paintings to Academies, 113; policy of shutting galleries, 113–14; Assisi, 166; see also Florence; Rome

Jacob, Gen. Sir Ian, Director General BBC, 142
Japan, invitation to KC, 168; language barrier, 168, 170, 172–3, 181; architectural blight, 169; temple art, 171–2, 174; portraiture, 172; Kamakura period, 172; sculpture, 172; aesthetic philosophy, 174–5; Shinran sect, 175; calligraphy, 175; Lady Ohtai, 175, 176; Zen temples, 175–6; television films, 176; good and bad taste, 178; sand gardens, 178; religious life, 179; tea ceremony, 179; Kabuki theatre and No drama, 179–80; position of women (the Geisha), 181; landscape, 181–2; national characteristics, 182–3; Samurai violence, 183; KC's television programmes, 208; Hakone, 182; Kyoto, 173, 182, Nishi Hongwan-ji temple, 171, the Myako, 173, 174, 176, Chishaku-in temple, 174; Nishi Hongan-ji, 175; department store, 177, 178; Nara, 170; Yamato Bunkakan gallery, 170; Horyu-ji, 171; Shaka triad, 171; Todai-ji, 171, 172, 177, 178; Kofuku-ji, 172, Yakushi-ji, 172; Shoso-in, 172; Sambo-in, 174; Tokyo, Old Imperial Hotel, 169 and n.; Mt Fuji, 182; Osaka, 170, 173, 182; artists: Hiroshige, 183; Hokusai, 168, 182; Kyonaga, 180;

Sharaku, 181; Unkei, 172; Utamaro, 168
Jarves, Alan, sculptor, 32
Jefferson, Thomas, Monticello, 220–1
Joad, 'Professor' Cyril, and Brains Trust, 47–8
Jones, Tom, 135; and Pilgrim Trust, 24; character, 24–5; and CEMA, 26; at Coleg Harlech, 25

Karsavina, Mme, 46, 54–5
Kelly, Sir Gerald, and young artists, 23; and KC, 23
Keynes, John Maynard (later Lord), 56, 133; and Arts Council, 26–7, 130, 131; and John Christie, 131; character, 27; death, 129, 133; Chairman, Covent Garden, 133
King, John, architect of Garden House, 204
Kipling, Rudyard, xii, 182; *Kim*, 161
Klee, Paul, 54, 116, 121
Kleiber, musical director Covent Garden, 132
Knowles, David, character, 196–7; and 'Civilisation', 211
Korda, Sir Alexander, 12, 37; and Film Division of MOI, 12

Lambert, Constant, 46, 167
Lassimonne, Denise, 27
Lawson, Mr and Mrs Levi, *see* Conway, Lady
Leavis, Dr Frank, 64
Lee of Fareham, Lord (Uncle Arthur), 4, 31, 49; and National Gallery pictures, 3; and Lloyd George, 36
Lee, Sir Kenneth, Director General MOI, 11, 15
Leigh, Vivien, 192; character, 59, 60–2; at Notley, 59–60, 61, 62; attacks of tuberculosis, 59, 62; and part of Anna Karenina, 60; 'manic depressive', 60–1; KC and, 62; Films, *Caesar and Cleopatra*, 39, 40, 59; *Doctor's Dilemma*, 58, 59; *Gone*

# Index

# Index

# Index

# Index

Redentore, 109; San Giorgio, 109; San Moise, 110; San Marco, 109–10; porphyry Emperors, 92
Verdi, Violette (m. to Colin Clark), 191; Director of Ballet, Paris Opera, 191n
Vienna, Kunsthistorisches Museum, 3

Wagner, Richard, projected *gesamt kunstwerk*, 212
Waley, Arthur, 20; translations from Chinese, 84
Wallace (later Agar), Barbie, 56, 57, 86, 184
Wallenberg, Count, 49
Walton, Sir William, 233; friendship with Jane, 36–7, 57, 192; music for *Major Barbara*, 37; for Sadler's Wells ballet, 46; marriage, 192–31; *Belshazzar's Feast*, 131
War Artists Committee, 55
Webster, Sir David, and Covent Garden Opera, 131–3
Wells, H. G., 30; 'Autobiography', xii
Wharton, Edith, xii, 89, 199; Sainte Claire le Château, Hyères, 114, 115; KC reviews a Life of, 241
Wheldon, Sir Huw, 210

Whitley, J. H., Chairman, BBC, 135
Wilde, Johannes, 3–4
Williams, William Emrys, and CEMA, 26; 'Art for the People' Scheme, 26; and Arts Council, 129
Williams-Ellis, Clough, at Portmeirion, 8
Wilson, Sir Horace, 24
Winterbotham, Hiram, 32, 70
Wolstencroft, and ITA, 139
World War II, KC and, 1 ff; Dunkirk, 19; Battle of Britain, 20; projected German invasion, 30–1; Hitler attacks Russia, 36; buzz-bombs, 57–8; V2s, 70; Germans leave Paris, 70; conclusion and aftermath, 74–5; Italian entry, 103; Pearl Harbour, 103
Worth, Irene, 192, 200
Wright, Frank Lloyd, Old Imperial Hotel, Tokyo, 169

Yashiro, Yukio, with KC in Japan, 168, 170, 171, 172; and Old Imperial Hotel, 169 and n; and the Myako, 173
Yeats, Jack, 54
Yeats, W. B., 54, 88, 222, 244; Edith Sitwell's debt to, 66

H2